THE ELIZABETHAN WOMAN

CARROLL CAMDEN

The
ELIZABETHAN
WOMAN

REVISED EDITION

PAUL P. APPEL, PUBLISHER
MAMARONECK, N.Y.
1975

33611

Library of Congress Catalog Card Number: 52-5665

International Standard Book Number: 0-911858-30-X

*The booke of God maketh mention of Women of divers
kindes, but all of them ... may be reduced to one of these
heads; either the Mysticall, Naturall, or Matrimoniall,
Woman. The Mystical Woman, is foūde in the Scriptures
to be the embleme or representation of good & evill ...
The next is the Natvrall Woman, by whome we vnder-
stand the man foeminine, or the female of man-kinde ...
The last is the Woman Matrimoniall, & her alone we call
a Wife, beinge a Woman vnder marriage, either only
initiate, in tearmes of contract or betrothing, ... or com-
pleate, and consummate called ever a Wife.*

John Wing
THE CROWNE CONIUGALL

*T*he nature of woman and her place in the scheme of things have fascinated writers in all generations. For those who try to understand the Elizabethan mind, a knowledge of this one half of mankind is indispensable, for woman is not just a peculiar variant in the formation of man. As the Elizabethans clearly recognized, woman's nature as well as her body differs greatly from that of the male of the species. The Elizabethan woman, moreover, was even a special representative of her sex. The rise of the middle-class, with its own culture, together with the changing attitudes implicit in the Reformation, brought forth a new kind of woman who could not be ticked off and classified in the same easy way as her medieval sister. Mere man was somewhat bewildered, and he did not like the sensation. The middle-class version of Renaissance erudition had taught him to expect all sorts of good results from the simplified directions of the learned, to be found in handbooks. But here close to hand was a subject which baffled him. The wealth of books on all phases of femininity must have been partially designed to satisfy man's curiosity concerning this new woman, just as the guides to knowledge were teaching him to partake of the new learning.

In this book, then, we endeavor to learn the nature of the Elizabethan woman, philosophically and actually. We try to discover what role she was intended to play and how her education prepared her for it. We follow her through her marriage and into her duties as a wife within the household; and we consider the Elizabethan version of the eternal feminine as she dresses herself, prepares her face, and relaxes in play. At the last we examine both sides of several controversies to discover their contributions to the problem of the Elizabethan woman. Throughout, we shall take a thoroughly sympathetic view of both the feminine and the Elizabethan ways. The time has passed, if it ever existed, when we could smile at the beliefs and practices of our Elizabethan ancestors; too often we have discovered, with the smug air of the scientific explorer, what the Elizabethans well knew.

Although the original spelling has been retained in the quotations, the general reader should have no difficulty with the passages. It may be well, however, for him to keep in mind two or three simple rules: an initial u was often written v (use : vse), and an internal v was often written u (every : euery); y and i are interchangeable; and sometimes the nasals m and n may be indicated by overscoring the preceding vowel (woman : womā). Long titles have frequently been shortened, except where the full title has some significance; some titles have had capitals added. Although the bibliographical material has been presented in a rather unconventional fashion, the curious reader should have little difficulty in finding the references. I have felt that a sprinkling of footnotes at the rate of one or two to the line, makes for unpleasant reading as well as for a typographically distasteful page. Therefore the plan I have followed is to gather together the references for one or two paragraphs and to list them in order; since about half of the passages have their authors named within the text, it should be easy to find any particular reference. Except for the last chapter, the notes consist almost entirely of bibliographical references. The word *Elizabethan* has been used conventionally to cover the period roughly from 1540 to 1640, but I have not hesitated to go a few years beyond these limits in certain instances.

The remaining task, that of presenting formal thanks, is most pleasant. I should like to express my appreciation to the staffs of the Folger Shakespeare Library and of the Henry E. Huntington Library for their many kindnesses in making available their invaluable collections of books. In particular I should like to thank Miss Mary Isabel Fry, Reference Librarian of the Huntington Library, for help in securing some of the illustrations; Dr. Giles E. Dawson, Curator of Books and Manuscripts of the Folger Shakespeare Library, for his patient and scholarly aid of many kinds; and Professor Carl R. Woodring, of the University of Wisconsin, for kindly assisting me at an early stage of the work. To my colleagues at The Rice Institute go my profound thanks for their contributions: to Professor Joe D. Thomas for his careful assistance in reading proof; to Professor William S. Dix, the Librarian, for his assistance in securing books and film; and especially to Professor Alan D. McKillop, who read the manuscript and who submitted to unending questions, small and large, with forbearing fortitude. I am unable to indicate the full extent of my debt to Professor Hardin Craig; not only has he made invaluable suggestions at several stages of the study, and discussed with me various problems of interpretation, but at the last moment he answered my importunate plea for a reading of the manuscript, giving enlightening advice and counsel to the great advantage of the book.

The Rice Institute
Houston, Texas
October 22, 1951

CARROLL CAMDEN

10

Contents

Illustrations

Many of the illustrations have been reproduced through the courtesy of the Henry E. Huntington Library; these have the name of the library in parentheses. Those marked (Planché) are from James Robinson Planché, *A Cyclopædia of Costume*, London, 1876.

CHAPTER I

The nature of woman

Orlando: *Can you remember any of the principal evils that he laid to the charge of women?*
Rosalind: *There were none principal; they were all like one another as half-pence are, every one fault seeming monstrous till his fellow-fault came to match it.*

As You Like It

Court lady with
farthingale, apron,
and fan

The lot of the Elizabethan woman may justly be compared in many respects to that of her modern American sister. European visitors to the United States today often comment on the freedom of the American woman and the adulation which she receives from the American male. In the same fashion, continental visitors to Elizabethan England were aware of a vast difference between the treatment of women in England and the treatment which prevailed in other European countries. Frederick, Duke of Württemberg, visited England in 1602, and wrote that 'the women have much more liberty than perhaps in any other place,' and that there was a proverb among other nations which ran: 'England is a paradise for women, a prison for servants, and a hell or purgatory for horses.' [1]

Working on the assumption that as virtue will not take a surface in art, so neither will the praise of woman make as interesting reading as the dispraise, a large number of Elizabethan writers turned out books in the main current of the traditional anti-feminist literature. Even they, however, insisted that though women be a burden to men, yet the men cannot get along without them. Robert Greene expresses the thought in saying: 'The Philosophers whose sayings haue beene holden as Oracles, haue sette down this for a principall, that howe perfect a woman be eyther in vertue, beautie, or wealth, yet they are to men necessarie euils.' [2]

Women are considered as creatures set apart from men in many ways. Man is the agent, woman the patient, is one way of wording this idea. Indeed, writes William Bercher, even the place of gestation is different for man and for woman, since everyone knows that man is formed in the right side of the mother's body and woman in the left. And since in the creation of the individual it is the woman who bears the man, 'if a man bee a little world woman is a great world, for the greater contains the lesse and not the lesse the greater.' In the original creation of mankind, insist a large number of writers, woman was clearly the superior of man; theological arguments to sustain this thesis were varied and ingenious, being based on personal interpretation of Biblical passages. Was not woman created from a more refined substance than man, since she was formed from Adam's rib, whereas man was made from 'slyme and earth'? In fact, argues William Austin, the bone of which woman was formed was not bare, senseless bone, but must have been bone with adherent flesh, since Adam himself said: 'This is bone of my bone, and flesh of my flesh.' Further, even the fact that woman was created last has some significance; thus, an evolutionary pattern is traced by a writer who details that first were created the minerals, then the vegetables, then the fish, birds, and man, followed by 'the last, for whom the first was made' – woman: '*Every worke* being still *more perfect* then other, still ending in the *most perfect* of all, he *rested* as having finished all *in her*, beyond *whose perfection* no creature more could be *added, created,* or *imagined.* But, though she were *last in time* brought forth: *Agrippa* is of opinion, that God determined her creation *first of all.*' [3]

Physiological differences between the sexes are considered at length. Popular writers all wanted to be heard on just why and how and to what degree women differed from men in constitution and mentality. John Donne sees woman as an eternal mystery, saying that women are like the sun, having a motion of their own which their husbands are unable to fathom. More prosaic authors point out that women's temperament is cold and moist, whereas men's is hot and dry. According to Ludovicus Vives, if the fertilized egg finds sufficient heat in the uterus, then a man child is brought forth, but if not, the child is female. Of course this coldness and moistness means that woman is phlegmatic, while man is choleric; her element is water, while his is fire. Since the moon is cold and moist, it follows by analogy that woman is under the direct influence of the moon, as is evident by her periodic difficulties, which are in time with the period of the moon's orbit. And as the moon shines brightest the more remote it is from the sun, reasons a gentlewoman in *The Knight of Malta*, so a wife is never freely merry or truly pleased except when farthest off from her husband. Moreover, as everyone knows, it is heat which makes a man bold and hardy, as can be seen in the effect on man when alcohol heats the liver, as Falstaff has duly noted in his famous apostrophe to sack; but the coldness

18

of woman makes her naturally fearful and timorous. And since women are weak physically, they must be weak morally and mentally. Spenser feels that there are 'phantasies in wavering womens witt,' and a character in *The Warres of Cyrus* insists that 'womens wittes are weake.' A warning comes from John Donne that one must not hope to find a mind in a woman, while Vives believes that the thought of woman is swift and unstable. It is therefore the conclusion of John Knox that it is as repugnant to nature that a weak, sick, and foolish woman should rule, as it is that the blind should lead those who can see. On the other hand, one of William Bercher's characters argues that this coldness of woman makes her more temperate in her desires and more weak in appetites. And it therefore follows that woman is governed by reason and understanding, while man is ruled by his appetites and senses. Moreover, there are two kinds of knowledge, one coming from nature and one from study; woman is obviously the superior in the natural form, because she matures earlier, and she could be superior in the other form if only she were permitted to test herself in the schools and in other places of mental exercise hitherto reserved for men. [4]

Other characteristics which set off women from men are the small stature, the thick hair, and the soft flesh. Not only is this last variation significant in itself, but by analogy soft flesh indicates a soft nature. 'The disposition of the minde is answerable to the temper of the body. A woman in the temperature of her body is tender, soft, and beautiful, so doth her disposition in minde corresponde accordingly; she is milde, yeelding, and vertuous; what disposition accidentally happeneth vnto her, is by the contagion of a froward husband.' Furthermore, a woman is constantly busy about trifles and always finding honor in such occurrences as having famous men as neighbors or having great princes speak to her. But most of all, woman is more subject to sickness and disease, feebleness of body, and miseries in general than any other of God's creatures. Not only does she suffer grief in her monthly purgings, but in carrying and bearing children she suffers danger and pain, so that the love of the mother is necessarily greater than the love of the father. Woman is also subject to such diseases as stomach troubles, rheumatic catarrhs, the gout, pimples, the falling sickness, the iliac passion, scurvy scabs, dropping distillations, etc. [5]

Of course, woman is also different from man because, contrary to the usual custom in nature, it is the female of the human species who is beautiful. Indeed, the beauty of woman is more praised and esteemed than any other beauty. The reason for this situation is probably that beauty is the only dowry of woman. It appears to be the order of nature that what is lacking in one sex is supplied in the other; and since man is endowed with wit, judgment, and a mind almost divine, all of which make him fit for contemplation and speculation, so in recompense woman is given bodily beauty that she may be superior to man in this respect.

The curious fact about these observations, and the ones which are to follow, is that we do not find any objective realization that woman is being seen through the eyes of men; this is especially noticeable to the modern reader when it is freely acceded, and even blindly assumed, that women are beautiful; they constitute the beautiful sex, in apposition to man, who is freely granted great virtues; indeed, he has all the best of things; but beauty? no, that belongs to what is still called the fair sex. Perhaps what we have here is another example of the eminent practicality of the Elizabethans; it was probably well to hold that women are desirably beautiful. Elizabethan authors insist, however, that this natural beauty must be nurtured and cared for before it can become beauty to the fullest extent; and it is for this very reason that princesses and women of honorable birth are generally fairer in body and mind than those born to a more modest scale of life, because their diet makes the blood more pure and their vital spirits more lively, and because their way of life, free from troublesome 'molestations,' gives more time for high thoughts and honorable imaginations. A simple view is expressed by Araspas, who tells Cyrus that to him a woman's beauty is like fire; and she uses this gift of nature to blind man's reason and provoke him to pleasure. Interestingly enough, Elizabethan writers feel that the decay of this flowering beauty does not set in as soon as the girl becomes married. On the contrary, Erasmus relates that he has seen some women who were pale and droopy until they married, whereupon the friendly fellowship of a husband made them so fair that one would think that their beauty failed to flower until the period of wedded bliss, Puritan, or otherwise. Greene may well have read this passage, for Mme. Castilla makes the same remark to Mamillia. [6]

The Elizabethan ideal of feminine beauty, which we have been examining, requires first of all that the *tout ensemble* be that of red and white. In beauty as well as in all things, the Elizabethan period was one of violent contrasts; and it was no exaggeration to say that the fairest women are 'as white as snow and as red as blood.' Edmund Spenser, in his description of Belphoebe (who probably represents Elizabeth), says that the effect is that of 'roses in a bed of lillies shed,' while Marston's Passarello puts it more bluntly by saying that the picture conjured up is that of red barberries served up on white meat. The face itself should be 'rounde and ruddie,' with a smooth, high, and white forehead, 'large, square, [and] well extended.' Under small, graceful eyebrows, marked as with a pencil, the lamp-like, gray eyes are alluringly full and set wide apart. But although the eyes are alluring when one gains a sight into them, they are ordinarily downward cast in a modest and simple regard. The cheeks not only show the rose and lily in combat, but should be dimpled as well, as should be the chin. Of course the lips will be coral, or 'lyk cherryes charming men to byte.' The neck must be snowy white, straight, round, and like an ivory pillar holding the head up high; the ears, round and well compact. The space between the shoulders should be wide. The breasts must be high, fair, and round, resembling budding lilies or young fruit in May, and should be spread with small, blue veins. The hands are to be small and white, with long and straight fingers, the nails of which are red. The body of this nonpareil will be small, dainty, and straight, with slender waist and rather large hips; she will have straight legs, and a fine, little foot, with a 'clean' (high?) instep. Of course the hair was then, too, a woman's glory, and a prime requisite for beauty in Elizabeth's day was golden yellow hair resembling the beams of the sun; it should be naturally curly as well. One interesting book on the beauty of women emphasizes that the voice is a part of feminine beauty, and that laughing and sneezing must be done quietly:

Womans beaulte that pourchase wyll praysyng
Wold that the woman set her besy cure
To maynteyne in hyr selfe a low laughyng
To laugh ouer hygh besemeth no creature
Beaulte yet cōmaundeth afterwarde
Unto all women thys poynt secondely
To haue alwayes a lowely regarde
Not ouer moche but moderately
That woman hath the bent of beaultyes bowe
That can regarde in helth and in dysease
Whan she shall neese to make the sounde but lowe
To do otherwyse yt may no person please.

Nor must a beautiful woman take a superior air and conduct herself in
a proud manner – beauty is as beauty does:

Womans beaulte eche person reproueth
Yf so be that she bayre the countenaunce
More eleuate or hygh than yt behoueth
Hyr beaulte tourneth but all to dysplesance.

Further, it is well for a beautiful woman to remember that beauty does
not last. 'A little cold pinches it, a little heat parches it: it is, at the most,
but skinne-deepe; subject to more casualities than there be Faces'; and
when beauty is gone, all is gone – gather ye rosebuds. Since physical
beauty is but skin deep and is but fleeting, it is best for a woman to concentrate upon inward beauty:

That outward Beautie which the world commends,
Is not the subject I will write vpon
Whose date expir'd, that tyrant Time soone ends;
Those gawdie colours soone are spent and gone:
But those faire Virtues which on thee attends
Are alwaies fresh, they never are but one:
  They make thy Beautie fairer to behold,
  Then was that Queenes for whom prowd Troy was sold.
As for those matchlesse colours Red and White,
Or perfit features in a fading face,

Or due proportion pleasing to the sight;
All these doe draw but dangers and disgrace:
A mind enrich'd with Virtue, shines more bright,
Addes everlasting Beauty, gives true grace,
   Frames an immortall Goddesse on the earth,
   Who though she dies, yet Fame gives her new birth.

The painter Giovanni Paolo Lomazzo insists that nothing in the world can beautify a woman more than cheerfulness and contentment; and Du Bosc, the author of *The Compleat Woman*, adds that modesty is also a potent charm, and without it beauty has no soul. Indeed, inward beauty will actually produce outward beauty. Not only will a noble mind make a woman beautiful, but (following the familiar Platonic principle) the fact that a woman is beautiful is a guarantee that she is chaste and has a fair soul, 'that very same bewtie which we see in sweete Gentlewomens faces, being no other thing, then the right glittering luster, and glorious brightness of a victorious & triumphant soule.'[7]

The subject of the dispraise of women is as ancient as the sex, but the popularity of such diatribes in the English Renaissance was due to many factors: medieval monasticism and the attitude of such church fathers as Tertullian, the problem of female rulers, the opposite side of the coin which first showed the woman of the Petrarchan sonnets, and the desire of the reading public for some satiric fare, different from the avalanche of religious books. Writers of this stamp had many interesting things to say about women, some of them original. The anonymous *The Praise and Dispraise of Women* records that Plato was uncertain whether he should place woman among the reasoning creatures or among the beasts, while Tasso believes that 'euery Woman would willingly bee a Man, as euerie deformed wretch, a goodly and faire creature: and euerie Idiot and Foole, learned and wise.'

A more important problem, however, was the question of a thousand year's standing: do women have souls? Since women are Biblically responsible for the existence of sin in the world, how can such creatures possibly contain even a small amount of the divine nature? In John Donne's

Iuvenilia appear certain paradoxes and certain problems; problem VI reads: 'Why hath the Common Opinion afforded Women soules?' in which the author argues that woman's loving has always destroyed man. And the author of *An Almond for a Parrat* states that he heard a sermon preached at Lichfield denying that women had souls. At any rate, it was agreed that many miseries were brought into the world by women and many cruelties done by them. Nashe, in *The Terrors of the Night*, insists that women will not let their husbands alone, even haunting them after death, and he concludes that 'women are borne to torment a man both aliue and dead.' A popular pun much in evidence is that woman derived her name from the fact that she was a woe to man. The author of *The Schole-house of Women* believes that there was some error in the statement that woman was made from man's rib; that what really happened was that a dog got hold of the rib from which woman was intended to be made, carried it off and ate it, and that God then took a rib of the dog to complete the work, as is evidenced by the fact that wives always bark at their husbands. Another writer gets from Boccaccio the story that when God became angry with human beings he sent three scourges: sickness and disease, travail and pain, and women, the last being the greatest scourge of all because they are stirrers up of argument and strife. The Reverend William Whately enlarges on this theme and concludes by saying that every woman has at least a thousand faults, though good bringing up may conceal them, good instruction may diminish them, and good nature keep them secret for a while. In fact, there was but one good woman, and the devil carried her away. A character in the comedy *Swetnam, the Woman-hater* announces that a woman is an angel at ten, a saint at fifteen, a devil at forty, and a witch at eighty. [8]

The particular faults of women, as listed by anti-feminist writers, are legion, beginning with the all-inclusive one that though men are full of faults, women have only two: everything they say, and everything they do. First of all a woman is obstinate and perverse; there is nothing a man can do to please her, or to draw her from her opinion. If a man loves her too much, she condemns him, since too much of anything is loathsome;

The shrew tames her husband

if he does not show his love constantly to the degree that she expects, she thinks he bestows his love elsewhere.

For the women they have no spurrs that can make them go no bands that can holde them no bridle that can staye them no lawe that can subdue them no shame that can reteigne them . . . he is yll bested that must rule them or correct them . . . yf they be advysed of any thynge theye beleve yt not. yff anye councell be geven them they never take yt yf they be threpned [threatened] they langwyshe. yf they be cheryshed they be prowde. yf they have no solace they envye them that have yt, yf a man wynke at them they becum shamless. yf they be chastysed they be more poysened. And thear was never woman that cowlde pardon iniurye or acknowlege benefyte. take the most Symple woman that is and she wyll sweare she knowethe as mutche as any man alyve....And yf any man will speake a gaynste them. they take hym for a mortall enemye.

Or to sum up the matter, the one thing above all others that a woman wants is to have her will, though when she has it she abuses the privilege by not knowing when it should be used.

Another proverbial complaint about women is that they talk too much:

> *Things that be bitter, bitterer than gall*
> *Physitians say are alwayes physicall:*
> *Then womens tongues, if into powder beaten,*
> *And in a Potion or a Pill be eaten,*
> *Nothing more bitter is.*

Since women talk too much, of course they are unable to keep a secret; poets imagine Echo to be a woman,

> *Because that sexe keepes nothing close they heare:*
> *And that's the reason magicke writers frame*
> *There are more witches women then of men;*
> *For women generally, for the most part,*
> *Of secrets more desirous are then men,*
> *Which hauing got, they haue no power to hold.*

Every man knows, too, that women love clothes, and that they go to church only to show them off. So consuming of time and money is this feminine fancy, that if a man lacks enough affairs to keep him busy, he should get a woman and a ship, 'for there are not any two things in the world that require more trimming.' This vice, added to woman's covetousness and her desire for all kinds of novelties and curiosities, can be counted upon to make a husband's life miserable. Dame Parnell, a character in Ercole Tasso's *Of Mariage and Wiuing*, works on her husband by telling him she has nothing to wear comparable to what her friends have, and she ends her complaint with a tear or two:

Well (saith Dame Parnell) yet happie is such a Gentlewoman, for she hath a husband that maketh much of her indeed: O what a fine gown she had vpon her this morning, the very lace and fringe about it, is worth more then any three of the best that euer I yet wore, since I was first borne: And what rich iewels and great orient pearle had shee about her necke? but her Rings, her Girdle, her Purse, her rich Furres, so sweetely perfumed, they past, and were the richest of all that euer I saw. Well may she shew her selfe amongst the proudest, and walke where she pleaseth, not a litle vnto her credit: but I poor soule, cannot with mine honor looke out of doores, nor suffer any to come and visit me, so much am I fallen out of reparations, for want of good apparell. . . . And having so said, and wringing out two or three little tinie teares (and those God he knoweth with much ado) they begin a fresh skirmish as their fashion is, and proceed with theyr second peale of rayling in this sort. [9]

To get what she wants, a woman will do or say anything; thus she is deceiving, dissembling, and lying. In *The Faerie Queene* the old Malbecco is married to the young Hellenore, and fearing for his rights, he keeps her in a bower away from the sight of men, refusing to allow any knight to enter. The teller of the story, however, says that women must not be handled in such a manner, because, if for no other reason, it is fruitless; for who knows not 'that womans subtiltyes can guylen Argus, when she list misdonne?' In Nicholas Ling's compilation appears a poem stating that woman habitually dissembles, going on to say that a man who can find constancy in a woman can find anything in a woman. Women are also of small discretion, and are jealous; some say that women are no more jealous than men, but if so, at any rate jealousy is worse in them because of their natural weakness; and red-headed women are given to this passion especially.

Perhaps the vice most often laid at woman's door is that of eroticism. Elizabethan writers begin by quoting Proverbs, 'Who shall find a virtuous woman?' and go on to speak of women's 'insatiable lust' and 'lewde behauiour,' calling them 'incontinent,' 'insatiable, & vnsatisfied,' and more hot than goats; they continue that 'wyman be more desyrous of carnall lust then men,' and that apparently they are born on the earth more to 'enterteine and nourish voluptuousnesse and Idleness' than to be trained in matters of importance. Edgar's remark in *Lear* comes to mind ('O undistinguished space of woman's will!'), as does Lear's famous speech concerning the erotic nature of women no matter how virtuous they may look; and Monsieur in Chapman's *Bussy d'Ambois* speaks of 'the unsounded sea of women's bloods,' and says that even Cerberus is unable to see 'the damned looks hid with the veils of women's virtuous looks.' Thus Spenser comments that women often seem to prefer the personified Lechery, though more handsome men may be present, and ends by questioning: 'O who does know the bent of womens fantasy?' It is no wonder, believes a character in *Swetnam, the Woman-hater*, that women are greatly inclined to lustfulness, for from early childhood you will see them delight in playing with babies and pretending they are married, 'in imitation of the wanton ends their riper yeeres will ayme at.' In an interesting essay, entitled 'The Naturall Disposition of Most Women,' Leonard Wright records most of these complaints against women which we have been examining: 'Most women by nature, are sayd to be light of credit, lusty of stomacke, vnpatient, full of words, apt to lye, flatter & weep; whose smiles are rather of custome then of curtesie, and their teares more of dissimulation, then of grief, all in extremes, without meane, either louing deerly, or hating deadly, desirous rather to rule, then to be ruled, despising naturally that is offered to them, and halfe at death to be denied of that they demaund. They are aptly compared to the Musician, who being intreated, wil scant sing, *Sol, Fa:* but vndesired, straine aboue *Ela.*' In the Folger Shakespeare Library is a manuscript ballad, dating from about 1500, which gives a delightful account of man's grumbles about women, relating that they are always gadding about, are inconstant and deceiving, constantly changing their minds, and loving only themselves; they have the ability to amend their ways, but they will not. The poet ends each stanza with the words of fearful man when faced with female ire:

> *Thes wamen all*
> *bothe great & small*
> *they wandre to & fro*
> *nowe here nowe there*
> *they wot not were*
> *but I will not say so*

they Ruͦne they Range
theyr myndes do change
they make ther frend yᵉ foo
as louers trewe
Euery Daye a newe
but I will not saye soo

wythin their brest
their loue Doth Rest
who lyst to proue shall know
for all their bost
all Daye almost
but I will not saye soo

now whot nowe colde
ther ys no holde
but as the wynd Doth blowe
when all is done
they will change lik the mone
but I will not saye soo

they loue they leyue
they will Disteyue
as Dyse that men do throwe
who vsyth them myche
Shall never be Rych
but I will not saye soo

Gyue this give that
all thyng they lack
and all you may bestowe
onez ought of Syght
farewell good nyght
but I will not saye soo

thus one & other
takyth after the mother
as cockes by kynde do crow
my song ys endyd
the best maye be amendid
but I wyll not saye soo [10]

29

Just as there was a cult for the dispraise of women, there were also numerous writers who defended women against the diatribes of the satirists. A character in a dialogue by Sir Thomas Elyot points out that none of the honest philosophers wrote anything against women. And Anthony Gibson, writing in 1599, paraphrases Plato in saying that 'womens society hath made ciuill the moste outragious condition of mens liues.' An author who calls herself Mary Tattle-well insists that 'none but Mungrill Rimers speake against Women,' and she is supported again by Elyot, who says: 'Poetes wrote againste women in wanton ditties, to content men with newe fangled deuises.' A woman, indeed, is just as a man is: a reasonable creature with a flexible intelligence which may be guided in the right paths by nurture and counsel; it is simply that her body is different. 'In the *sexe*,' writes William Austin, 'is all the *difference*; which is but onely in *the body*. For, she hath the *same reasonable soule*; and, in that, there is neither *hees*, nor *shees*; neither *excellencie*, nor *superiority*: she hath the *same soule*; the *same mind*; the *same understanding*; and tends to the *same end* of eternall salvation that *he Doth*.' And thus it is that the Salic law, which excludes women from the French crown, as being too eccentric, is to be condemned and to be considered as quite unjust. Of course men are stronger than women, but strength is no criterion, for if it were the horse and the ox would be better than man. Actually, man can not do without woman, because she is man's best helper, taking care of his needs in meat, drink, and clothing, as well as being his companion. In Greene's *Orpharion*, Arion sings a song listing some of woman's aids to man:

> *Women . . . are harbours of mans health,*
> *Pleasures for night, and comforts for the day:*
> *What are faire women but rich natures wealth?*

> *Women are sweets that salue mens sowrest ills,*
> *Women are Saints, their vertues are so rare:*
> *Obedient soules that seeke to please mens wills,*
> *Such loue with faith, such Iewels women are.* [11]

A large number of Elizabethan books are taken up with stories of various women who have shown exemplary characteristics. Legends of good women were as popular in the Renaissance as in the Middle Ages. John Alday's translation of *The Praise and Dispraise of Women* relates stories of brave women, clever women, prudent women, chaste women, constant women, and women who first brought religion to men. Richard Ferrers ransacks not only the Old and New Testaments to find stories of constant women, but even Ovid, Thucydides, Domitian, Pliny, Strabo, Sallust, Eutropius, and many others. Illustrative stories of the female virtues are grouped by Thomas Heywood under each of the nine muses. A long list of women who have accomplished some great good is provided by Anthony Gibson; he mentions such females as Semiramis, Penthesilea, Deborah, Thea, Judith, Hester, Medea, etc. Much later, in the middle of the seventeenth century, *The Ladies Vindication* still feels that man needs to be reminded of their good deeds, and furnishes more women from the Bible and from history as examples of various types. Other writers point out that the nine muses, the twelve sibyls, the four cardinal virtues, and the three graces are all female, and that the arts, the sciences, and the virtues are apostrophized as feminine. Sappho is said to be the equal of men in poetry; the alphabet is supposed to have been invented by a woman; and man is further reminded that Christ, after His death, first appeared to women.[12]

Besides, if any women are bad, it is the men who have made them so. Some accuse women of lying, but though this be a fault which appears in even the best of wives, yet it is because they have learned to lie in saving the reputations of their husbands. If women are proud, it is ten to one that men have made them so by flattery, 'perswading us that our beauty is incomperable, our complexions of white and red, like Straberies and Creame; our cheekes like damaske Roses covered with a veile of Lawne, our lips are Corall, our teeth Ivory, our haires Gold, our eyes Chrystall, or Sunns, or Load-stars, or Loves Darts: our glances Launces, our voyces, our breathes perfum'd Musicke, our vertues Immortall, and our whole frame, feature, and composure Celestiall.' Nor is it proper to condemn a whole sex just because a few are bad, especially when it is only the bad that are put into books. Men write about bad women because we expect men to be bad and women to be good; it is the exceptions which are attractive, and it is these that are put into print. The tactics are changed from defense to attack by Jane Anger, who printed *Protection for Women* in 1589, as she argues that it is the men who are really bad, anyway. 'We haue rowling eies, and they railing tongues: our eies cause thē to look lasciuiously, & why? because they are geuen to lecherie.' She goes on to say that men are deceitful, lustful, and malicious, and that if women do bring woe to men, yet men bring care, poverty, and grief to women. Men, she insists, lie in bed without any cares and like to dress in rich apparel, and yet it is the women who by their careful diligence make possible the ease of men. Continuing this consideration of the notable virtues of women, Anthony Gibson gives the physician Vigo as his authority for the statements that the eyes of a dead virgin have such efficacy against charms that if the apple of the eye be laid under a brass candlestick, all apparitions will vanish; and that many diseases are cured merely by the sight of the women who come to visit the patients.

The difficulties that women have with men, come chiefly from the very kindness and considerateness of their natures, for thus they lay themselves open to slander. If men thought that women would stand up to them, argues Jane Anger, they would soon draw in their horns. But they have been so used to the good nature of women that they take advantage of feminine goodness. The greatest faults that women have, she says, are that they are too credulous and too honest; 'for could we flatter as they can dissemble, and vse our wittes well, as they can their tongues ill, then neuer would any of them complaine of surfeiting.'[13]

There are several particular virtues of women which are praised by the defenders of the sex. In *The Royal Exchange* is found a list of four attributes which belong to women: beauty of face and proportion of body, chastity of mind, honesty of manners, and 'a familiar curiousness,' which probably means a well-known exquisiteness of character. As opposed to those detractors of women who would have them lustful, other writers single out

The housewife and the hunter

the chastity of women for praise, for chastity is the chief ornament of
women; and women should be heedful of this virtue, because there is
little difference between being unchaste and being thought unchaste. In
the *Entertainments at Sudeley*, Lyly's character Melibaeus asks why it is the
man who always does the wooing, and he receives from Nisa the answer
that it is because men are the least chaste and most amorous, while women
are indifferent to these foolish affections. Indeed, nature herself recognizes
that chastity is woman's chief virtue, and strives to protect it even after
death; both Vives and Heywood relate a fact they got from Pliny that
when a man drowns he floats belly up, while a drowned woman floats on
her stomach.[14]

A becoming virtue of women is their liberality. This virtue naturally lies more in women than in men because women are more easily moved to pity, mercy, and charity. They are constantly visiting hospitals and prisons to give aid to miserable men. And further, they have been responsible for the founding of many schools and hospitals.

The vice of frequently changing the mind, so often commented on in the dispraise of women, is defended by William Bercher as a virtue. Wise men have often praised the changing of the mind; a captain of a ship would be foolish not to change his mind when the tempestuous wind is against him; 'to stonde allwaies styff and obstynate in one opynyon is rather vyce then vertue.' Continuing in this vein, John Donne entitles his first paradox 'A Defence of Womens Inconstancy.' He agrees that women are inconstant in this sense, but argues that everything worth while changes – the heavens, the stars, the elements, etc. If your mistress were so constant that she never changed her smock, you would complain of her sluttishness. And if you have not a mistress and should get one, it will be only because she is inconstant and mutable. Donne suggests that a far better word would be *variety*, since the word *inconstancy* has been poisoned with too many slanders; variety makes the world delightful, 'and a Woman for that the most delightfull thing in this world.'

Women are also praised for certain other good qualities, such as prudence, justice, temperance, fortitude, humility, and modesty; many stories can be found which illustrate these. Thomas Carter, in his *Christian Common VVealth*, lists eight virtues which all women should claim, and Elizabethan parents had these in mind when they tried to actuate their hopes for their girl-children by naming them Faith, Hope, Prudence, Temperance, Charity, Constance, etc.[15]

Thus it is evident that the nature of woman is a problem which has many facets. This nature is clearly different from that of man; sometimes woman is praised for that difference and sometimes condemned. This appraisal of women from the Elizabethan point of view, so far leaves much out of account. We have heard of them as paragons of virtue and as the sources of all that is deplorable, but little of them as human beings or as partners with men, equally responsible with them for the conduct of affairs. Later we shall see that companionship is an ideal in marriage, and we presume that it was not infrequently achieved. What is apparent at this point is that there was an avid interest in the sex, as evidenced by the hundreds of books and pamphlets on the subject of women. And several explanations of this fact come to mind. Books are rarely issued about perfectly understood and readily accepted matters: everyone knew about men – what they were capable of doing, what they were supposed to do, and what they did; indeed the whole world was run by men. But women were still a mystery, or had convinced the men that they were, and their rapidly changing status made men wonder about them even more. They had suddenly moved out of the milieu in which they had been kept by the church for many centuries, and, as we shall see, had come crowding into the economic and intellectual spheres. It is no wonder, then, that men were questioning the true nature of this somewhat new woman of the Renaissance.

CHAPTER II

Education

And toward the education of your daughters,
I here bestow a simple instrument.

The Taming of the Shrew

Family religious instruction

An Elizabethan girl was brought up in far narrower surroundings than a modern one. She had little opportunity for the self expression advocated by our child psychologists. In 1598 Robert Cleaver writes that parents have four particular duties toward their children: to instruct them in the fear of the Lord; to rear them to love virtue and to hate vice; to be examples of godliness to them; and to keep them from idleness. Girls are to be under the strict authority of their fathers at all times, and must obey them implicitly, even in matters of marriage. For example, in Robert Greene's *Perimedes the Black-Smith*, Gradasso, the father, has decided to marry his daughter, Melissa, to Rosilius rather than to her choice, Bradamant. '*Melissa* noting with a secret mislike hir fathers motion, yet for feare durst not oppose hir selfe against his determination, but told him that as she was his Daughter, so she was bound by the law of nature to obeye him as hir Father, and his will should be to hir as a law, which by no means she dared to infringe.' Later, she tells Bradamant of her decision: 'Rather had I marrye *Rosilius*, and so wed my selfe to continuall discontent and repentance, then by being lose in my loues, and wanton in my thoughts disobeying my fathers commaund, to disparage mine honour and become a by-word throughout all *Aegipt*, for Ladyes honors are like white lawnes, which soone are stayned with euerye mole.' Even after marriage the daughter is still under the rule of her father to a large extent. If her parents die, she is ordinarily put in ward; but this state should not exist past the age of fourteen, and if it continues, she may at age sixteen have legal action against her guardian for the recovery of her inheritance. [1]

Although the father's authority is supreme, there is still a question concerning the best person to instruct a female child in the ways of life. If the parents are in modest circumstances, the mother will be the one who will naturally have the instruction of the child in her care. A very popular work on the education of a young gentlewoman was written by Giovanni Michele Bruto, and the English translation was published in 1598 with the Italian and French versions printed alongside 'for the better instruction of such as are desirous to studie those Tongues.' In the version as Englished by W.P., the author tells of a number of fathers who, in order to satisfy their pleasures, have given their daughters 'amorous and impudent' songs to memorize and repeat at gatherings. He states further: 'I am of opinion that there are not many fathers to whome ... men should commit the care of their children, and lesse number of mothers; because their wisdome and vertue is often ouercome...by the great affection they beare vnto them.' Such thinking had long been current in England, and the result of this reasoning was the system known as 'placing out,' by which the parents would place their children in the household of some acquaintance, or else the custom of employing a gentlewoman 'of grauitie and wisdome, of good conscience and behauior' to supply the place of the parents and teach the youngster the principles of Christian living and the manners of society. Lyly, on the other hand, insists that the entrusting of the care of the child to the custody of a 'hirelying' should be eschewed. Bruto goes on to say, however, that the gentlewoman should be selected with great care, always remembering that it will be impossible to find a perfect one: 'You must doe, as if you were to choose an excellent painter that should paint the Hall and Chambers of your house, to whome you shall shew the patterns of Albert Dure, Raphael Vrbin, Michel Angell, or Iules Romain (who in our time haue beene and alwayes shall be esteemed most excellent painters), not looking that hee should doe the like, but that seeing such notable patternes, shee should striue to follow them.' The gentlewoman who is to guide the child must also always show a pleasant and merry countenance, and must not be influenced by the petty annoyances which naturally fall to the lot of a governess. The chief duty of this gentlewoman is to rear the child from an early age in the delights of virtue and to instruct her in religion; perhaps the strongest influence in the life of the sixteenth century Englishwoman was religion, and its teachings naturally made her defer to the wishes of the father and later of the husband. The wise matron into whose hands the daughter is placed will teach her virtue, prudence, temperance, and generosity. Of these, virtue or chastity is the most important; it is 'the flower of manners, the honour of the body, the ornament and splendour of the feminine sexe, the integrity of the bloud, the faith of their kinde, and the proclaimer of the sincerety and candour of a faire soule.' And chastity is its own protection, since no man will steal that which he can neither keep nor restore again. [2]

Many practical suggestions are made for the guidance of the governess. First of all, the child should be kept away from all men, since our love naturally continues toward those with whom we have passed our youth. She should also be kept away from serving maids, since she will undoubtedly delight in their tales and prattlings. Vives would permit her to play with girls of her own age, if the mother or governess or some other female adult is present; but Bruto would deny even this, stating that she must be kept away from all children, even though they be of her own age and sex. Then too, the parents must never kiss or embrace their daughter, or permit others to do so. Vives acknowledges that in olden times kinsfolk were permitted a chaste kiss, but he feels that this type of greeting should be avoided; he says further that at the present time the kissing even of those who are not kin is quite common in England and France, but that he considers any kiss or embrace (even that of the parents) to be 'the foulest dede of all.' The young lady must never be permitted to give or receive gifts: 'A womā yᵗ gyueth a gyft, gyueth her selfe: A womā yᵗ taketh a gyfte, selleth her selfe. Therfore an honest womā shal nother gyue, nor take.'

From the foregoing injunctions, it is evident that the young lady is supposed to lead a Spartan existence as far as companionship, affection, and free intercourse with her own age group are concerned, although it is difficult to say just how far practice jibes with theory, here or elsewhere. At any rate, this severe attitude extends to the food and the furnishings provided: her bed should be clean, but hard; her diet must be simple and not delicate, consisting of common, unspiced food, not exotic; her only drink should be water. Her clothing too must be simple, but 'without fylthe and without spotte.' She must not envy her equals nor try to surpass them in costly apparel lest she be accused of pride and ambition, it being just as bad to be envied as to envy. Although some indulgent parents may smile at their daughter's childish escapades, they are warned that they must not condone any unseemly deed, either by words or by laughing. Neither the parents nor the governess should be too easy on the girl, and they must never permit her to be idle. Some authorities recommend that the rod must not be spared, and one of Lyly's characters (Lucilla) remembers the rigor and the whip of her parents. But Bruto insists that the young gentlewoman must never be beaten or even struck, calling this means of chastisement beastly to a 'franke and honest mind.' If there are some small faults which need disciplining, he continues, and if the governess feels forced to leave her ordinary course of speech (which he still feels should be unnecessary), the correction should be administered more with mildness than with rigor. [3]

It behooves the parents or the governess to teach the young lady civil behavior and good manners, because 'A well nurtured and mannerly maiden is as a polished stone of a Pallace, and the honour of hir fathers house.' Books of good manners had been popular since the beginning of printing; Jacques Legrand's *Book of Good Maners*, for example, was first published in 1487, and ran through six editions in twenty-eight years; Erasmus' *Booke of Good Maners for Chyldren* first appeared in English in 1532, with editions also in 1540, 1554, and 1578. Much later, William Fiston's *The Schoole of Good Manners* was first printed in 1609, and was issued again in 1629. These books taught in general that children should be courteous toward their equals, and kind and loving to all. More particularly, children must know how to greet those who approach them; they must learn to rise when their elders and their betters pass by them; they must stand while their betters are sitting; they must know how to curtsy 'in token of humilitie and subiection'; and they must always 'give place to their betters. They must be especially careful in their speech, knowing when to speak and when to be silent. Children must let their elders and betters speak first, and must never interrupt. They must use fair speech toward everyone, and in speaking of themselves they must be humble and not use 'sesquipedals.' Every Christian must be greeted lovingly by them, and they must indicate that they are thankful for all kindnesses shown to them. Such handbooks of conduct for children also provide specific information, such as how to take pie, how to blow the nose, etc. They contain such miscellaneous information as: 'It is good Manners to salute another when he neezeth, saying, *Christ helpe you*'; they also furnish guides to feminine behavior, such as: 'Nowe if the men syt a parte, and talke to gether beholdyng her, yet let not her thynke, that they talke of her, nor loke at her.' In Ben Jonson's *The Case is Altered*, Aurelia gives her sister some evidences of good breeding, ending in a *double entendre*:

> *I would I had some girles now to bring vp;*
> *O I could make a wench so vertuous,*
> *She should say grace to euery bit of meate,*
> *And gape no wider then a wafers thicknesse:*
> *And she should make French cursies, so most low,*
> *That euery touch should turne her ouer backward.* [4]

Moreover, the daughters of the family must be taught the practical pursuits which pertain to the running of the household. When a learned young lady was presented to King James I, and her knowledge of Latin, Greek, and Hebrew praised, James asked: 'But can she spin?' Similarly, in Lyly's *Euphues* Livia writes to Euphues: 'I haue wished oftentimes rather in the countrey to spinne, then in the courte to dawnce, and truely a distaff doth better become a mayden then a Lute, and fitter it is with the nedle to practise howe to liue, then with the pen to learne how to loue.' Writing in the same vein, Richard Mulcaster says: 'I thinke it, and knowe it, to be a principall commendation in a woman: to be able to gouerne and direct her household, to looke to her house and familie, to prouide and keepe necessaries, ... to know the force of her kitchen,' and states that these principles must be taught to the young woman. Specifically, the young woman of every class or station in society should learn cookery, not elaborate dishes, but the simple fare of the home; 'let no body lothe the name of the kechyn.' Some twenty books of cookery were printed before 1640, besides those containing recipes mixed in among other matter, and two works were given over to the art of preserving. The young woman must also be taught such household pursuits as spinning, carding, weaving, sewing, milking, butter-making, cheese-making, and so on. She must know all the processes of turning flax and wool into clothing; and she must be thoroughly acquainted with the dairy; she must know how to govern the house and how to dress meat and drink. Bruto gives a pretty clear picture of the extent of her knowledge when he writes:

Our gentlewoman shall learne not only all manner of fine needle-worke . . . but whatsoeuer belongeth to the distaffe, spindle, & weauing: which must not be thought vnfit for the honour and estate wherin she was borne . . . And which is more, to the end that being become a mistres, she shal looke into the duties and offices of domesticall seruants, and see how they sweepe and make cleane the chambers, hall, and other places: make ready dinner, dressing vp the cellar and buttery: and that she be not so proud that she shold disdaine to be present when they lay their bucks, & when they bake, but to be present at all houshold workes.

'Laying bucks' is a detail of washing clothes, in which the clothes are put into a vat to be steeped in lye. The young lady had at her disposal several books on sewing and carving, printed before 1600, such as five editions of *The Booke of Carving and Sewing*, five editions of *Murrels Two Books of Cookerie and Carving*, *A Booke of Curious Strange Inuentions, called the First Part of Needleworks*, *A Schole-house for the Needle*, etc. It is not surprising that no detailed mention is made of silk in these manuals, as it was just coming into use among the gentry. Nevertheless, there were a number of works on the culture of silkworms, and the overworked housewife might be found, in her spare time, reading such a book as Olivier de Serres' *The Perfect Use of Silkewormes* (1607). [5]

Writers in general are agreed as to the necessity of training young women in religion, duty to parents, good manners, and the care and supervision of the household. But all are not agreed concerning the advisability of educating young women in the arts and sciences or in general learning. Some authors compare a woman with education to a madman with a sword: he handles it not with reason, but only as the violent fits of illness

*Embroidery pattern for Queen Elizabeth's smock:
her favorite pattern of oak leaves and acorns*

Preparing and serving a meal

45

impel him. In a similar vein, Greene has one of his characters ask another: 'Many gentlewomen to please their louers which were Poets, left the socke and the needle, & tooke in hand pens and bookes: now tell mee if these strange Metamorphoses be not meere points of follie?' Bruto, on his part, argues that learning and the 'humane Arts' are bad for young ladies because they induce those evils which are fundamental in human beings even from their birth, for reading gives too many examples of corrupt manners and too many of pleasures and delights. He goes on to say that although those who favor education for women insist that the learning be all directed toward chastity and purity, yet once a woman knows how to read in English and foreign tongues nothing can prevent her from reading books of love, Ovid, Catullus, Homer, Virgil, and others, and learning all about the loves and adulteries of human beings and of the gods. He further argues that there are only two reasons for indulging in learning: for recreation, and for profit; but woman was given by nature to man to serve as a companion in his labors, and she should therefore be so busy in running the house that she has no time for recreation, not to speak of the fact that studies which bring pleasure can only be granted to women with the danger that they will have the beauty and glory of their delicate minds injured; and as far as the profit is concerned, they cannot profit by something which will do them harm, and they have no need for the profit anyway, since they are neither to govern estates or commonwealths nor to teach the laws of philosophy. [6] Bruto's reasoning seems to be of the circular variety; having wound himself up in a veritable cocoon of ratiocination, he remains a prisoner of his own tenuous theorizing.

Most of the writers, however, who touch on the subject of the education of women urge that formal education be included as essential. Ludovicus Vives, for example, begins his argument by stating that there are several advantages to be derived from education: some writings increase eloquence, some make the reader subtle and crafty, some merely delight and please, and some instruct and inform the mind in the knowledge of natural things. He believes especially that women should concentrate on the knowledge of natural things, but adds that such works as will make a person better are as necessary for women as for men. Further, women want to be educated because they are naturally discontented with their position in life and will try to better it by whatever means are proposed to them. Vives' attitude seems quite consistent: having recommended a severe upbringing, he permits a woman to have a mind and recommends the improvement of it. In urging that young maidens be educated, Richard Mulcaster gives four reasons: in the first place, it is the custom of the country for English girls to receive formal education beyond the elementary; then, it is the duty of parents to educate them; third, their natural abilities make them apt – 'their owne *towardnesse*, which God by nature would neuer haue giuen them, to remaine idle, or to small purpose'; and last, many good results have been obtained from educating girls, as can be seen from those that are well trained, particularly Queen Elizabeth. Mulcaster's statement that formal education for maids was customary is interesting, and indeed it would seem that early in the sixteenth century intellectual pursuits became very fashionable, even for the young middle-class women. Mrs. C. C. Stopes believes that higher education for women became respectable because of the influence of Queen Katharine of Aragon, the daughter of Isabella, whom she calls the most learned woman of her time. When Katharine came to England she met Margaret, Countess of Richmond and Derby, who founded lectureships, schools, and colleges, translated two French books, and commanded the translation of others. [7]

Other arguments for the formal education of women were also set forth by the advocates of such learning. First of all, the point that education makes women immoral is not borne out by the facts, says Vives, because all lewd and evil women are unlearned, and because he has never seen a woman of learning or knowledge who was unvirtuous. Furthermore, if the parents will do right by their daughters, they will educate them so that they will be attractive to marriageable young men. If the girl is not educated, she will talk with young men of nothing that is not either foolish or filthy. It is especially important, if the parents are not wealthy, that they shall make every effort to train the daughter in intellectual pursuits so that she may appeal to some young man of good station and then marry well. Another proposition is that a girl must be educated so that she may later fill the duties of a wife, and thus supply the defects she may find in her husband, as many have done to such good effect that their husbands have blushed at their own ignorance. When Sir Thomas Elyot's character Candidus asks Zenobia what good her knowledge of letters did her after her marriage, she replies that it taught her to please and delight her husband while he was alive; and after his death her learning helped her to manage her affairs, even to choosing a tutor for her children. Finally, learning is a preparation for motherhood: 'Is it either nothing or but some small thing, to haue our childrens mothers well furnished in minde, well strengthened in bodie? ... it is too much to weaken our owne selues by not strengthning their side.' [8]

Before Henry VIII came to the throne there were two common methods of female education: placing out, and the attendance at nunneries. The placing out system continued even into Elizabethan England, as is evidenced by the case of Margaret Dakins, later Lady Hoby, who received her education in the household of the Countess of Huntingdon. According to Fuller, convents taught the girls and maids to read and to perform household duties, and instructed them in a little Latin, music, and church history. During the Elizabethan age, girls were taught either at home or in the elementary school. In the latter half of the sixteenth century, schools, usually in the form of day schools for both sexes, were set up by religious refugees from the continent. In at least one instance, the establishment took on something of the nature of a boarding school. During this period little girls were admitted to some of the regular grammar schools. There were also the domestic schools of Sir Thomas More, Sir Anthony Cooke, and Henry Fitzalan, 12th Earl of Arundel. There was no precedent, however, for the attendance of young women in the universities. Greene's 'shee conny-catcher' indicates some of the training given by these elementary schools, as she accounts for her degraded condition; she received good schooling, but her parents spared the rod and made her wanton: 'after I grew to be six yeeres olde, [I] was sette to Schoole, where I profited so much that I writ and read excellently well, playd vpon the virginals, Lute

48

& Cytron, and could sing pricksong at the first sight; in so much, as by that time I was twelue yeeres olde, I was holden for the most faire, and best qualitied young girle in all that Countrey, but with this, bewailed of my wel-wishers, in that my parents suffered me to be so wanton.' [9]

If the teaching is to be done at home, great care should be given by the parents to the selection of the tutor. There seems to be some difference of opinion concerning the sex of the tutor; Bruto, apparently fearing the effect of the opposite sex upon a green girl, insists that the guide to learning must be a woman; Vives, on the other hand, believes that 'a woman shulde not teache leste whan she hath taken a false opinion & beleue of any thyng she spred hit in to the herars by the autorite of maistershyp and lyghtly bringe other in to the same errour'; but Mulcaster says that the teacher may be of either sex. If a male teacher is selected, it is true that some danger is run from the fact that the tutor may be a lover in disguise. Such a situation arises in *Euphues*, where Camilla pretends that Philautus is her tutor, and gives him a copy of Petrarch requesting him to construe her lesson for her when she really wants him to find there a letter; Philautus takes the Petrarch home that the interpretation may be the better. In *The Taming of the Shrew*, Petruchio presents Hortensio to Katherina as a tutor for Bianca, saying that he is 'cunning in music and the mathematics, to instruct her fully in those sciences, whereof I know she is not ignorant.' [10]

The training of the young woman who plans to study the humane arts and the sciences should be begun early and should continue at least until she is thirteen or fourteen years old; if the family can afford it, Mulcaster believes it is well to continue past this age and to add travel; he suggests that girls study drawing, writing, logic, rhetoric, philosophy, languages, and housewifery. Of the subjects usually included in polite learning, it is obvious that reading is the most important, since all other subjects are dependent upon it. In Jacques Du Bosc's *The Compleat Woman*, as Englished by N. N., can be found an interesting essay entitled 'Of Reading.'

It is certaine that *Reading, Conversation*, and *Musing*, are three the best and most excellent things of the world. By *Reading* wee treat with the dead; by *Conversation* with the living, and by *Musing*, with our selves. *Reading* enricheth the memory, *Conversation* polisheth the mind, and *Musing* frames the judgement.

But of these noble Occupations of the soule, to say here, which is the most important, wee must confesse that Reading setteth the other two aworke; and without it, Musing is fruitlesse, and Conversation unpleasant. It is even necessary for all *women*, what kinde of spirit soever they be of, while it affords a certaine lustre to such as have it in an eminent degree, and lessens much their *imperfection* who have it not so great; it makes the one tolerable, and the other admirable. And truly Reading shewes many things which reason by it selfe can never discover; it makes us have more soliditie in our thoughts, and more sweetnesse in our discourse; it finisheth that which nature but begins.

It is then in this comparable Schoole, where they learne what is excellent, for the entertainement of good companies, and for remedie of the evill; and where *womens* being tired with many importunat visitors who talke but of Hunting, and Hawking, and Warres of the *Netherlands*, finde a counterpoyson for that which persecutes them.

Certainly these are cogent arguments for instructing girls how to read, and are applicable today. Even Bruto finally comes around to admitting that women should not 'bee debarred from the commodity of reading and vnderstanding, because it is not onely commodious to a wise and vertuous woman, but a rich and precious ornament,' though he insists that they must never be permitted to read love poems and amorous tales, particularly mentioning the stories of Boccaccio. He goes on to tell us that when men read such works 'it is rather for the pleasantnesse of the stile, with the great varietie and harmonie of wordes magnificall, braue and singular that are therein, than for the matter,' while apparently the women are interested only in the amorous content. Vives suggests that the young student learn by heart the *Distichs* of Cato, the *Sentences* of Publilius Syrus, and the *Seven Sages of Greece* collected by Erasmus. He advises reading the Old Testament, the Gospels, the Acts and Epistles of the Apostles, St. Jerome, St. Cyprian, St. Augustine, Ambrose, Hilary, Gregory, Plato, Cicero, Seneca, and similar writers; also included are Anacreon, Sappho, Propertius, Lucan, Erasmus, and More's *Utopia*. As proper reading for the young female, Bruto offers the Bible and Plutarch, remarking that she shall read of and admire the women of the Troianes, Sabines, Phociennes, Argiues, and the virgines of Rome. And shall learne a singular example of pietie towardes her countrie, by Megistone, Aretaphile, Policrite, and of those godly women Iudith and Hester, and of loue towardes their husbands,... And to conclude... she shall find examples of all vertues, religion, holines, & loyaltie, in so many sacred virgins whose names are renoumed amōg vs, ... who both by shedding of their blood & loosing of their liues, induring most incredible and accustomed torments, haue giuen vnto the world most certaine testimonies of their faithes.

As for the kind of reading actually done by the women – one of Jonson's characters (Mrs. Polish) relates that Mrs. Steele read the Bible in the original languages; Imogen in *Cymbeline* read the tale of Tireus and Philomel; and Gabriel Harvey speaks of a female pamphleteer who has read Homer, Virgil, Plutarch, Agrippa, and the divine archetypes of Hebrew, Greek and Roman valor. [11]

Books which were to be completely eschewed by the daughter of the household are clearly set forth by Vives. As examples of the works he has in mind, he names *Amadis of Gaul, Florisando, Tirante the White, Tristan and Isolde, Celestina* ('yᵉ baude mother of noughtynes'), *Lancelot of the Lake, Paris and Vienna, Ponthus and Sidonia, Melusina, Flore and Blanchefleur, Lionell, Pyramus and Thisbe, Parthenopex of Blois, Ipomedon, Libeaus Desconus, Guy of Warwick, Bevis of Hampton, The Golden Ass,* and others. He also states that the unsavory conceits of Lucian, of Poggio, and of Aeneas Sylvius Piccolomini (Pope Pius II) are full of filth and viciousness. He particularly objects to books which are too romantically remote from reality, such as those in which one man kills twenty by himself, and another thirty; one receives a hundred wounds and is left for dead, only to be made whole and strong enough on the next day to kill two giants, and finally goes off loaded down with more gold, silver, and precious stones than a galley could carry. None of these books, however, can compare in their lasciviousness with Ovid's books of love, believes Vives, although Ovid is carried around in the hands and learned by heart; indeed, some schoolmasters not only teach Ovid to their scholars, but even make expositions and interpretations of the lines. [12]

Is it becaufe that thou art onely faire,
Oh no fuch gracefull lookes banifh difdaine,
How then, to feede my paffions with difpaire,
Feede on fweet loue, fo I be loued againe.
Well may thy publike fcorne, and outward pride,
Inward affections, and beft likings hide.

Breath but a gentle aire, and I fhall liue,
Smyle in a clowde, fo fhall my hopes renue,
One kind regard, and fecond feing giue,
One rifing Morne, and my blacke woes fubdue.
If not, yet looke vpon the friendly Sunne,
That by his beames, my beames to thine may runne.

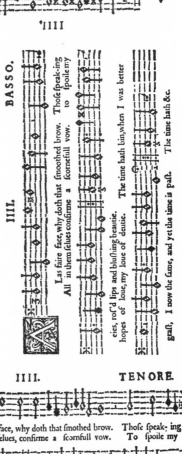

An opening from Francis Pilkington's *The First Booke of Songs or Ayres* (1605), showing arrangement for four persons, grouped around the book, to sing from one copy

53

An accomplishment which the Elizabethans much admired in their females was singing and the playing of musical instruments. That our Elizabethan ancestors loved music is attested by the large number of works dealing with some branch of music. Robert Burton indicates the efficacy of music in love, and laments the fact that although young maids work hard to accomplish the musical arts, yet they are inclined to let them drop when they are married. Anthony Gibson goes so far as to say that a woman's voice is a natural harmony. That most men consider it a great ornament for a woman to sing and play on divers instruments is admitted by Bruto, and he will permit women to practise music as long as they use their ability to good and honest intent, saying that music deserves a place among the rest of the liberal arts. The trouble is, he continues, that music is a kind of secret bait that leads to great mischief. He thinks that music is all right for men, serving as a recreation for those who are wearied with important affairs, but argues that since music opens the gate to many vices, it is more to be avoided by women, because the danger is insidious in its apparent innocence. He concludes by asking: 'should wee then be so well persuaded of a weake and delicate young gentlewoman, tenderly bred vp, that as not to feare, that shee not only hearing but learning so pleasant an art, should not in time become licencious, delicate, and effeminate?' [13]

The art of conversation, as we have seen, is a highly praised accomplishment for a woman to have. Even Bruto believes that 'speaking the Latine tongue with a sweet and pleasant stile' is an attainment which a young lady should develop, as well as the proper speaking of her own language. Her speech should be simple and not ornate, warns Vives, since speech of this latter sort indicates the vanity of the mind. Du Bosc wants women to appear intelligent in conversation, but is afraid that most of them who have anything to say are tedious and irksome, probably because 'their spirit hath not heat enough, to digest what reading giveth them; ... They are such slaves to their memory, as almost they have not the use of their judgment.' Most important of all is that a woman recognize her own humor, reform it if ill and polish it if good. An interesting and enlightening (though somewhat tongue-in-cheek) passage, which summarizes the

accomplishments of an educated woman, may be found in Jonson's
Volpone as Lady Politic Would-be discusses the subject with Volpone; she
begins the matter, modestly saying:

> *I have a little studied physic; but now*
> *I'm all for music, save, i' the forenoons,*
> *An hour or two for painting. I would have*
> *A lady, indeed, t' have all letters and arts,*
> *Be able to discourse, to write, to paint,*
> *But principal, as Plato holds, your music*
> *(And so does wise Pythagoras, I take it)*
> *Is your true rapture: when there is concent*
> *In face, in voice, and clothes: and is, indeed,*
> *Our sex's chiefest ornament.*

Volpone replies that a poet who is as knowing and as ancient as Plato has
said that silence is the greatest female grace; and the Lady angrily retorts:

> *Which o' your poets? Petrarch, or Tasso, or Dante?*
> *Guarini? Ariosto? Aretine?*
> *Cieco di Hadria? I have read them all . . . .*
> *Here's Pastor Fido –. . . . All our English writers,*
> *I mean such as are happy in th' Italian,*
> *Will deign to steal out of this author, mainly;*
> *Almost as much as from Montagnié:*
> *He has so modern and facile a vein,*
> *Fitting the time, and catching the court-ear!*
> *Your Petrarch is more passionate, yet he,*
> *In days of sonnetting, trusted 'em with much:*
> *Dante is hard, and few can understand him.*
> *But for a desperate wit, there's Aretine;*
> *Only his pictures are a little obscene –* [14]

Perhaps the proof of the efficacy of formal education for women is to
find out what they have done with it. Elizabethan writers in favor of such
education give examples both from ancient and from modern life. Sappho
of course is mentioned, as are the Queen of Sheba, the daughter of
Pythagoras, Arreta the mother of Aristippus, Corinna the poet, Cornelia
the wife of Scipio Africanus, Diorus, Marcella, Tyanea, Istrina the mother

of Aripithis, and Cornelia the mother of Gracchus. The old story even crops up of the woman who became a pope; according to one writer, Pope Joan was really a Dutch woman named Gilberta who went in men's apparel to Athens with an English monk of the Abbey Fulda, later went to Rome, and still later became pope. Her disguise was discovered when, having been got with child by 'some of hir Cardinalls,' she fell in labor while in a procession and disgraced everyone. The authorities for this ridiculous story, surely one of the silliest ever told, are given as follows: Platina, *Life of the Popes;* Sabellicus, book I; Eneardus, book IX; Raphael Voletarenus, book XXII; Bergomenseus, book XI; and Boccaccio.[15]

During the Elizabethan age cultural interests became quite fashionable for women, so that the educated woman became a kind of ideal, and the principles of her education were those of the humanistic scholars. Later, these principles were modified by the schools of refugees from the continent, mentioned earlier in this chapter, and by the influence of the Puritans; the result was that education became more widely spread and a good bit more practical. The position of women was raised by the attitude toward marriage found in the German Reformers, who began the rehabilitation of women after their degradation at the hands of the church. But the status of women was even more improved by Queen Elizabeth, who had the support of the Protestants, who ruled her country with masterful command, and who was looked upon as a paragon of learning. A contemporary work speaks of her as knowing Latin, Greek, Hebrew, French, Dutch, Spanish, and Italian; and Julius Caesar Scaliger said she was better educated than any of the great men of her time. She received lessons, mainly in Latin, from Edward's tutor, Sir John Cheke; and Roger Ascham taught her such Greek literature as the orations of Isocrates, the tragedies of Sophocles, the crown orations of Demosthenes and Æschines. By the time she was twelve years of age, Elizabeth had studied French, Spanish, Italian, Flemish, mathematics, astronomy, politics, history, geography, and architecture; later she studied other languages, rhetoric, philosophy, and divinity. Nor was she alone in the field as a feminine scholar. Katharine of Aragon began the fashion of the English bluestocking, and had Vives' *Instruction of a Christian Woman* dedicated to her; her daughter, Mary Tudor, was instructed in Latin by Dr. Linacre, an early humanist. Princess Mary knew Latin, French, and Spanish, and had as her educational guide Ludovicus Vives, who lectured at Oxford in 1523, and she presumably read some of the works which he advised for women; she was also interested in botany and in dialing, could dance, play cards, and play the virginals; she acted in plays of Terence and in the court masques. Sir Anthony Cooke, one of the learned tutors of Edward VI, gave his daughters a remarkably liberal education, equal to that which men received; it consisted, among other studies, of Greek, Latin, Hebrew, Italian, and French. These young ladies were the wonders of the age, and were especially singled out for praise by William Bercher in his *Nobylytye off Wymen*; they were Mildred Cooke Cecil, Anne Cooke Bacon, Katherine Cooke Killigrew, and Elizabeth Cooke Hoby Russell; Thomas Lodge dedicated his *A Margarite of America* to this last daughter, calling her the English Sappho, and Geoffrey Fenton dedicated his *Monophylo* to her. Bercher also speaks of the Howard sisters, particularly Jane, who knew Greek and Latin and could compose verses; of Jane, the daughter of the Duke of Somerset; and of Jane and Mary, the two daughters of the Earl of Arundel. John Aylmer, who replied to John Knox's work against female rulers, and who later became Bishop of London, was the guide to Lady Jane Grey's education; she knew Latin, Greek, Hebrew, Arabic, Chaldean(?), French, and Italian, and studied philosophy; she also played instrumental music and was noted for her sewing. Marie Stuart knew Greek, Latin, and French, and the eminent Ronsard urged her to try her hand at poetry; she played several instruments, danced well, and did not neglect her needlework. Mary Arundel translated wise sayings from the Greek and Latin; Joanna Lumley translated the Greek of Isocrates' *Archidamus* into Latin; while Elizabeth Fane wrote psalms and pious meditations. Sir Thomas More's daughter, Margaret Roper, was educated in the liberal arts and sciences, Greek, and Latin, as were her sisters, Elizabeth and Cecelia. Other names which come to mind as examples of well-educated women are Mary Sidney, Margaret How Ascham, Jane

Countess of Westmorland and daughter of John Fox, Dorothy Leigh, Lord Maltravers' daughters Mary and Jane, Elizabeth Jane Weston, Arabella Stuart Seymour, Esther Inglis, Catherine Tishem, and Elizabeth Legge.

The education of a young lady under the Stuarts is illustrated by Anne, Lady Halkett, who records in her *Autobiography* that her mother employed tutors for her in writing, French, playing on the lute and virginals, needlework, and so on. In addition she and her sister 'were instructed never to neglect to begin and end the day with prayer, and orderly every morning to read the Bible, and ever to keep the church as often as there was occasion to meet there, either for prayers or preaching.' [16]

Nor were the women of the age content to keep their learning hid away from public view. Over fifty women wrote some eighty-five compositions during the years from 1524 to 1640. Fifty-eight of these books were printed separately, while the others appeared in anthologies, liturgies, and other collections. The nature of these printed pieces is rather interesting: they include three translations of non-religious works, sixteen translations of religious works, thirty original non-religious compositions, and thirty-six original religious compositions. It would seem, therefore, that the male authors of antifeminist literature can find little here to support their views that women are frivolous and inclined toward the gayer side of life, since more than sixty percent of their printed efforts are given over to religious subjects. The other compositions are such works as Elizabeth Carew's *The Tragedie of Mariam*, Jane Anger's *Protection for Women*, Anne Dowriche's *The French Historie*, Christine Du Castel's *Boke of the Cyte of Ladyes*, Mary Fage's *Fames Roule*, and Rachel Speght's *A Mouzell for Melastomus*, this last being one of the replies to Joseph Swetnam's malevolent attack on women. [17]

CHAPTER III

The choice of a wife

Hearing thy mildness praised in every town,
Thy virtues spoke of, and thy beauty sounded,
Yet not so deeply as to thee belongs,
Myself am mov'd to woo thee for my wife.

The Taming of the Shrew

Courtship

Since the married life is accepted as the one most conducive to happiness and to the living of a godly and productive life, the choice of a spouse is one of the most important decisions which the Elizabethan male has to make. Sir Thomas Overbury argues that although he had little part in creating the man he is, yet he can improve himself through posterity by the careful choice of a wife:

> Myselfe *I cannot chuse*, my wife *I may.*
> And in the choise of Her, *it much doth lye,*
> To mend my self in my posterity.

Those authors who give advice on the selection of a wife begin by pointing out that the regret of having married is not only an indecent thought, but is just as surely a foolish one. And since married life can be hell, it behooves the young man to exert great effort in finding the one who will be 'more then a friend, lesse then trouble: an equall with him in the yoke. Calamities and troubles shee shares alike, nothing pleaseth her that doth not him. She is relative in all; and hee without her, but halfe himselfe. Shee is his absent hands, eyes, eares, and mouth.' There is no greater joy that a man can have than a loving, kind, and honest wife.[1] Of course it is obviously true that men often fail in finding a good wife, and Thomas Nashe suggests that this failure is due to the small field of choice when men are restricted to the good women only, the implication being that most women are bad.

Prospective husbands are warned to go slowly in choosing their mates, therefore. If it is necessary to eat a bushel of salt with a man before selecting him as a friend, how much more care must be exerted in choosing one's second self. Before even setting foot out of doors to see the young lady, the young man should diligently inquire of her reputation – whether or not she wears her own hair, etc. – 'for by the Market-folke thou shalt heare how the market goeth.' Nor should he believe everything he sees; just as

> *With womens teares be not thou mov'd at all,*
> *For as they please they keep or let them fall,*

so too some women are like painted cloth in showing the good side to prospective husbands, but having another side which is at first not evident. The careful young man should make all diligent inquiry, not however taking his wife merely upon the recommendation of others. [2]

The matter of good parentage in a prospective mate looms large; Elizabethans were frank in their esteem of good breeding, and equally frank in appraising worldly goods. Wealth and culture vie for first place in the eyes of a man searching for a wife; good parentage is essential, since this parentage will be passed on to the children. What a woman ought to be, because of her heritage, however, does not always follow; her own attributes are what count in a happy marriage. Of course, the financial position of the parent comes into the discussion. Richard Brathwait reasons that a good dowry will not make a good wife any worse, while it will certainly make a poor one more palatable; the man who makes a poor bargain is that one who gets neither a good wife nor a good dowry. Swetnam agrees with him, in pointing out that a man who marries a wife for good looks is likely to treat her like 'kitchinstuff,' while if a wife brings a good dowry the husband will always find something in his wife to be in love with. And anyway, asks a writer, with customary waggery, how can a man be kept in his usual style of elegance if his wife bring not a good dowry? Robert Burton suggests that the mother of the young man is likely to consider that the most important virtue of the chosen girl should be a good ancestry, while the father respects only wealth, thinking by that means to recover the fortune he has lost by folly and indiscretion. Stating that such is the custom of the times, Alexander Niccholes puts the seal of society's approval on the requirement that the girl to be chosen must always have money: 'It is a fashion much in vse in these times to choose wiues as Chapmen sell their wares, with *Quantum dabitis?* what is the most you will giue? and if their parents, or guardians shall reply their vertues are their portions, and others haue they none, let them be as dutifull as *Sara*, as vertuous as *Anna*, as obedient as the Virgine *Mary*; . . . these may be adiuncts or good additions, but money must be the principall, of all that marry.' This insistence on wealth, think many writers, is the cause for the failure of many marriages, since the wife who brings wealth to the union will be full of pride and will feel that the husband must give her first place and be forbearing to her to such an extent that her obnoxious actions will cause the husband to seek strange women. [3]

Next in importance in the prospective wife is usually her degree of education. The education she has received should enable her to talk about all kinds of places, persons, and fashions, and should cause her to associate only with those who will improve her knowledge of and her practice of goodness; she will then, of course, be well stored with wit or intelligence, although not necessarily 'learned by much Art.' Nor should the Benedick forget that 'wit in a woman is like Oyle in the flame, which either kindleth to great virtue, or extreme vanity.' [4]

In general, the wife should be the same age as the husband, or rather close to it. A character in *The Flower of Friendshippe* insists that the difference in ages should never be more than four or five years. Some writers disregard the age of the husband, but say that the wife should always be young, not merely because a young woman is more likely to bear children, but also because it is easier to teach a young woman the ways of the husband. Others, however, condemn parents who marry twenty-year-old girls to men who are sixty or older. In *Euphues*, on the other hand, Camilla writes to Philautus that the prospective bride should certainly not be too young: 'Corne is not to be gathered in the budde, but in the eare, nor fruite to be pulled from the tree when it is greene, but when it is mellow, . . . nor young Ladies to be sued vnto, that are fitter for a rodde then a husbande, and meeter to beare blowes then children.' The author of *A Discourse of the Married and Single Life* takes a somewhat cynical point of view as he says that it really makes little difference what the age of the bride is: if she is young she will be importunate to have fancy clothes, and if she is old her constant giving of advice will be simply intolerable. [5]

The couple about to be married should further be of the same status in society. Those of high degree should never marry those of low degree; otherwise the peace of marriage will be disturbed at the start. Pierce Penilesse learnedly relates that in Denmark 'it is death... for anie but a husbandman to marry a husbandmans daughter, or a Gentlemans childe to ioyne with any but the sonne of a Gentleman,' and implies that such a regulation would be advisable in England. Alexander Niccholes even goes so far as to say that merchants and mariners should choose a wife phlegmatic in humor as more in keeping with the cold and moist condition of their employment. The name character in Geoffrey Fenton's *Monophylo*, however, puts in an objection that the approval of society is not always on the side of reason, arguing that 'if I chance to settle in affection with a mayde of base condition, and by a tollerable suggestion of nature, proceede with hir in holye maryage, shall I not runne into a popular obloquie, as proclayming in me an act and example of wilfull folly? . . . But if in a greedie desire of golde and transitorie drosse, I practise a Ladie of equall place and value to my selfe, then that blind ignoraunce commendes and congratulates with me, as esteeming that for my benefite, which in deede conuertes to my extreme displeasure.'

It is also advisable and even imperative, believe many writers, that the married couple be of the same religion; for, as Nashe's Pasquill puts it, you cannot have much love and sympathy for a spouse whom you believe to be damned. [6]

A widow in the Elizabethan age could scarcely hope to marry, if we are to believe most writers on the subject, for it is the practically unanimous opinion that a widow should be immediately eliminated from any list of acceptable mates. And this conclusion is a logical one from the premise that a man should marry a young girl and train her up in his ways, since a widow has been trained to the conditions of another man. 'If thy wife be a widdow, shee will alwaies be either praising or praying for her first husband.' Swetnam believes that a widow will be the cause of a thousand woes, and *The Court of Good Counsell* condemns second marriages as 'cole-worts twice sodden.' Alexander Niccholes has recourse to the *double entendre* in his statement: 'He that marryeth a Widdow, hath but a reuersion in taile.' On the other hand, we know that marriages to widows were regularly contracted, and indeed Cornelius Agrippa argues that there is no impediment to second marriages, even though the objection is supposed to go back to Joseph, the husband of Mary. In a curious work, entitled

64

Elizabethan view of Oriental courtship

The Parliament of Women. With the merry Lawes by them newly enacted. To live in more Ease, Pompe, Pride, and wantonnesse: but especially that they might have superiority over their husbands: with a new way found out by them to cure any old or new Cuckolds, and how both parties may recover their credit and honesty againe, the women enact one law which proclaims that old bachelors must marry widows who have no means of support, and conversely that rich widows must marry younger sons who have no income. [7]

Little is said about romantic love in connection with marriage. Young Elizabethans are constrained by a severe sense of duty, of obligations to God and to His representatives in their lives – their parents. While romantic love certainly agitates the hearts of youths and maidens, it does not provide the free passage to marriage which we take for granted; indeed it is hardly considered, at least by those actively planning a 'sensible' marriage. Of course, there must be love after marriage, because the wife owes love to her husband, but the emphasis here is upon duty. It is somewhat surprising, therefore, to find William Gouge recommending that a young man should choose for his wife someone he loves. On the other hand, such an eminent authority as Vives believes that before marriage, love with the intended bride is ill advised, and he says: 'I would not counsel yᵉ to mary her, wᵗ whome thou hast bene in amors withal, whom thou flatterdest, whome thou didst serue, whom thou calledst thy hart, thy life, thy maistres, thy light, thy eyes, wᵗ other suche wordes as foolishe loue doth perswade.' [8]

Whether or not the prospective bride should be beautiful is indeed a matter of some speculation for the Elizabethans, but there is no unanimity. The Reverend Stephen Geree states that 'next to *birth* that which commends a woman is *Beauty*, wherewith men are much taken,' but he hastily goes on to say that the beauty of holiness is the best beauty. Brathwait puts beauty first in his list of requisites; Tasso lists it second. In speaking of the beauty of women, Daniel Tuvil quotes the following stanza from *The Faerie Queene*:

> *Nought vnder heauen so strongly doth allure*
> *The sense of man, and all his minde possesse,*
> *As beauties louely baite, that doth procure*
> *Great warriors oft their rigor to represse,*
> *And mighty hands forget their manlinesse,*
> *Drawn with the power of an hart-robbing eie,*
> *And wrapt in fetters of a golden tresse,*
> *That can with melting pleasance mollifie*
> *Their hardned harts, enur'd to blood & cruelty.*

But perhaps it is supererogation even to mention this subject, since men have always expected beauty in their loved ones, at least in their own eyes. Imogen is considered beautiful by all who see her; so are Desdemona, Juliet, and innumerable others.

Beauty, however, can be somewhat onerous in a wife. Elizabeth

Grymeston gives the proverb: 'A faire woman is a paradise to the eie, a purgatorie to the purse, and a hell to the soule,' while Niccholes speaks disparagingly of those who choose their wives for lust, looking no further than the carnal beauty which may be observed in outward shape and lineaments, gait, gesture, countenance, and behavior, and he then quotes the Italian proverb:

> *Whose horse is white, and wife is faire,*
> *His head is neuer voide of care.*

We learn elsewhere of one cause of this care; it is that a beautiful woman will always be a proud one, since pride accompanies beauty as the shadow does the body. Yet an ugly woman should equally be avoided since she will cause the husband to seek wives of other men, 'with danger of life, honour and soule.' Vives believes in the mean as the best: 'It is a greuous thyng to suffer her that is foule, and a harde thynge to kepe her that is fayre. And therfore they counseyled men to take those, which were neyther to fayre nor yet to foule. And to choose those that were of the meane sorte.' Another writer, Anthony Gibson, argues that even though beauty may be preferred, there is no reason why it must be blond beauty, and that no reasonable person can say that 'beauty hath any perticuler colour, a proportion definite, or a grace imaginary: for nature... hath made an Ethiopian or Moore perfectly blacke, to be as faire as the whitest in our Europe.' He believes that a woman who can write to her lover as follows, must be judged most fair:

> *My Loue, I am a little blacke,*
> *But say that I were much more black.*
> *Mine eyes browne, my face like browne,*
> *Admit my necke and brests more browne.*
> *My haire and skin all black to be,*
> *Sauing my teeth of Iuory:*
> *Inuironed with a curroll fence,*
> *Which breaths more sweet then frankinsence ...*
> *Must I for this my louely browne,*
> *Haue my Loue on me to frowne?*

Are not my eyes as piercing still,
And able Marble hearts to kill?
Or can my Loue be ere the lesse,
My minde being made of gentlenesse?

The poem concludes by saying that at night you cannot tell the difference between blonde and brunette anyway! [9]

The young man in search of a wife must particularly search for virtue. 'All loue is a certeyne affection to y^t thing, that is goodly & fayre, there is nothing more goodly then virtue, the which yf a man might behold & see with his bodely eyes vnto it self, but it is seene with the inwarde eye of the mind, and draweth those that beholdeth it to beneuolence, & to embrace and loue it.' In Greene's *Francescos Fortunes*, Ragadon counsels himself thus: 'a woman that is faire and vertuous maketh her husband a ioyfull man; and whether he be rich or poore, yet alwaies he may haue a ioyfull heart.' Thus it behooves all women to be especially careful to be modest in appearance and in manners. Since a book is often censured by what the title promises, an honest heart is of little avail in the avoidance of the world's censure, if immodest looks first strike the eye. As Herodotus says, when a woman puts off the garment of shamefastness, she walks naked. 'How charie ought all Virgins to be? how carefull and cautelous in all . . . deportments? to be wary in their words, and weighty in their writings, that their countenances bewray no lightnesse, their eyes no loose-nesse: that their carriages be not complementall, but courteous: their gestures not grosse, but gracious: their language fashionable, not frivolous: and to the name of Virgin still remember to add that best becomming attribute and character, Vertue.' Barnaby Rich laments the fact that the age has departed when bashful modesty in a virtuous breast was the best lure a woman could have. One practical guide to the reputation of a woman is to notice if men speak often of her, for 'the most honest woman is least spoken of,' or as Tuvil versifies Thucydides:

Those of women still are counted best,
Of whom in praise or dispraise mē speak least.

Rich, indeed, observes that a virtuous woman is unlikely to have anyone speak

Elaborate gown with trunk sleeves

even in her favor, unless it be a member of her immediate family: 'I haue seldome seene an honest woman to haue many frinds that will take hir part, that will speake for her, that will quarrell for her, that will fight for hir; there be not many that wil bestow giftes on her, that will lend her mony, that will send in daily prouision of capons, conies, partriges, pigeons, wine, sugar, spice, and send other acates, both costly and dainty: you shall not see an honest woman supported, vnlesse by a father, a brother, or by a husband.' [10]

The Elizabethans recognize a vice proverbially belonging to women, when they warn against the woman who talks too much. Since 'silence becommeth a woman,' a man 'should rather chuse a wife by his eares then by his eyes.' Thomas Carter tells of the suffering that too much talking can bring to the husband: 'The apostle warneth them not to be false accusers, and this toucheth busie bodies of our time, which wil goe pratling to carrie newes... so that many times the men smart for the womens tongues and neighbors liue at great varience one with another which otherwise would liue in loue and peace together.' A rattling tongue is often characteristic of a shrewish wife; such a woman is called a scold, aptly enough. Quiet speech, on the other hand, indicates a good disposition. A proper wife, therefore, will let her speech be simple, since affected and ornate speech shows the vanity of the mind. [11]

Such a consideration serves to introduce another vice which seems to be peculiar to the women, if our authorities can be trusted: namely, pride. Never choose for a wife a woman who is proud; she is always a care to her husband and is unable to love effectually because she is always suspicious. A proud woman is characterized thus by Nicholas Breton:

> She that can haue her breakefast in her bed,
> And sit at dinner like a maiden Bride,
> And all the morning learne to dresse her head,
> And after dinner, how her eye to guide,
> To shewe her selfe to be the childe of pride,
>   God, in his mercy, may do much to saue her:
>   But what a case were he in that should haue her!

70

Perhaps the best description of a proud woman is that which is given in Arthur Dent's *The Plaine Mans Path-way to Heauen:*

Yet we see how proud many, especially women, be of such bables... for when they haue spent a good part of the day tricking and trimming, pricking and pinning, pranking and pouncing, girding and lacing, and brauing vp themselues in most exquisite manner, then out they come into the streetes, with their Pedlers shop about their backe, and carrie their crests very high, taking them selues to bee little Angels: or at least, somewhat more then other women; whereupon they do so exceedingly swell with pride, that it is to be feared, they will burst with it as they walke in the streetes. And truly we may thinke the very stones in the street, and the beames in the houses do quake... at their monstrous, intolerable, and excessive pride: for it seemeth that they are altogether a lumpe of pride, a masse of pride, euen altogether made of pride, and nothing else but pride, pride.

A well reared young woman, on the other hand, will wear simple attire, and will eschew foreign fashions and all fantastic dress. [12]

The perfect wife should be wise and of a serious turn of mind. In choosing her, the young man should 'looke not upon the feature of the body, but search into the fancies of the mind; and take her not for her outward person, but her inward perfection.' And this is the accepted point of view; but Gunophilus, in Lyly's *The Woman in the Moone*, believes that the best wife is not a grave one: 'Grauity in a woman is like to a gray beard vpon a breaching boies chinne, which a good Scholemaister would cause to be clipt, and the wise husband to be avoyded.' Not many, however, can be found to agree with him. This seriousness in a woman will most likely find its expression in religion. The Elizabethans were a very religious people, and surely the wife would be expected to conform in these matters. William Whately cautions the young man in search of a wife to choose not the finest body, sweetest face, largest dowry, or most exalted position, 'but the holiest heart, the richest soule, the beautifullest spirit.' Richard Brathwait concurs, and says that a woman should not spend time in eyeing herself in a mirror, but rather in examining 'the glasse of her life.' Whether or not she should be a Puritan, naturally depends upon who is writing the advice. In Jonson's *Bartholomew Fair*, Quarlous paints for Win-wife the terrors of marrying into a Puritan family, and asks if Win-wife could 'brooke the noise made, in a question of *Predestination*, by the good labourers and paineful eaters, assembled together, put to 'hem by the Matron, your Spouse; who moderates with a cup of wine, euer and anone, and a Sentence out of *Knoxe* between.' But Thomas Carter, naturally, sees nothing wrong with such a course: 'if there bee any amongest you which maketh conscience of these things, and so striue to liue according as they ought to doe, are not such disdayned and scorned of the rest, & brāded by you with the name of Puritane & holy sister? but where is your purity and holinesse while you thus deride others in their well doing?' [13]

Somewhat in the nature of a summary, Robert Cleaver gives a list of six feminine characteristics which the young man of 1598 should consider highly desirable in the woman of his choice; since the same list was presented by Matthew Griffith thirty-five years later, perhaps it will be worth while to repeat these six items. First comes *the report*, or the reputation of the young woman; second, *the look* or outward appearance; third, *the talk* – what she talks about, how she expresses herself, and whether she knows when to keep silence; fourth, her *apparel;* fifth, *company*, or the people with whom she associates; and sixth, her *education.* [14]

Once the young man has selected the girl of his dreams, the next problem is how to woo her. First of all he should do it himself and not trust his case to an ambassador. Then, if the young man is a courtier, he will probably kiss her pumps, hold the cloth for her, and praise her cleverness, as Fastidius Briske does in *Every Man Out of His Humour.* Sybilla, in *Sapho and Phao*, advises Phao to 'write, and persist in writing; they read more then is written to them, & write lesse then they thinke. In conceit studie to be pleasaunt, in attire braue, but not too curious; when she smileth, laugh outright; if rise, stand vp; if sit, lye downe. Loose al thy time to keepe time with her.' Of course the wooing will depend in large part upon the kind of woman she is. In Greene's *Planetomachia*, Cupid suggests that if the lady is beautiful, she will be won with praises, if coy – with prayers, if proud – with gifts, if covetous – with promises; and no matter how self-willed she may be, or cruel, or wilfully froward, she will be caught by one of these lures. If we are to take Barnaby Rich's word for it, the wooing of a woman (apparently a lady of the court) can become pretty complicated:

If his braine be not too barren, he must indite louing lines, and amorous verses in the praise of his mistresse: He must borrow colours from Lillies, and Red Roses, to beautifie her cheekes, her teeth must be of Pearle, her breath Balme, a *Pallas* for her wit, a *Venus* for her chastitie, her tongue the tongue of an Adder, her taile, worse then the taile of a serpent; he must lerne pretilie to lispe out, sweete Mistresse, kinde Mistresse, he must kisse her prettie hand, the handle of her fanne, her Nosegay, the nether skirt of her Petticote, he must play with her little Puppie, he must adore the point of her Busk, the seate that she sits on, the ground that she treads on, yea the verie strings that serues to tie her shooes. [15]

But let us look at the other side of the picture. Is the feminine counterpart not to have an opportunity of some sort to survey the field? And when she does survey it, what virtues should she seek for in the husband-to-be? Surely she is expected to be as particular as possible in her choice; and as she is the subject of thousands of pages of speculation, her importance is undeniable. In *Bartholomew Fair* Grace Welborne states unequivocally that she must have a husband she can love. A mother in one of Greene's works says that a son-in-law should be of proper age, from a similar status in society, handsome enough to please the eye of her daughter, have enough virtues to please both herself and her daughter, and enough money to support them. The improvident Greene clearly had this last requirement on his mind, since a rich merchant in *Greenes Never Too Late* tells his daughter that to marry a man who cannot maintain her is to buy a dram of pleasure with a pound of sorrow. Perhaps the most complete advice for the young lady is supplied by Leon Baptista Alberti. According to him, she should choose a man neither too young nor 'ouer-wearied with yeares'; but if one or the other must be chosen, let it be the older man, since young men are sudden, rash, indiscreet, and suspicious. He cautions against choosing one who is too rich, too handsome, too negligent, too base, too holy, too important, too fortunate, or too unfortunate: 'As little wisedome is it, to loue such as are slothfull, dull spirited and couragelesse, who through want of better wit or exercise, make an arte or occupation of their loue, gadding abroad with frizled lockes, embroidered garments, & other open marks of their lightnesse, onely to procure their own scorne and derision.'

He particularly recommends a man who is learned, wise, modest, and virtuous. The writer who uses the pseudonym of Esther Sowernam is perhaps a little more practical when she advises the young girl to get the name on the dotted line, and make the man show the ring: 'Some [men] will pretend marriage, another offer continuall maintenance, but when they haue obtained their purpose, what shall a woman finde, iust that which is her euerlasting shame and griefe, she hath made her selfe the vnhappie subiect to a lustfull bodie and the shamefull stall of a lasciuious tongue.' [16]

Having been informed of what kind of man to choose, however, the young lady must be further instructed how to take her part in the courtship. The helpful Alberti observes that nothing can be counted on to prevail sooner upon the reluctant male than 'a sweete carriage of countenance, as also a comely, discreete, and modest presence: one piercing looke heates and enkindles the dullest desire, one modest amorous glaunce awakens sleepie thoughts, fetcheth fire from the flint, and makes the hart as yeelding, as your own can craue enioying.' He goes on to advise that one lover at a time should be the rule; and concludes that golden jewelry, pearls, periwigs, and cosmetics will not be nearly as effective as 'faire & comely demeanour, humanitie, gentlenesse and modestie.' One who signs himself Erastophil believes that it is wise to play hard-to-get, and philosophizes about the subject thus: 'Were there no *difficulty* in the *obtaining*, there would be no *pleasure* in the *injoyment*, for it is *that* which *renders* the *fruition* so much the *sweeter*, so *miserable* is our *Lot* here, that we cannot *relish* the least *contentment*, unlesse it be *seasoned* with the *bitternesse* and *acerbity* of *misery*.' Another stratagem is suggested in *Loves Pilgrimage;* Philippo is weary of his feminine friends who have anticipated such Victorian ladies as Sweet Alice, who fainted away at a frown, in that fainting has become a religion with them:

> You do pick
> *Your time to faint when some body is by: . . .*
> *Inform me but of one that has been found*
> *Dead in her private chamber by her self,*
> *Where sickness would no more forbear, than here*
> *And I will quit the rest for her.*

Of course there is no guarantee that any or all of these methods are infallible. In *The Wild-Goose Chase*, Rosalura and Lillia complain that every direction has been followed, but as yet there are no results:

Rosalura:	*We expected Husbands*
	Out of your Documents, and taught behaviours;
Lillia:	*We follow'd your directions, we did rarely,*
	We were Stately, Coy, Demure, Careless, Light, Giddy,
	And play'd at all points: This you swore would carry.
Rosalura:	*We made Love, and contemn'd Love, Now seem'd holy*
	With such a reverent put-on Reservation
	Which could not miss according to your Principles. [17]

CHAPTER IV

The marriage contract, marriage, marriage customs

God, the best maker of all marriages,
Combine your hearts in one, your realms in one!
As man and wife, being two, are one in love,
So be there 'twixt your kingdoms such a spousal,
That never may ill office, nor fell jealousy,
Which troubles oft the bed of blessed marriage,
Thrust in between the paction of these kingdoms,
To make divorce of their incorporate league.

King Henry the Fifth

Betrothed couple

Never prone to ignore the proposing and answering of simple as well as complex questions, the Elizabethans ask themselves just exactly what marriage is and what the marriage relationship should be. We learn first that the state of wedlock is 'an hye and blessed order ordeyned of God in Paradyse,' and that it is a relationship 'wherin one man and one woman are coupled & knyt together in one fleshe and body in the feare and loue of GOD.' No marriage is consummated on earth, either, that was not made in heaven, nor none made blessed here unless made there 'in mercy.' Marriage, furthermore, must be a marriage of minds rather than of bodies, since that is the only way to 'increase vnto Christ,' or 'increase vnto the cōmon welth.' The old English proverb must always be remembered that 'there belongeth more to marriage then two payre of bare legges.' Nor must the couple become discouraged if this marriage of the minds does not immediately make itself evident; 'but as in Musique are many discords, before there can be framed a true Diapason: so in Wedlock are many iars, before there can be established a perfect friendship.' Anthony Sherley puts his conception of marriage into verse:

Marriage *is Gods Indenture which he drawes*
Twixt Man and Woman: tis lifes Obligation;
It is Loues Piller: this the Chayne of Lawes;
Tis the good euill, *the* bitter delectation.

Wedlockes hell, is when the husband throwes
His frownes, his brawles, his curses, and his blowes,
On his Wiues head: yet spendes the amorous charmes
Of smiles and kisses in a Strumpets armes. [1]

There are many kinds of marriage, but all are not good. There may be a marriage of love, or of honor, or of labor – in which there is a disparity of age, or a marriage of grief. Under the last heading would come enforced marriages, where the requirements of the parents are paramount to the wishes of the child. If the father gives his daughter in marriage for money, the husband is likely to confront her with this fact upon all occasions; or the situation may be vice versa. The mother, on her part, may wish her child to marry into a family of good breeding, rather than of wealth. [2]

There are four ends of marriage, or four reasons why marriage was instituted. First, it is designed for the procreation of children; God creates men and women, endowing them with a natural desire to be fruitful; and it is these children who are 'the verye sure bande and last knot of loue Matrymonyall.' The next reason is that marriage is a way of avoiding fornication, of subduing and slaking the lusts of the flesh, 'for matrimony excuseth an innocente manne from synne, from fornicacion, frō aduoutry, and from any other vnlawful fleshely desyre.' Third, it is not good for man to be alone; therefore marriage provides for mutual society of the parties concerned, giving them the help and comfort which they need of each other, so that they can perform their duties in this world 'in better and more comfortable manner.' Last, marriage was instituted by God so that the 'holy seed' could be procreated and 'the Church of God may be kept holy and chaste.' Most writers touching on the subject mention at least three of these four reasons, but Nixon adds some original and thoughtful reasons for marriage. His four reasons are: that God instituted it, that it is a kind of ingratitude to deny to our posterity that which ourselves got from the past, that we achieve immortality by means of our offspring, and that by this institution we may increase our kinsfolk, our friends, and our allies. [3]

Since the state of marriage is very different from that of single life, especially for women, many writers think it well to examine the advantages of matrimony over virginity. Thomas Becon points out that not only is the state of virginity inferior, but the tradition of vowing chastity comes from the Pope while matrimony comes from God. From this fact he concludes that marriage which is contracted after a vow of chastity has been taken is nevertheless quite valid, and may not be dissolved by any earthly authority.

Not only has God ordained matrimony, but history bears witness that mankind has favored it throughout ages. The truth is, says Robert Cleaver, that those who talk most against marriage are the ones who are the greatest

The bride

offenders against marriage because of the unchaste lives they lead. Another writer urges that the argument of these loose livers that marriage is too expensive and will beggar the man, is invalid, for if he is unable to maintain an honest wife, how can he support his mistress? Boaistuau writes that there is nothing so conducive to the pleasurable life as marriage: 'If a man wyll remayne solitarie in his house, his wife keepeth him cōpanie, doeth cherishe and comfort him and causeth him more easilye to digest the incōmodity of his solicitude, if he wil go to the fieldes, she cōducteth him with eye, so far as she can see him.' Perhaps the best summary of arguments in favor of marriage is given by Robert Burton:

But what do I trouble myself to find arguments to persuade to, or commend marriage? behold a brief extract of all that which I have said, and much more, succinctly, . . . pathetically, perspicuously, and elegantly delivered in twelve motions to mitigate the miseries of marriage, by Jacobus de Voragine, . . . 1. Hast thou means? thou hast one to keep and increase it, – 2. Hast none? thou hast one to help to get it. – 3. Art in prosperity? thine happiness is doubled. – 4. Art in adversity? she'll comfort, assist, bear a part of thy burden to make it more tolerable. – 5. Art at home? she'll drive away melancholy. – 6. Art abroad? she looks after thee going from home, wishes for thee in thine absence, and joyfully welcomes thy return. – 7. There's nothing delightsome without society, no society so sweet as matrimony. – 8. The band of conjugal love is adamantine. – 9. The sweet company of kinsmen increaseth, the number of parents is doubled, of brothers, sisters, nephews. – 10. Thou art made a father by a fair and happy issue. – 11. Moses curseth the barrenness of matrimony, how much more a single life? – 12. If nature escape not punishment, surely thy will shall not avoid it.

Burton remarks that all of Voragine's items are valid, and concludes that it is best to marry, even though the outcome is never certain. [4]

The opposite point of view, however, is supported by many Elizabethans, and they present many arguments. First of all, an unmarried man is free and can do as he pleases, but marriage changes all that. This interruption of freedom is the first of *The fyftene Joyes of maryage*.

> *The fyrst Joy of maryage is this*
> *As whan a man of tender yeres is*
> *Flourynge in youth | pleasaunt fresshe and gay*
> *Then in this worlde | nothynge may hym dysmay.*
> *Ne other mynde | desyre nor appetyte*
> *Conforte | lykynge | pleasure | Joye | ne delyte*
> *Hathe he except how he may tye his poyntes*
> *And make his vysage and his lymmes fayre*
> *He brussheth oft his goune | and other gayre*
> *His hede he combeth smothe ryght as hym lyketh*
> *Wherof the heres | pruneth he and pyketh*
> *And maketh hym as clenly as he can*
> *That folke may say there gooth a goodly man.*

The young man's complaint is paralleled by that of the woman, as Mamillia, in one of Greene's stories, tells her friend her views: 'But sure eyther you know more then all, or else say more then you know: for not onely the common people, but also the most learned hath thought maryage to be such a restraint of libertie, as it feeleth no sparke of freedome: for both the body is giuen as a slaue vnto the will of an other man, and the minde is subiecte to sorow, and bound in the caue of care: so that euen the name of a wife importes a thousand troubles.' It is surely easier to live the single life; marriage not only corrupts 'good and great spirits,' but robs the commonwealth of many good things which might be produced, because that marriage has exhausted the energies of those who might have accomplished them. A man who has the wisdom and foresight to govern the whole world finds that he must give up his time to governing a woman and a few children. [5]

There are also other inconveniences to marriage. A man who has conducted his home to please himself finds that he has to make many changes in his housekeeping. He has to bear with the imperfection of servants which his wife has introduced into the household but cannot control. 'Whosoeuer marries, must looke for more trouble and aduersitie, then in single estate . . . The married estate is more encumbred with troubles and afflictions, then the vnmarried.' He must submit to the insolence of his wife and to the pangs of jealousy, whether or not it is justified: 'It were better for him to put the halter about his neck, and to cast himself into the Sea his head downward, to end his miserable life, then to live always in the pains of hell, and to suffer without intermission on his side the tempest of jealousie, of malice, of rage, of madness, of brutish obstinacy, and other miserable conditions: and therefore one sticks not to say, That he that invented this knot and tie of marriage, had found a goodly and beautiful means to be revenged of man.' He finds that marriage is very expensive, and discovers that he should have paid heed to Erasmus, who advised that it is a wise thing for a man to marry unless he cannot afford it. Indeed the situation of a married man is so onerous that both Anthony Nixon and Pierre Boaistuau quote Diponares to the effect that there are only two good days in marriage: the wedding day and the day the wife dies. With all of these obvious inconveniences which the state of marriage brings upon a man, it is not surprising to learn that 'marriages in these dayes, are rather made for fornication than for continencie, not so much in hope of issue, as for gaine of money, more for lucre than for loue.' After all, there must be some reason why a man 'cometh out of Heaven's benediction into the warm sun,' or from a good estate to a poor one. [6]

Various aspects of the marriage contract absorb the interest of a large number of Elizabethan writers. One point of conflict between the Catholic and the Protestant forces is the question whether marriage is really a contract or verily a sacrament. The Catholics, of course, believe it to be a sacrament, and that therefore any questions appertaining to it are to be determined by ecclesiastical judges only. The Protestants, naturally, argue that matrimony is a contract and that all matters with regard to the contract – such as impediments in the contract, degrees of kindred, and so on – are the exclusive prerogative of the civil magistrates. William Perkins states that originally these matters all rested with the civil magistrates, and that 'the ancient Church' did not consider itself the final authority; in questionable situations it did not rest on its own decrees, but had recourse to the 'seate of Iustice,' submitting itself to the laws and constitutions of the state. [7]

There were two definite parts to marriage: the contract or spousals (espousals), and the marriage itself, in which the contract is made manifest. Enough time should elapse between the two for the minister to proclaim or publish the banns (announcements), so that if anyone could offer any lawful impediment to the marriage, an opportunity could be had. These banns were usually asked on three successive Sundays or other festival days. They must be a day apart, but need not be a week apart. If both parties were born and now live in the same parish, the banns are asked in that parish; but if otherwise, the banns are asked in more than one parish. If anyone knows any impediment to the marriage, he must come forward with the information and present it. It is then the duty of the curate to make an investigation. [8]

This espousal or contract is 'a voluntarie promise of marriage, mutually made betweene one man and one woman, both beeing meete and free to marry one another, and therefore allowed so to do by their Parents.' And there are two necessary conditions for the contract: choice, and consent of the parties involved. Perkins calls this free and full consent of the contractual parties 'the very soule and life of the contract.' Elizabethans are agreed, however, that this consent means for the most part that the children accept the choice of a mate made by their parents. One author answers the question of whether the election of the parents is to be considered superior to the affection between the two children, by saying that the parents must be obeyed, while Griffith answers the question of just what is a holy contract by saying: 'It is a *Mariage-desiring* promise betweene two persons, with consent of Parents, and parties.' Bullinger quotes Moses in his argument that a father has complete control over his daughter's marriage; and we learn further that it is the obvious duty of the father to provide marriages for his children. Children who marry without their parents' consent 'offēd greuously.' If a virgin proceeds to espouse herself without her father's consent, she is 'vnhonestly espoused,' but she is lawfully espoused just the same. ⁹

According to two Elizabethan dramatists, however, wise parents may defer to the wishes of the child. In Lyly's *Midas*, the protagonist says to Martius that if anyone can satisfy certain conditions, 'he shal haue my daughter to his wife, or if she refuse it, a Dukedome for his paines,' clearly showing that the refusal lies in his daughter's hands. Similarly, in the anonymous *Sir Clyomon and Sir Clamydes* the King of Denmark accepts with good grace the choice his daughter has made. It is quite proper for him to do so, too, for no one should be compelled by force to make a marriage contract. Writes Henry Cornelius Agrippa: 'Wherfore they moste greuously offende, what so euer they be, parentes, nere kinsfolke, tutours, and gardians, whiche, ... beyonde all due obedience to parentes by goddes commaundement (by a certain tyranny) restrain and make bonde (whiche to this sacrament oughte to be geuen) the free consent of their sonnes and dougters, and compel them to be maried to suche as they hate, without any consideracion of

age, loue, cōdicion, maners, and specially of goddes commaundemente.'
He further relates that there are certain worldly rulers who will even force
their subjects to marry, and then will take over the dowries for their own
coffers. Another writer calls forced marriage 'the extreamest bondage that
is,' while Thomas Heywood states in strong language that such marriages
are ruinous to both parties: 'How often have forced contracts beene made
to add land to land, not love to love? And to unite houses to houses, not
hearts to hearts? which hath beene the occasion that men have turned
monsters, and women devills.' Likewise, in *The Merry Wives of Windsor*,
Fenton censures Mrs. Page for planning to marry off her daughter Ann to
one she does not love:

> *You do amaze her. Hear the truth of it.*
> *You would have married her most shamefully,*
> *Where there was no proportion held in love.*
> *The truth is, she and I (long since contracted)*
> *Are now so sure that nothing can dissolve us.*
> *Th' offence is holy that she hath committed,*
> *And this deceit loses the name of craft,*
> *Of disobedience, or unduteous title,*
> *Since therein she doth evitate and shun*
> *A thousand irreligious cursed hours*
> *Which forced marriage would have brought upon her.*

In fact, a popular play on this theme was written by George Wilkins, *The
Miseries of Inforst Marige* (1607), in which the hero's misfortunes are due
to the machinations of a designing uncle, who brought about an unhappy
marriage. [10]

This marriage contract of which we have been speaking 'is a mention of
mutuall promise of future mariage, before fit and competent Iudges and
Witnesses.' It is called the spousal or espousal, and can be compared to
the modern engagement. There are two types of espousals: *in verbis de
futuro* and *in verbis de praesenti*. If the ceremony takes place with the words
'I shall take thee to my wife,' or 'I will take thee,' then we have the *de futuro*
espousal. T.E. writes in *The Womans Lawier*: 'The first beginning of Marriage
(as in respect of Contract, and that which Law taketh hold on) is when

Wedlocke by words in the future tence is promised and vowed, and this is but *sponsio*, or *sponsalia*.' Later he explains: 'Though this *Sponsalia* be alwaies made with intent that Matrimony should insue, yet the Contracter cannot therunto be compelled, vnlesse there were another thing ioyned to the contract of Spousals, neither are they compellable to marry, though an oath accompanied the promise, vnlesse it were made pure and without condition.' In other words, even though an oath has been made and even though a priest be present, the *de futuro* espousal is not binding upon either party. It is simply a statement of intention to have the marriage performed in the future. Two young people can make such a type of contract, or it can be made for them as children by their parents. William Perkins, in his important work entitled *Christian Oeconomie*, points out that even in the *de futuro* type, if the parties use the words of the future but at the same time intend to bind themselves for the present, then 'the bond is in conscience precisely made before God, and so the Contract is indeed made for *the present* time before God,' and he feels that such a promise should be lived up to. He agrees, however, that if one of the parties has a just cause or thinks he has a just cause why he should change his mind, he may void the contract; and such a contract is superseded by a contract made in words of the present, even though the *de futuro* espousal 'were formerly made, & confirmed by oath.' The only exception admitted is when the parties 'do lie together before the condition (though honest & appertaining to mariage) be performed; then the contract for time to come is, without further controuersie, sure and certaine. For where there hath been a carnall vse of each others bodie, it is alwaies presupposed, that a mutuall consent, as touching Mariage, hath gone before.'

The espousal *in verbis de praesenti* is quite different, however, for here the key words are 'I doe take thee.' The approved form of the marriage contract *de praesenti* is given by Robert Cleaver in his *A Godlie Forme of Householde Government*: 'I. N. doe willingly promise to marrie thee N. if God will, and I liue, whensoeuer our parents shal thinke good, & meet: till which time, I take thee for my only betrothed wife, and thereto plight thee my troth. In the name of the Father, the Sonne, and the holy Ghost:

So be it.' Perkins clearly indicates the importance of this type of espousal when he says that by the use of these words 'the mariage is begun, though not in regard of fact, yet in regard of right and interest, which the parties haue in each other in deed and in truth.' Jean Bodin describes the validity of such an espousal more strongly in these words: 'If by consent of the man and woman, contract of mariage be made by words of the present time, before they know one another; for that, the law calleth iust marriage.' Perkins states that this is the reason why 'persons betrothed in Scripture are termed man and wife,' while Griffith, in lifting this passage from Perkins, omits the reference to occurrences in the Bible, saying baldly: 'And hence alone it is that the *Parties betroathed* are call'd *Man*, and *Wife*.' T. E. proceeds to the ultimate step by stating that 'the full Contract of Matrimonie, is when it is made by words, *de praesenti*, in a lawfull consent, and thus two be made man and wife existing without lying together, yet Matrimonie is not accounted consummate, vntill there goe with the consent of mind and will Coniunction of body.' To put it differently, the parties to a *de praesenti* espousal were in effect actually married, though not so in name. And the church and state both recognized such a union as valid, providing an interesting situation whereby marriage could actually take place without the sanction of either the church or the state. It is quite obvious, then, that the marriage contract itself is the important consideration, not the actual marriage service. Thus it is that no license to marry can be issued until two responsible people serve as sureties for a bond lodged at the Consistory Court guaranteeing that neither of the parties has a precontract with a third party. And quite properly so; Henri Estienne, in *A world of wonders*, relates the story of an Italian lady who hired two murderers to kill her husband, and when they failed she took her dagger and killed him herself; he continues: 'Now the hatred which moued her to commit this murther, was conceiued vpon a rumor blazed abroad in the citie, and whispered into her eares, that before he maried her, he had contracted himselfe to another citizen. A weightie reason no doubt.' [11]

The likelihood has often been observed that such a precontract as the *de*

Title page showing early form of espousal

praesenti took place between William Shakespeare and Anne Hathaway in the summer of 1582. At any rate, such a spousal does take place in the poet's *Twelfth Night*, as, in the presence of the priest, Olivia apologizes thus to Sebastian:

> *Blame not this haste of mine. If you mean well,*
> *Now go with me and with this holy man*
> *Into the chantry by: there, before him,*
> *And underneath that consecrated roof,*
> *Plight me the full assurance of your faith;*
> *That my most jealous and too doubtful soul*
> *May live in peace.*

The priest, however, is to conceal the espousal until that time when they feel it is proper to hold the marriage ceremony itself. Later, when this episode is referred to, we have a brief description of the *de praesenti* ceremony in the words of the priest:

> *A contract of eternal bond of love,*
> *Confirm'd by mutual joinder of your hands,*
> *Attested by the holy close of lips,*
> *Strengthen'd by interchangement of your rings;*
> *And all the ceremony of this compact*
> *Seal'd in my function, by my testimony.*

Thus we see that the hand-clasp, the kiss, the exchange of rings, and the testimony of the priest, or other witnesses, are all part of the formal espousal. That the espousal *de praesenti* is tantamount to marriage, is clearly shown in the following passage from John Webster's *The Duchess of Malfi*, as the Duchess speaks to Antonio:

> *I have heard lawyers say, a contract in a chamber*
> *Per verba de presenti is absolute marriage.*
> *Bless, heaven, this sacred Gordian, which let violence*
> *Never untwine.*

The problem is not a simple one, however, and perhaps should not be disposed of so summarily. In *The Tempest*, the Duke warns Ferdinand and

Miranda against premarital relations; in *Measure for Measure* another Duke advises Mariana differently, while at the same time taking a somewhat opposite view of the Claudio-Juliet relationship. Nor must we forget that the legal status is not necessarily consonant with the moral one. [12]

It is interesting to note that the marriage ceremony of today, at least in the Protestant churchs, includes both the *de futuro* and the *de praesenti* espousals, as well as the marriage service. That such was also the case in the Church of England ceremony in 1686, is clearly indicated by the publisher in that year of Henry Swinburne's manuscript, *A Treatise of Spousals*, which had been written about 1600; he states: 'In our Publick Office of Marriage, Spousals and Matrimony are united, and performed in one continued Act; When the Minister demands, *Wilt thou have this Woman to thy wedded Wife, &c.* And the Man answers, *I will*, and so the Woman *vice versa*, there's a Specimen of *Spousals de futuro*. When the Man repeats the words, *J. N. take thee N. to my wedded Wife, &c.*, and so the Woman *vice versa*, there's the form of *Spousals de praesenti*, which in Substance are perfect Matrimony . . . When the Minister adds his Benediction, and pronounces them to be Man and Wife, then 'tis a perfect Marriage to all constructions and purposes in Law.' [13]

In spite of often recorded statements that child marriages were common in Shakespeare's day, they actually have no standing under the law. They can only be considered as being in the nature of *de futuro* espousals. According to William Perkins, a marriage 'which is made betweene two persons that are vnder age, is to bee holden and accounted as vnlawfull. And though it should be done by consent or cōmandment of Parents, yet it is of no moment. This alwaies remembred; except it be ratified by a new consent of the parties after they be come to age; or that they in the meane time haue had priuate and carnall copulation one with the other.' If one of the parties is of full age, however, 'the vnder-aged may not break off consent, either before, or when they be come to perfect yeares, but must rest in expectation of the accomplishment of the contract, when hee or she shall be out of their minoritie.' The proper age at marriage will be taken up later in this chapter; suffice to say here that the chief object of the socalled child marriage is that by its means the parents may provide for their children in case of death; and certainly one of the regular duties of the parents is to make advantageous marriages for their children. Other reasons for child marriages are: to bring about peace by uniting two families or two countries; to avoid having the crown take over the estates of children, as provided for by feudal laws; and at times, to increase the coffers of the parents by the marriage settlements, if the child be seven years of age. Presumably, however, in most cases the parents are simply considering the welfare of their children. [14]

Clandestine marriages, besides being very common, are quite legal in most cases, though severely frowned upon. In essence, these marriages are simply secret marriages. [15] In William Harrington's *The Comendacions of Matrymony*, published in 1528, we find: 'If ye man & woman or theyr proctours do make matrymony secretly by them selfe without any recorde or but with one wytnesse y^t is called matrymony clādestinat which for many causes is forboden by the law. And they which done make suche matrymony are accused in ye dede doynge notwithstondyng that matrymony is valeable and holdeth afore god.' Clandestine marriages might be made in private homes or secret places, in the night, without a lawful minister, or in a church but with an insufficient number of witnesses. They are therefore marriages 'contracted so priuily that they cannot bee lawfullie proued by witnesses.' It is recorded in the *Calendar of State Papers* that Queen Elizabeth was highly displeased over the secret marriage of Thomas Shirley, the son of her treasurer for the wars in the Low Countries, with one of her ladies in waiting, Frances Vavasour. An important problem in connection with clandestine marriages is whether or not the issue of such marriages are legitimate. The Council of Trent in 1563 decreed that if the marriage be not performed in the presence of priest and witnesses, it is void; the Council of Lateran, too, made the same decision; but such edicts had no effect upon the Church of England. William Harrington concurs in stating that if there is anything wrong with a marriage, such as only one witness or none being present, the banns not lawfully asked, or one party already married, the children born to the couple are bastards.

ln *The Triall of Bastardie* (1594), however, William Clerke makes the categorical statement that without exception the issue of such marriages are legitimate. [16] Nevertheless it is apparent from the foregoing that for many reasons a marriage could be declared invalid, and no doubt this was very convenient at times. It was easy enough to bring pressure to bear on the clergy, particularly when persons of wealth and nobility were involved. As is well-known, Queen Elizabeth had marriages of her court ladies invalidated on occasion, when she did not approve, and there was little to be done about it. Thus many children were bastardized; what this could mean Elizabeth knew from bitter experience. Many times noble children were political pawns, and a sure weapon against them was a question as to the legality of their birth. The simplicity of the marriage service in our society makes it well nigh impossible to question the legality of a bona fide marriage or the status of any children.

Several questions arise concerning the eligibility of prospective candidates for marriage. First naturally comes the question of the proper age of the parties; 'the ciuill law, and common law also, set downe twelue yeares for the floure of a females age, and fourteen of a males.' But although these ages are the legal ones for marriage, it is always recommended that the couple be older. Geoffrey Fenton, for example, says that although the Romans declared the same legal ages as those in England, it is wrong to have more respect for the ability of the body than the capacity of the mind. The age of fourteen seems to have been a popular one for the marriage of girls. We remember Juliet's age; and Overbury's character of a true woman relates: 'Shee is *Marriageable* and Foureteene at once; and after shee doth not liue, but tarry.' Similarly, in *The Magnetick Lady*, the witty Mr. Compass speaks to Parson Palate of a young lady 'who strikes the fire of full fourteene, to day, ripe for a husband.' The evils of early marriage, however, and consequent early childbearing, are obvious to the Elizabethans. Alexander Niccholes, for example, remarks that 'forward Virgins' consider the age of fourteen or even thirteen as the best for matrimony, following the example of their mothers, but 'the effects that, for the most part, insue thereafter, are dangerous births, diminution of stature, breuity of life, and such like, yet all these paines will they aduenture for this pleasure: ... so are there others that as much offend in the contrary, by passing ouer their youth for certaine cautionary worldly respects, to salute this society with their age.' According to Vives, women ought to be at least eighteen years of age before they bear children, or otherwise they do so with great peril and danger. In Sir Thomas Elyot's *The Defence of Good Women*, when Zenobia says that she was twenty at her marriage, Candidus says she waited too long; Zenobia replies that from the age of sixteen to twenty she was improving herself by studying moral philosophy. Leicester's protege, Robert Laneham, says that in a pageant presenting a country wedding before Queen Elizabeth, both the bride and her maids were thirty or over, but this age was surely unusual. [17]

There are several impediments which will prevent a valid marriage, and will serve later as grounds for annulment. William Harrington undertakes to name fifteen such impediments: error of person (when the one you marry is not the one you thought her to be), error in condition (where the social status has been misrepresented), prohibition by a formal vow of chastity, cognation or cousinry or consanguinity (where there is not a just and lawful distance of blood), affinity (marrying a relative of one with whom you have had sexual relations), right of public or common honesty (marrying one of your dead wife's relatives), cognation spiritual (marrying anyone connected with your baptism – godparents, children of godparents, officiating clergy, etc.), adultery, murder, diversity in religion, forced matrimony, taking of holy orders, precontract, impotence, and madness. Harrington then goes on to name other impediments which may prevent a marriage, if known, but will not annul a marriage: certain times of the year, interdiction of the church, simple vow of chastity, adultery with relatives of betrothed, murder of spouse in order to marry again, rape, christening one's child, murder of a priest, solemn penance being undergone, and holy orders taken by a woman. Perkins adds to these lists that Christians must not marry pagans (diversity of religions), both parties must be in good health, a girl must not marry one who has a mistress; and he says that if a man is espoused to a woman who is later shown to be with child, he may void the contract. Most of the impediments just mentioned may be found in a rollicking scene in Jonson's *Epicoene* as Otter, disguised as a divine, and Cutbeard, disguised as a canon lawyer, annoy Morose with their loud cavilling, and harass him in his attempts to be divorced from Epicoene; Cutbeard says that there are twelve impediments to marriage:

Cut. The first is *impedimentum erroris.*
Ott. Of which there are several species.
Cut. Ay, as *error personae.*
Ott. If you contract yourself to one person, thinking her another.
Cut. Then, *error fortunae.*
Ott. If she be a beggar, and you thought her rich.
Cut. Then, *error qualitatis.*
Ott. If she prove stubborn or headstrong, that you thought obedient.

Morose thinks this last will make him a good case until Otter points out that it applies only *ante copulam*, not *post copulam*. Cutbeard continues:

Cut. The next is *conditio:* if you thought her free born, and she prove a bond-woman, there is impediment of estate and condition ... Well, then, the third is *votum:* if either party have made a vow of chastity ... The fourth is *cognatio:* if the persons be of kin within the degrees ... The fift is *crimen adulterii:* the known case. The sixt, *cultus disparitas*, difference of religion ... The seventh is, *vis:* if it were upon compulsion or force ... The eight is, *ordo;* if ever she have taken holy orders ... The ninth is, *ligamen;* if you were bound, sir, to any other before ... The tenth is, *publica honestas;* which is *inchoata quaedam affinitas.*
Ott. Ay, or *affinitas orta ex sponsalibus;* and is but *leve impedimentum* ...
Cut. The eleventh is, *affinitas ex fornicatione.*
Ott. Which is no less *vera affinitas* than the other, master doctor.
Cut. True, *quae oritur ex legitimo matrimonio.*
Ott. You say right, venerable doctor: and, *nascitur ex eo, quod per conjugium duae personae efficiuntur una caro –* ...
Cut. I conceive you, master parson: *ita per fornicationem aeque est verus pater, qui sic generat –*
Ott. *Et vere filius qui sic generatur –*

Morose, who is quite bewildered by this learned talk and pretty weary of it all by now, asks: 'What's all this to me?' But Cutbeard, paying no attention to him, goes on:

Cut. The twelfth and last is, *si forte coire nequibis.*
Ott. Ay, that is *impedimentum gravissimum:* it doth utterly annul, and annihilate, that. If you have *manifestam frigiditatem,* you are well, sir ... or if there be *morbus perpetuus, et insanabilis; as paralysis, elephantiasis,* or so – ... it is in the canon, master doctor ... That a boy, or child, under years is not fit for marriage, because he cannot *reddere debitum.* So your ... *impotentes,* I should say, are *minime apti ad contrahenda matrimonium* ....
Cut. But then there will arise a doubt, master parson, in our case, *post matrimonium:* that *frigiditate praeditus* .... Who cannot *uti uxore pro uxore,* may *habere eam pro sorore.*

This erudite discussion goes on and on, but we shall leave it here. Suffice to say, Morose gets absolutely no help from it in his efforts to avoid the noise of marriage either by divorce or by annulment. [18]

When once the couple is married, however unfortunate the relationship may be, the marriage sacrament can rarely be broken. Agrippa states emphatically: 'Nor cā it be laufull for any cause, the wife to forsake hir husbande, or the husbande his wife, because it is laufull for no man to departe from him selfe, nor no man to leave hym selfe. For she which is made of a mannes ribbe, of fleshe, the same fleshe, and the same bone of bones for an helpe vnto the man: God neuer wolde hir to be separate frō the man, but for fornicacion: whiche one onley cause, God did excepte.' Here Agrippa is clearly speaking of separation, but he goes on to say that the sacrament must not be broken by any 'sacietie or lothsomnesse,' not by old age, not by a sickness such as the pestilence, leprosy, or any other contagious disease, not by a crime, not by heresy. Nor can marriage be dissolved for barrenness; and indeed it is quite proper for old men to marry, even if they are past the age for children. Barren people, further, are not included in the impotent group, 'For though procreation of children be one end of marriage, yet it is not the only end: and so inuiolable is the mariage bond, that though it be made for childrens sake, yet for want of children it may not be broken.' Nor should it be broken for desertion, say some

Gascoigne offering his book to Elizabeth

Gossiping at the Market

authorities. In *A Bride-Bush* (1617, 1619, 1623), William Whately says that 'the sinne of wilfull desertion doth likewise dissolue the bond of Matrimony,' although in *A Care-cloth* (1624) he retracts his former statement. But according to Perkins, if a man voluntarily absents himself from the country for a year, the wife may crave of the public magistrate a dissolution of the covenant and marry another, unless the one to whom she was contracted be heard from in the meantime. [19]

There is no unanimity concerning the effect that adultery on the part of a man or woman will have upon marriage. As noted above, Agrippa considers it grounds for divorce. At first Whately thinks so too, but later changes his mind, as he did in the case of desertion. John Dove, in *Of Diuorcement*, states that Melanchthon believed that a man could put away his wife for adultery and marry another, but argues that Melanchthon is wrong. Dove believes, however, that adultery is grounds for separation, along with agreement of both parties, as well as disease:

> For there are three departures from the marriage bedde which are lawfull, two priuate, the third publike: The first with the consent of both parties, one dispensing with the other. ... The second in case of necessitie, it is lawfull for the man to dispense with himselfe, as if the woman be infected, with a contagious disease, that he cannot doe the office of an husband without manifest daunger of his life, and it is no fraude because it is not voluntarie. The third, if the wife be an adulteresse woman, because it is a publike scandall, he may by publike magistrate be separated from his wife for her chastisement vntill shee shew manifest tokens of amendment.

Perkins accepts adultery as grounds for divorce, but others disagree. The problem of divorce was dealt with extensively during this period, beginning with the famous act of 1540 (32 Hen. VIII, ca. 38). It was the intention of this act to stabilize marriages, since 'mariages have been brought into suche uncertainty thereby that no mariage could be so surely knytt and bounden but it shulde lye in either of the parties power and arbitre ... to prove a precontracte a kynnerede an alliance or a carnall knowledge to defeate the same.' This act declared, therefore, that 'mariages being contracte and solemnised in the face of the churche and consūmate with bodily knowledge . . . shalbe . . . taken to be lauful good juste and indisso-luble, . . . notwithstanding any precontracte . . . not consūmate with bodily knowledge . . . any dispensation prescription lawe or other thinge . . . . And that no reservation or prohibition, Goddis law except, shall trouble or impeche anny mariage without the Leviticall degrees.' The law, however, was generally ineffective because the words 'Goddis law except' provided a loophole for the church. A similar act of 1607 again tried to correct the condition, but to no avail, and the Puritan-Anglican controversy on divorce raged throughout the period. Milton's tracts on the subject are famous. The debate went on and on, and it can scarcely be said that the present divorce laws in England or America provide the ideal solution. Since the problem of divorce has been investigated widely and is a special study in itself, it has not been thought expedient to give an extended account of the question here. It need be said only that divorce, and especially divorce for adultery, was a considerable problem. That the question can be settled privately and independently of divorce is indicated by a story of Henri Estienne, 'that a woman dwelling neare *Narbone* being in bed with her husband, cut off his priuities, for that he had defiled the mariage bed.' Another current question has to do with the authority and rights of a husband who finds that his wife has played him false. According to William Heale, whom we remember as a defender of women against husbands who beat their wives, 'a husband taking his wife in adultery might lawe-fully kill her, yet not without the guilte of hainous offence.' And with this enigmatic statement we shall leave the subject. [20]

An important social custom connected with marriage is the bringing of a bride's dowry. Although T. E. states that the dowry is 'not of the essence of Matrimony which is made by consent,' it was customary for the wife to bring from her parents what money they could provide. The amount, of course, would be dependent upon the finances of the parents, but it was surely easier for a girl to become married if she could provide her husband with a sizeable dot. Placentia Steele, in *The Magnetick Lady*, apparently came to her husband with sixteen thousand pounds—perhaps three quarter of a million dollars in value of today. This money was at the disposal of the husband, and Robert Greene records, though we may not believe his self-condemnatory *Repentance*, that he left his wife and child after he had spent all the marriage money she brought. According to *A discourse of the married and single life*, if there are no children, 'thou must restore halfe of thy wiues dowry.' [21]

The marriage ceremony itself is very colorful. It takes place in the 'face' of the church or the church porch, or as the Wife of Bath says, at the 'chirche-dore.' It must be in the clear light of day, 'after the toune be rysen and with honoure and reuerence.' The ring used in the ceremony is placed on the third finger of the left hand. If a ring was used in the espousal, it is now transferred from the right hand to the left and becomes the wedding ring. Whetstone says of it: 'The Rynge that is geuen by the Hus-bande, and put on the Wiues finger, ought to be of Gould, to witnes, that as gould is the most precious of Mettalles, so the loue of the married, exceedeth all other loues.' The bride's gown or 'marrying smocke' is white, and may be of any material from 'home-spun Cloath' to the very finest silk. The bride is likely to wear a small cap and gloves, and is sure to provide all of her friends with two-penny gloves. In Jonson's *The King's Entertainment at Welbeck*, the bride 'was drest like an old *May-Lady*, with Skarfes, and a great wrought Handkerchiefe, with red, and blew, and other habiliments. Six Maids attending on her, attir'd with Buckram Brides-laces beguilt, White sleeves, and Stammell Petticotes, drest after the cleanliest Countrey guise.' A delightful description of an early wedding is given by J. C. Jeaffreson in his *Brides and Bridals* (1872):

To the church-porch... the espoused woman of pre-Reformation times, with loosened locks falling to the waist, came on her wedding day, preceded by minstrels and vase-bearer, conducted by bride-knights or pages, attended by maidens, surrounded by her kindred, and followed at a distance by her father.... If she had previously gone through no ceremony of public betrothal, the earlier part of the proceedings at the porch corrected the omission.... The marriage followed immediately on the utterance of her wish for it.

She stood at the groom's left hand.... Firmly pressing with his grasp the un-reluctant hand,... the groom said, 'I, * *, take the * *, to my wedded wyf, to have and to holde, fro this day forwarde, for bettere for wers, for richere for porere; in sykeness and in hele; tyll dethe us departe: if holy chyrche it wol ordeyne; and therto I plight the my trouthe.' The hands of the spouses having been momentarily separated, the fairer and gentler of the two caught the other's large hand with a nervous grasp, and said 'I, * *, take thee, * *, to my wedded husbonde, to have and to holde, fro this day forwarde, for better for wors; for richer for porere; in syknesse and in hele; to be bonere and buxom, in bedde and at borde, tyll dethe us departhe, if holy chyrche, it woll ordeyne; and therto I plight the my trouth.'

Next came the use of the ring .... Together with the ring the groom put gold and silver on the officiating priest's book; and after the symbol had been duly consecrated before the assembly, ... he took it up with the thumb and two next fingers of his right hand, and placed it with peculiar ceremoniousness on the particular finger of the bride which it was destined to adorn. 'With this rynge I the wed, and this gold and silver I the give, and with my body I the worship, and with all my worldely chatels I the endow,' he uttered, following the priest's voice. Having thus spoken the words of endowment, he placed the ring momentarily over the extremity of the thumb of the right hand, saying, 'In the name of the Father'; then applied it as briefly to the end of the second finger, saying, 'And of the Son'; then put it to the tip of the third finger, saying, 'And of the Holy Ghost'; and lastly, pushed it home on the fourth finger, with a sonorous ejaculation of 'Amen.' The ceremony of placing the ring on the bride's ring-finger was followed by the priestly utterance of benediction – 'May you be blessed by the Lord, who made the Universe out of nothing!' which was followed by the recital of verses of the 68th Psalm, and the delivery of other blessings, that terminated the proceedings at the church-door.

Now that the wedding is over the bridal group may move into the body of the church for prayers, sermon, or mass. 'Before leaving the church,' writes Powell, 'the bridal party partook of wine, bread, and sweetmeats, blessed by the priest, who also gave the groom a benedictional kiss, which the latter conveyed to the bride.' The guests, however, did not kiss either the bride or the groom. [22]

The wedding celebration takes place at the home of the groom, with a feast, drinking, profane songs, sonnets, jigs, dancing, and other diversions of this sort. The clergy objected very much to such entertainment as 'publique incendiaries of all filthy lusts,' saying that Christ should be at each marriage and at each marriage feast. Nevertheless, the custom of bride-ale continued. In *Epicoene*, Madam Haughty complains bitterly to

Marriage ceremony

Morose about the lack of customary gifts and entertainment at his wedding, saying that he has let his 'nuptials want all marks of solemnity': 'We see no ensigns of a wedding here; no character of a bride-ale: where be our scarves and our gloves? I pray you, give 'em us. Let's know your bride's colours, and yours at least . . . no gloves? no garters? no epithalamium?

no masque?' The union of Florimell and Marinell in *The Faerie Queene* provides us with an extended description of the kind of celebration which takes place among the nobility, with feasts and banquets, masques and disguises, and particularly with incidental jousts and a tournament. [23]

The consummation of the marriage was of importance for many reasons. It could turn either form of espousal into actual marriage and could legalize the marriage of under-age children. Marriage is properly consummated, according to Perkins, 'by three sorts of actions; one of the parents of the Bride and Bridegroome, the other of the Minister in publike, the third of the persons coupled together.' Further, this first coming together should never take place until the couple has first knelt in prayer in the secrecy of their chamber and commended themselves to God. The recommendation of Ludovicus Vives is perhaps even harder to follow: 'After yᵘ hast married thy wife, go thy waye into thy chamber, and abstaynyng thre dayes from her, geue thy selfe to prayer with her, and in the fyrst nyght thou shalt burne the liuer of the fyshe, and the deuil shalbe driuen awaye. The seconde nyghte thou shalte be admitted vnto the companye of saynetes. The third night shalt yᵘ obtaine the blessyng of God, so that whole children shalbe borne of you. And after the third nighte be past, take thy wyfe vnto thee in yᵉ feare of god, and moore for the desyre of children, then bodelye lust.' With such a beginning, it is much easier for the couple to have a proper religious attitude toward each other, and to perform the chief duties of married people toward each other – which are communion, chastity, and cohabitation. This last word clearly means living together in all the various relations of the family life. [24]

Since practically the whole of a woman's life is to be given over to obedience and submission to her husband, the widow presents a somewhat special problem for the Elizabethans. The older widow should employ herself with religious works; she is not likely to be bothered with attentions from men. The younger widow needs to be very circumspect in all that she does; since she is considered fair game by many men, she must be more careful even than young maidens. She should leave her home only rarely, and must then be accompanied by a woman of repute. Whether or not she should marry again is debatable. Those who follow St. Paul think that she should, on the theory that she will thus avoid her greatest danger of sin, since as Becon insists, young widows have been proverbially known for their tendency toward unchastity. Tasso thinks, however, that it should 'seeme conuenient that that woman or man, that haue beene diuorced by death from that first band of Matrimonie, ought not to be knit vnto a second.' If the widow remarries, she should wait for at least a year of mourning, although, as William Heale writes in *An Apologie for Women*, 'a widdow that remarrieth within her yeere of mourning, is by the law free frō infamie, but by the lawe also adiudged vnworthie of matrimonial dignity.' Nevertheless, there are apparently many who find themselves unable to wait the year out. For example, in Robert Greene's *Morando: The Tritameron of Love*, the author moralizes thus over Panthia's conduct: 'The call of a Quaile continueth but one quarter, and a widdowes sorrow onelie two monethes: in the one sad for her old mate, and in the other carefull for a new match.' [25]

Some special legal questions arise in connection with women. Most of the ones mentioned here derive from T. E.'s important work, *The Lawes Resolutions of Womens Rights: or, The Lawes Provision for Woemen*, which bears the running title, *The Womans Lawier*. The author of this book points out that women have no representation in Parliament; neither make laws, nor consent to them, nor abrogate them. Since all women are either married or to be married, there is little recourse for them except to subject themselves to their husbands and depend upon them. As we have seen, the husband has pretty complete control over his wife; but he has none over his mistress, nor over his betrothed. Even if the betrothal is a *de praesenti* one, and the law calls it just marriage, the man does not control the woman's goods, unless the woman has followed her husband and lives with him. If it happens that the woman dies before the nuptials are celebrated, the prospective husband does not share in her wealth, except by her last will and testament. Once married, however, the status changes completely: 'If before Marriage the Woman were possessed of Horses, Neate, Sheepe, Corne, Wool, Money, Plate and Jewels, all manner of moueable substance is presently by coniunction the husbands, to sell, keepe or bequeath if he die.' Even the jewelry and clothing which a man gives to his wife are still his own to dispose of as he wills. Matthew Griffith, writing in *Bethel: or, A Forme for Families,* does not accept this generally held view, but he seems not to be on good legal ground. According to him, 'Some hold that a wife hath no power to dispose of any thing, meerely of her selfe, but only by allowance; as if all things were the womans only in communion to use, but her husbands only in discretion, to dispose. But if the wife have right, and power over her husbands body, much more sure over his goods: and if she have but only the use; then what is her preferment above childe, or servant? Others (as wide on the other side) think that the wife hath right, and power, over her husbands goods to give, when, and what, and to whom she pleaseth.' Griffith clearly feels that the goods and possessions are held in common and are to be disposed of in common. In *Of Domesticall Duties,* however, Gouge writes of those 'humane lawes which refraine wiues from disposing goods, without or against their husbands consent.' In connection with these legal matters, T. E. names several ages in the life of a woman, in which her status changes in the sight of the law:

The learning is 35. Hen. 6. fol. 40. that a Woman hath divers speciall ages, at the 7. yeare of her age, her father shall have aide of his tenants to marry her. At 9. yeares age, shee is able to deserve and have dowre. At 12. yeares to consent to marriage. At 14. to bee *hors du gard:* at. 16. to be past the Lords tender of a husband. At 21. to be able to make a foeffement: And *per Ingelton* there in the end of the case, a woman married at 12. cannot disagree afterward, but if she be married younger, shee may dissent till shee be 14.

The age of 7. yeares, when *Bracton* wrote this aide, for making a sonne a knight, or marrying the daughter, was . . . measured by the indigence of the Lord, and opulence of the tenants: But *West.* 1. *Cap.* 35. in the third yeare of Edward 1. the Law was made certaine, the Lord shall have aide of his tenants, as soone as his daughter accomplished 7. yeares age for the marriage of her. *Viz.* xx. s. of a whole knights fee, and xx. s. of xx. l. land in soccage, and so forth, according to the rate more or lesse.

He quotes further a statute of the fifth year of Elizabeth's reign that if a woman between the ages of twelve and forty be unmarried and out of work, she may be forced by two justices of the peace in the country (or the head officer and two burgesses in the city) to serve and be retained by the year, week, or day in any work they think proper and for whatever wages they approve, under penalty of being committed to prison until she will serve. Further, if a girl is a ward of the lord, and then marries, she is then no longer a ward, even though she become a widow; she may not remarry, however, unless she has the lord's assent. In reference to the aid of tenants in providing funds for marriage, it is an interesting note that James I had recourse to such a legal custom. If the feudal lord could demand contributions from his tenants, then the sovereign could levy such contributions on his subjects. When James was faced with the problem usually belonging to fathers of brides, he issued writs for the payment of a marriage tax. Although the marriage celebration itself cost £ 53,294, and the bride's portion amounted to £ 40,000 more, he received from the tax only £ 20,500. [26]

CHAPTER V

Domestic relationships

*Katherine, I charge thee, tell these headstrong women
What duty they do owe their lords and husbands.*

The Taming of the Shrew

Dinner scene

As always, we may expect a frank discussion from Elizabethan writers when we come to consider the fruits of a successful courtship, namely – marriage. There is a large and interesting literature on this subject of the matrimonial state, and it is clear in describing the duties of husband and wife toward each other, and toward any children they may rear, together with specific directions for managing a household. On the subject of matrimony, these writers breathe an air of maturity and sobriety which is often lacking in modern literature. The Elizabethans considered marriage bonds to be holy bonds, and that premise underlies all the discussion of the working partnership of husband and wife. In general the married state was conceded to be one of dignity and worthiness; it was not easy to keep the covenant. Today we insist that all go smoothly, at least on the surface; but the writers of that day did not seem to be concerned with covering up the unpleasant side of marriage. No ordinary couple felt ashamed, apparently, of a noisy quarrel, nor cared who heard it. Victorian shushing and curtain pulling are but lately come. On the other hand, a really good marriage, although it might include some such interludes as we have mentioned, stood on firm ground and achieved a working stability which is still not easily attained after the passage of four centuries of domestic trial and error. During an approximate century (1528 to 1633), over thirty works were published which dealt extensively with the organization of the household and with the duties of the wife and the husband within their little world. Over half of these works were issued in more than one edition, and five of them appeared in four or more editions.

The origin of these English books dealing with domestic conduct is pretty much in doubt. Professor Chilton L. Powell indicates that the prototype may be the brief treatise entitled *Of Weddid Men and Wifis and of Here Children also*, which has been ascribed to Wiclif; but the type did not become popular until one hundred years later, and then the first of these books were of foreign origin; *Of Weddid Men* was not published until the nineteenth century. The most extensive of the English treatises on the subject had four main divisions: the marriage state discussed from religious and secular points of view, legal aspects of the matrimonial contract, the relations of the husband and wife, and the government of the family. [1]

A conception common to most of these books is that the family may be considered as a small body politic: 'A familie may bee compared vnto a commonwealth: wherein there are diuers societies and degrees reciprocally relating, and mutually depending one vpon another. The highest degree of societie is between the husband and the wife; and this is as the first wheele of a clocke, that turneth about all the rest in order. The next societie, is betweene the Parents and the children. The third betweene the seruants one with another, and towards all other superiors in the familie.' In this commonwealth, it is the husband's office to give the proper orders, and it is the wife's office to see that they are obeyed. And since no state can remain long in existence if there is conflict among its inhabitants, so in a family there must be mutual love and agreement between the man and wife: 'Diuers houses are none other, but euen very Fencing-Schooles, wherein the two sexes seeme to haue met together for nothing, but to play their prizes, and to trie masteries. Hence it is, that many husbands and wiues doe fare almost alwayes, as *Iob* fared, when the Deuill had smitten his body with boyles and vlcers, cursing their Wedding-day, as much as he did his Birth-day, and thirsting after diuorce as much, as euer he did after death.' In a household which is correctly managed, the husband and wife will consider that all things are held in common between them, and neither will take the best. It is even possible to learn from birds and animals how husbands and wives should behave toward each other. For where there is mutual love, 'marriage is a merri-age, and this worlds Paradise.' Furthermore, there are three principles which if observed will produce the ideal relationship between husband and wife: first, they must have one heart, one will, and one mind, and must not upbraid each other for any imperfections; second, they must keep no secrets from each other; and last, they must keep no resentment unspoken but must tell their griefs. As a perfect example, an interesting picture of wedded bliss is presented by Robert Greene in *Perimedes the Black-Smith*, when we hear of the hero's own family:

And yet Fortune that she might not be thought to iniurious, in lieu of all her other disfauours lent him a wife of his owne conditions, whome he loued more then himselfe: for the poore woman although she was barren, and had no children, yet was she of a verie pure and perfect complexion, and withall of such good behauiour, first in loue and dutie to her husband, and then in friendly and familiar conuersation with her neighbours, that shee was thought a wife fit for so honest a husband. These two thus beloued of all the inhabitants of *Memphis*, prescribed them selues such an order of life, as diuerse men of great calling, sought to be carefull imitators of their methode: for suffring no priuate iarres to come within their . . . cottage, as a thing most preiuditiall to an Oeconomicall estate, no sooner had these two past away the day, he at his hammers, and she at the Bellowses, for boy they had none, but that sitting them selues to supper, they satisfied nature with that their labour did get, and their calling allow, and no sooner had they taken their repast, but to passe the rest of the euening merely, they fell to pleasant chatte between them selues, some time discoursing of what came first in their heads, with *Pro & contra*, . . . other while with merie tales, honest, and tending to some good end without either lasciuiousnesse or scurilitie, thus euer they passed away the night. [2]

The sociologists of today have cleverly discovered that it is wise for the young couple to live alone, but the Elizabethans knew this long ago. William Whately contends that two families cannot exist under the same roof in harmony:

Let mee commend vnto thy consideration, these two things following: When thou art married, if it may be, liue of thy selfe with thy wife, in a family of thine owne, and not with another, in one family, as it were, betwixt you both. And in all thy worldly dealings, trust no more then thou must needs; nor otherwise, then vpō due security. The mixing of gouernors in an houshold, or subordinating or vniting of two Masters, or two Dames vnder one roofe, doth fall out most times, to be a matter of much vnquietnes to all parties: Youth and Age are so far distant in their constitutions, that they wil hardly accord in their conditions; . . . let the young couple [have] another house, that they may learne to liue of a little, to know what is their owne, and how it becomes their owne, and to vse their owne to their owne best aduantage, that whatsoeuer come, they may neuer fall into that vnhappiest of all vnhappinesses, of either being tormentors of their Parents, or tormented by them. [3]

In general, the husband must remember that the action of his wife depends to a large extent upon his own actions: an 'inimical husband wil make a lascivious wife, and a riotous husband a voluptuous wife, a prowde husband a prowde wife, a modest and honest husband a modest and honest wife.' [4] The consensus is that the husband should bear a heavy burden of responsibility; society lays the blame at his door for any misbehavior of his wife.

The first duty which the husband has toward the wife is to love her. 'Loue is a naturall affection of the mind, inflaming all the powers of the Louer, with willing dutie towards the beloued.' This love must be the same love he bears to himself, for he must love her as himself in all points; this is the measure of mutual matrimonial love. Indeed, there is no time when it is not proper for a man to love his wife. The husband is to show his love for his wife in two ways: in protecting her from danger, and in providing for her maintenance both during his lifetime and after his death, as well as he can. Edmund Tilney, in *The Flower of Friendshippe*, makes a very practical point, namely, that a man should love his wife for self-protection if for no other reason, for 'the man, that is not lyked, and loued of his mate, holdeth his lyfe in continuall perill, his goodes in great ieopardie, his good name in suspect, and his whole house in vtter perdition.' [5]

The next duty of the husband is to rule or govern his wife in all duties that properly belong to marriage, using his knowledge, wisdom, and judgment to maintain himself in the place that God intended him to have; 'Nature hath framed the lineaments of his body to superiority, & set the print of gouernment in his face, which is more sterne, less delicate then the womans.' That the rule of the husband may not be easy is indicated in an anonymous play, *Swetnam, the Woman-hater;* here Scanfardo explains to his friend: 'The reason I would learne [duelling] is, because I am to bee married shortly: and they say, Then or neuer, is the time for a man to get the mastery.' To do so is rather difficult, however, for as Tasso tells us the wife has the same philosophy in mind, and is scarcely in the house for two days before she begins to give her orders and make her laws. Thus we see that theory breaks down in practice; apparently a nice balance of power

Mary Fitton, Maid of Honour to Queen Elizabeth

*Royal procession of Queen Elizabeth to the wedding of Anne Russell
and Lord Herbert at the Blackfriar's on June 16, 1600*

was maintained, with each establishment making its own rules. It is acknowledged by a female writer, Rachel Speght, that 'the *Man is the Womans Head*,' but she argues that this fact gives him no right to domineer over her or to treat her as a servant. Pierre Charron agrees; he believes that the husband should instruct the wife in her duty and her honor, and says that as far as mastery is concerned it is equally vicious to make her the mistress by subjecting himself to her, or to hold her merely as a servant. The ever-ready humor of the times is apparent when Otter, in *Epicoene*, facetiously denies that there is such a thing as a wife but only one who serves as various kinds of servants: 'Wife!... There's no such thing in nature. I confess, gentlemen, I have a cook, a laundress, a house-drudge, that serves my necessary turns, and goes under that title; but he's an ass that will be so uxorious to tie his affections to one circle.' [6]

When a husband speaks to his wife, he should speak softly; sweet and fair words are most important in increasing the perfect love in marriage. The husband must thus remember not to be fierce, rigorous, or hasty with his wife, if there is to be unity and concord in the home. *The Flower of Friendshippe* uses the figure of the garden, and says that there are certain herbs which nourish the flower of friendship in marriage; the first is to be advised in speech, and the second is to be courteous and gentle in conversation: 'Women for the most part, are froward of complexion, and tender of condicion, whereto the wise husbande must haue great regarde, and if he once reprehende them sharpelye, he must a hundreth exhort them louinglye.' It follows, then, that in dealing with a wife's infirmities, such as anger, waywardness, and the like, the husband must be wise and patient. He must always abstain from 'brawling, lowring, and grudging.' The husband who cannot control his temper is sharply admonished by William Whately: 'For to see a man so foolish and absurd, that hauing made himselfe the Gouernour of an houshold, he can beare no disorder of wife, children, seruants; no disaster in goods, cattell, dealings; without chafing, and fuming, and stormes, and without those pangs of a base and feeble mind, vaine wishes of hauing neuer knowne his wife, or so forth.... What was he, trow you, a reasonable man, or a bruit creature, that rushed so foresightlesly into marriage, as neuer to say to himselfe, that some of these things must needs befal al that are wedded?' The husband must always be merry and pleasant with his wife in order that she will be much in love with him at the beginning of marriage, so that if there should later be some slight disagreements they will be the result of sudden anger, soon gone, and not the result of any malice of long standing. Indeed, the husband should sometimes even permit his wife to admonish or advise him, and should give in to her when trifling matters are at issue. [7]

In his relations with his wife, the husband should be generous. He must yield to his wife's humble suit; he should often give her favors of his love; he should not be 'a very nygarde / and a chynche,' but should freely spend of his store to provide for her clothes. John Manningham saw fit to record in his diary that one Marrow, the sheriff of Warwickshire, 'useth his wife verry hardly' in not providing her with money or clothes, and in not trusting her in anything. From *Epicoene* we learn that a wife must be supplied with servants of all sorts: lady's maid, chamber-maid, page, gentleman-usher, French cook, and four grooms; and she must also have for her use a coach and four. Robert Cleaver even pushes generosity so far that he recommends that the husband must love his wife's relatives. He should be thus generous not only because it is the proper way to treat a wife, but also because 'except a woman haue what she will, say what she list, and go where she please, otherwise thy house will be so full of smoake, that thou canst not stand it.' It is pointed out by one author, whether in reproof or relief, that women are much more kindly treated than their ancestors. It is William Heale speaking, and he says that the canonists who made the laws in olden times were bachelors who knew nothing of the 'estate and mysterie of marriage,' and that they made their laws very strict: a wife lost her dowry if she gave a lascivious kiss; a wife was legally bound to follow her husband, wandering for his pleasure from city to city; a husband's mere suspicion of his wife's 'lightnes' could be responsible for her expulsion from the husband's company; and a wife was dignified only by the husband, but the husband was never graced by the wife.

The many duties of the husband toward the wife include not only kindness

114

A milkmaid

and forebearance, but correction of her faults. Altogether this model husband is delineated as a sanctimonious creature. Wives must be corrected with words rather than whips, and they can best be corrected thus. The husband must never open his mouth to tell his wife of a fault while he is 'hot & burning with violent passion.' Wives are better persuaded by reason than compelled by authority; they are better led by persuasion than constrained by severity. If a fault needs correction, the husband should admonish his wife for the smallest faults, and reprehend her for the greater offences. Further, the reproof must always be secretly administered, in private and never in public. The question of whether or not the husband has the right to subject his wife to physical punishment is debatable. In 1609 William Heale published a work the full title of which reads: *An Apologie for Women, or An Opposition to Mr. Dr. G. his Assertion. Who held in the Act at Oxforde. Anno. 1608. That it was lawfull for husbands to beate their wiues;* he insists that he has never seen it set down that a man was permitted by law to beat his wife. A work of 1568, however, states the opposite in recording that 'though the ciuill lawe giueth man the superioritie ouer his wyfe, that is not to offende, or despise hir, but in misdoing, louingly to reform hir.' But in 1632 was published *The Lawes Resolutions of Womens Rights: or, The Lawes Provision for Woemen. A Methodicall Collection of such Statutes and Customes, with the Cases, Opinions, Arguments and points of Learning in the Law, as doe properly concerne Women;* this author seems to have canvassed the situation more carefully, and it is his opinion that a husband has such a right but should not use it. To support his contention, he refers to Justice Brooke, who in the twelfth year of Henry VIII's reign 'affirmeth plainly, that if a man beat an out-law, a traitor, a Pagan, his villein, or his wife it is dispunishable, because by the Law Common these persons can haue no action'; and he concludes: 'God send Gentle-women better sport, or better companie.' Heale, however, reasons that a husband will naturally want to treat his wife well in order to escape a guilty conscience: 'A husband taketh his wife from her friends, disacquainteth her with her kindsfolkes, debarreth her from whomsoever was dearest vnto her; he takes her into his own hospitality; receiues her into his own protection, & himselfe becomes her sole Guardian. Wherefore then to beate and abuse her, is the greatest iniury that can be against the law of *hospitalitie.*' [8]

The thoughtful husband, further, will not do anything to make his wife jealous; for example, he will not bring his feminine friends into the home and then praise them before his wife for their beauty. He must realize, now that he is married, that what was formerly proper is now improper, and he must not give way to any 'raunging affections.' It scarcely need be mentioned that he will never have a mistress, even though Thomas Becon insists that 'matrimony now a dayes is so lytle estemed, and whoredome so commonly vsed.' In support of Becon, Manningham relates in his diary a dreary tale of the Earl of Sussex:

The Earle of Sussex keepes Mrs. Syluester Morgan (sometyme his ladies gentle-woman) at Dr. Daylies house as his mistress, calls her his Countesse, hyres Captain Whitlocke, with monie and cast suites, to braue his Countes, with telling of hir howe he buyes his wench a wascote of 10 l., and puts hir in hir veluet gowne, &c.: thus, not content to abuse hir by keeping a common wench, he striues to invent meanes of more greife to his lady, whoe is of a verry goodly and comely personage, of an excellent presence, and a rare witt. Shee hath brought the Earle to allowe hir 1700 l. a yeare for the maintenaunce of hir selfe and hir children while she lives apart.

It may be noticed here that under extreme provocation there is still no attempt to break the marriage. [9]

Conversely, the wise husband will not be jealous of his wife, remembering that where suspicion comes in, love goes out. And if he have occasion to mistrust his wife, perhaps he should better look closely to his own actions. Writing in 1568, Edmund Tilney discusses jealousy in words which remind us of *Othello:* 'The Stoike philosophers saye, that ieolousie is a certaine care of mans minde, least another shoulde possesse the thing, which he alone woulde enioye. There is no greater torment, then the vexatiō of a ieolous minde, which, euen as the moth fretteth the cloth, doth consume the hart, that is vexed therewith.' He goes on to say that there are two kinds of men who are commonly sick of this disease: those who are naturally evil in themselves, and those who, having gone astray in their youth, suppose that as other men's wives have misbehaved (as they well knew), just so will theirs.|

Naturally the husband must place no temptation before his wife by bringing male acquaintances into his home. While he may bring his best friends to the house, even here he should remember 'that a man may shewe his wife, and his sworde to his friende, but not to farre to trust them. For if therby grow vnto him any infamie, let him not blame his wife, but his owne negligence.' According to Heale, if a man is proved a cuckold, in Catalonia he must pay a fine, while in Paris he rides through the city in disgrace with a crier proclaiming before him: 'So do, so haue.' He adds that in England he has seen customs not much different. How to avoid the catastrophe of being cuckolded? In *Volpone* we find that one man has found the way by never letting his wife out of doors. As often cautioned, wives should never be permitted to dress frivolously; one of the risks of over-dressing is here remarked: 'Such gorgious & trimly decked wiues are gredy & desirous to wander abroade, & to be seene, and that is the frute of al ye cost and charge, & they that behold thē so gorgiously apparelled, are therby the more inticed & prouoked.' [10]

Since a chaste and loving life is earnestly commended among married couples, the manners and the talk must be chaste too. The husband should eschew 'fylthye handelynge, and all vnsemelynes.' Vives quotes Eusebius that 'thou shalt not onlye abstayne from vnclene sportes, but also frō playes, & filthye touchinges, lest thou shew thy selfe rather to be a louer then a husbande.' Euphues delivers the same advice to Philautus in a passage expanded from Plutarch's *Coniugalia Praecepta*. Certainly such immodest actions must never take place before company, at any rate: 'thou must neither chide nor play with thy wife before company; those that play and dally with them before company, they doe thereby set other Mens teeth on edge, and make their Wiues the lesse shamefast.' [11]

The good husband will take pains to be a companion to his wife; the contentment which should be found in marriage can exist only with love and friendship. If pensive solitariness is considered a miserable and un-

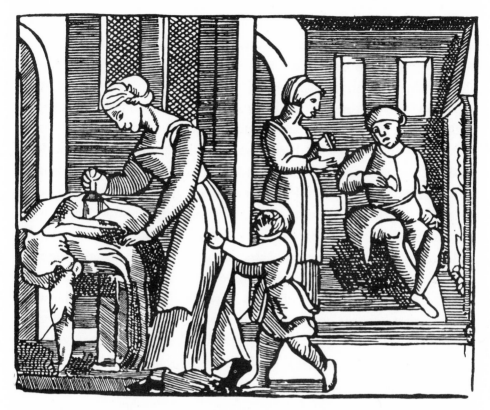

Household duties: cleaning clothes, caring for the sick

pleasant life, then company must make life happy and delightful; but there is no company more dear or joyous than that which exists between man and wife. And the husband should realize that his company is due to his wife. When the husband comes home, he must remember that the wife has had to stay within the house and be the housewife, and that she wants to hear the events that are taking place in the world; and if the husband relates interesting occurrences (although they must be none which will corrupt his wife's good manners), the wife is less likely to want 'to wander and raunge abroade.' As a sign of love, the husband should also tell his wife his secrets, because many men have found much comfort and profit by taking counsel of their wives; and if the secret is of an unpleasant nature, the telling of it will lighten his cares. A wife is expressly bidden to share her husband's troubles when he comes home at night. Obviously, these suggestions apply only if the wife is a wise one who can hold her tongue. While it is the husband's duty to give counsel to his wife, particularly if he is older and more experienced, it is conceded that a wife's advice is permissible at times.[12] The line between permissible advice and meddling in his affairs is admittedly a fine one.

It is rather interesting that three works specifically mention that a husband should see to it that his wife does not drink alcoholic beverages – even wine. Thomas Heywood blandly relates that kissing was first introduced to serve as a test of women's breath, since they were forbidden to drink wine.[13]

Besides the duties which the husband owes to his wife, he also owes many duties to his household. It must be understood, first of all, that the complete charge of everything lies in the hands of the husband. If anything goes amiss in the household, he will be held responsible by God, and also by his contemporaries. He must see to it that nothing unlawful or unseemly is done by any member of the household. He must therefore keep order and exercise discipline, and make corrections by rebuking or by chastising. It is the duty of the husband to provide meat, drink, and clothing for his family. He deputes this duty to his wife by furnishing her with the money with which to buy the necessaries, but he must also make certain that she does not spend too much. Or as Lyly puts it: 'Let all the keyes hang at hir girdel, but the pursse at thine, so shalt thou knowe what thou dost spend, and how she can spare.'[14]

While it is true that the husband governs the wife, he should realize that the wife has charge of running the house, and he must not meddle with it and thus be a cotquean: 'Those men are to be laughed at, who hauing wise and sufficient wiues, will (as they say) set their Hens to brood, season the pot, dresse their owne meate, teach the Chamber-maides, and take their wiues office from her.' Particularly, he should keep out of the kitchen and have nothing to do with his wife's maids. It is his province, rather, to govern the male servants, rebuking and correcting them when there is need. Similarly, the male children are under his specific care, and he must exercise due circumspection in making choice of some man to whom he may commit their instruction. It is further the duty of the husband to worship with the family, to instruct the family in religion, and to bring the family to church on Sunday, making sure that they behave themselves religiously there. The custom of entertaining preachers apparently has flourished for centuries, for William Perkins suggests the practice, listing it as the last of the five duties of the master of the family: 'To giue intertainment to those that are strangers, & not of the familie, if they be Christians, and Belieuers; but specially to the Ministers of the Word.' [15] It is probably needless to observe that Perkins was a minister himself.

As the first duty of the husband is to love his wife, so the first duty of the wife is to love her husband. Thomas Carter explains this duty by referring to the marriage ceremony itself: 'And as the ring is not of any mixt or base mettall, but of the most precious & pure mettal which may be: so it teacheth the woman that the loue shee must performe vnno [*sic*] her Husband, must bee pure, holy, and chast, it must allow no mixture.' This love and honor is owed to the husband because the wife must consider him as a divine and holy being. As a part of her love, then, she must give honor, reverence, and respect to her husband, since he is her lord and master. She must submit herself to him and acknowledge and revere him as the head in all matters. She must express her reverence towards her husband not only in her speech and gestures before him and to others in his presence, but in her speech behind his back she must be dutiful and respectful. She must express humility in everything she does. 'In a word the wiues maine dutie here is subiection.' [16]

As the oath taken by the wife in the marriage contract clearly specifies, the wife must obey the husband. This obedience or submission extends not only to the performance of duties required by the husband, but also to the abstinence from those activities which are displeasing to him. She indicates her obedience in many ways: she must come when he calls; she must take reproof meekly; and she must acknowledge her inferiority and 'carry her selfe as inferiour.' Furthermore, 'it nourisheth loue and concorde exceedingly, when the wife is readie at the becke and commaundement of her husbande.' [17] In order to answer an argument of John Knox, Bishop John Aylmer contends that 'a womā maye rule as a magistrate, and yet obey as a wife.' This subjection and obedience of the wife to the husband is not boundless or unlimited, however; according to Robert Cleaver, 'Yet must not this obedience so far extend, as that the husband should command anything contrary to her honour, credit and saluation, but as it is comely in the Lord.' The wife must obey in all things, believes Jean Bodin, except those which are 'repugnant vnto honestie.' A problem noted by one author occurs in many families: 'Namely, where the husband and wife are at oddes, which of them shall first begin to performe their duty, that is, whether the husbands loue bee the foundation of the wiues obedience; or the wiues obedience of the husbands loue. The wife will say, Let mine husband loue me as he should, and I will obey him as I ought. The husband he saith, Let her doe her dutie, and I will loue and maintaine her.' He goes on to say that the proper solution is to have the husbands and wives each perform their duties first; but he concludes that it is the wife's duty to avoid contention, even though the cause of the contention may be in the husband. This view is most widely held. If a woman considers that her husband has been choleric and hasty, she should overcome him with mild speeches; and if he chides her, she should hold her peace, even though she is not to blame; 'she must beare it patiently, and giue him no vncomely or vnkinde wordes for it: but euermore look vpon him with a louing and cheerfull countenance, and so rather let her take the fault vpon her, then seeme to be displeased. Let her be alway merie and cheerfull in his companie, but yet not with too much lightnesse.' For, as Eubola says, upon hearing Penelope's tale, 'obedience is a present salue against choller, and . . . the wife hath no better defensiue against an angry husband then submission with patience.' Of course it is very difficult for a wife to perform these acts of abnegation; in *The Unfortunate Traveller*, Nashe realizes this when he speaks thus of Diamante, the expelled wife of Castaldo: 'Hir husband had abused her, and it was verie necessarie she should be reuenged. Seldome doe they prooue patient martyrs who are punisht vniustly: one waie or other they will crie quittance whatsoeuer it cost them.' [18]

A good wife will be known as a silent woman. She will speak only with her husband or in the presence of her husband; she should be more seen than heard, for a silent woman is said to be a precious gift of God. Lampriscus, in *The Old Wives' Tale*, says that his first wife had a tongue which wearied him, sounding in his ears 'like the clapper of a great bell,' and that her talk 'was continual torment to all that dwelt by her.' And Penelope, in Greene's *Penelope's Web*, relates the story of the Ambassador of Corinth who, being asked how the ladies of his country behaved themselves, replied, ambiguously enough: 'They were silent, comprehending vnder this word all other vertues: as though that woman which were moderate in speech could also moderate her affections.'

A complementary virtue is that a good wife will never provoke her husband to anger, but will rather let her mood correspond to his. If the husband be sad, she must be sad; if he is merry, she will be merry. Indeed, often it will be found that love is completely lost between married couples before they have had time truly to know each other, and 'the maine reason of it is, because they obserue not one anothers qualities, and apply themselues accordingly.' A true wife should rather be 'like a *Turcoyse* stone, cleere in heart in her husbands health, and clowdy in his sickenesse.' The Second Gentleman in *The Knight of Malta* sums up what he considers the proper aspect of a wife, but then complains that such requirements are not at all fair: 'There is no wife, if she be good, and true, will honor, and obey, but must reflect the true countenance of her husband upon him; if he look sad upon her she must not look merrily upon him: if he look merrily she must not sorrowfully, else she is a false glass, and fit for nothing but her delight; if he weep, she must cry: if he laugh, she must show her teeth; if he be sick, she must not be in health; if he eat Cawdles, she must eat pottage, she must have no proper passion of her own; and is not this a tyranny?' [19]

How, then, can a wife get her way with her husband if she must follow these many precepts for the weaker sex? She works in devious ways to achieve her ends. By agreeing with all that her husband says, she may accomplish much, and it is often the part of wisdom to admit a guilt, at least for a time, even if she is really guiltless. 'The wise woman must consider, that hir husband chydeth eyther without reason, or hath good cause. If reason moue hym, then of dutie she is bound to obey, if other wise, it is hir part to dissemble the matter. For in nothing can a wyfe shewe a greater wisedom, than in dissembling with an importunate husbande. In a good example of the euphuistic style, Lucilla says much the same thing to Euphues: 'Though women haue small force to ouercome men by reason, yet haue they good Fortune to vndermine them by pollycie. The softe droppes of raine pearce the hard Marble, many strokes ouerthrow the tallest Oke, a silly woman in time may make such a breach into a mans hearte as hir teares may enter without resistaunce.' Another method of working (this time, before marriage) is to give a gentle smile: 'There are many young men which cudgell their wits, and beat their braines, and spend all their time in the loue of Women, and if they get a smile, or but a fauour at their Loues hand, they straightway are so rauished with ioy, yea so much, that they thinke they haue gotten God by the hand, but within a while after they will finde that they haue but the Deuill by the foot.' What chance has poor man, then, if he be so easily won both by tears and by smiles? What every woman knows is that she must let her husband think that he runs all affairs. Or to quote Epigram III in John Taylor's *A Iuniper Lecture*:

> *Megge* lets her Husband boast of Rule and Riches,
> But she rules all the Roast, and weares the Breeches. [20]

As we have earlier seen, it is very necessary for a woman to be circumspect and careful of her good name. Thus she must exercise discretion concerning what strangers come to the house, and also which of her gossips come there. She will remember that great talebringers are likely to be as great in carrying tales; 'the wise woman will be warie, whom shee admitteth into her house to sit long there, knowing that their occupation is but to marke and carrie.' The best way for her to preserve and protect this good name is to stay at home, for if she is naturally honest, her reputation will thus be made greater, and if she is naturally evil, the lack of evil opportunities will stop the mouths of her neighbors. That is the reason a wife is called a housewife and not a street-wife or a field-wife – to show that a good wife keeps to her house. Some women seem to think of their homes as prisons from which they must escape regularly, but they should rather think of their homes as pleasant abodes. In fact, 'the house shalbe vnto her in steede and place of a great & large citie, & she must go so sildom forth, that when she setteth her fote ouer the thresholde, she muste thinke y^t she goeth a pilgrimage. She must go onely to necessary places, seking no occasion to viset mother, parētes or any other frēdes.' Robert Burton quotes an unknown philosopher that a woman is to go out of her home only three times in her life: for baptism, marriage, and burial; but Burton thinks he is too strict. Another author re-emphasizes the restraint a woman must put upon herself. He postulates that there are only the following times that a wife is permitted to go out: to public holy meetings, to friendly meetings having to do with charity and good neighborliness, and with her husband when he requires her presence. This last means that she must dwell wherever her husband will have her dwell, and must follow him wherever he goes – even into exile and banishment – as a wife in *The Noble Gentleman* promises her husband. Upon the occasions when the wife goes to church, urges Thomas Becon, she must be very quiet and not disturb the congregation; if she wishes to ask her husband what the minister means, let her wait until she gets home. [21]

It is a corollary of staying at home, that the wife must keep her house neat and clean, so that there will be nothing to drive her husband out of doors. Nothing a woman can do will make her husband love her more than playing the good housewife. She must not be idle or permit her maids to be idle. Cassander, in *Euphues and His England*, advises his son Callimachus that a good housewife is a great patrimony. This theme is expanded by Pierre Charron, who says that the wife is to employ her time in 'the practice and study of housewifery, which is the most commodious and honourable science and occupation of a woman; this is her special mistris-quality, and which a man of mean fortune, should especially seek in his marriage. It is the only dowery, that serveth either to ruinate, or preserve families; but it is very rare. There are divers that are covetous, few that are good housewives.' [22]

Edmund Tilney's *The Flower of Friendshippe* insists that it is the duty of wives to be merry in bed. The remark sounds rather curious to our ears, and we naturally wonder what is meant. The answer becomes clear when we examine one of Lyly's 'Later Love-Poems':

> *In bed what strifes are bred by day,*
> *Our puling wiues doe open lay.*

The same complaint is made by Iago, who objects that his wife Emilia will never let him sleep when he gets to bed, but wants to talk to him continually. This complaint seems to be rather current in Elizabethan times. Thomas Heywood, for example, entitles one of his works *A Curtaine Lecture*, and relates that wives, when the husbands 'are willing to sleepe, whisper many private lectures in their eares, which they would not listen unto.' The nature of these 'lectures' is sufficiently indicated by a reference from Joseph Swetnam's important book:

Women are called night-Crowes, for that commonly in the night they will make request for such toyes as commeth in their heads in the day. Women know their time to worke their craft; for in the night they will worke a man like Waxe, and draw him like as Adamant doth Iron: and hauing once brought him to the bent of their Bow, then shee makes request for a Gowne of the new-fashion... for a Petticote of the finest Stammell, or for a Hat of the newest fashion. Her husband being ouercome by her flattering speech, partly hee yeeldeth to her request, although it be a griefe to him, for that he can hardly spare it out of his stocke; yet for quietnesse sake, hee doth promise what shee demandeth, partly because he would sleepe quietly in his Bed.

Manifestly the wives are taking undue advantage of their husbands to attack them when they are at the day's lowest ebb. The Proud Wife, in her *Pater Noster,* urges the young wife to make her requests either in bed or at the table. And Antoine de La Sale satirically points out that putting up with these curtain lectures and bed-requests is one of the fifteen joys of marriage. In *Christs Teares over Ierusalem,* Nashe goes so far as to insist that it is the

Domestic scene: the confinement

duty of the wife to discuss in bed various problems of housekeeping and of providing for the family. And he must be correct, for interestingly enough Desdemona, who is a paragon of wifely virtues, says that she will indulge in the custom, when she assures Cassio that she will serve as intermediary for him with Othello:

> If I do vow a friendship, I'll perform it
> To the last article: my lord shall never rest;
> I'll watch him tame and talk him out of patience;
> His bed shall seem a school, his board a shrift.

Furthermore, Robert Burton argues, in *The Anatomy of Melancholy*, that if the husband wants peace in the family, it is his duty to listen to these speeches: 'When you are in bed take heed of your wife's flattering speeches over night, and curtain sermons in the morning.' [23]

The Elizabethan wife must always put her husband first; she should work 'for his health, for his credit, for his wealth, for his happines in his estate more then for her selfe.' By economies and careful management she will take care of her husband's goods. 'A good woman is laborious, like the marchantes ship that seekes to bring in, shee bringeth in by her good foresight, by her care, by her diligence, and by the wisdome of her gouernment.' But even in forwarding the estate of her husband, she must not engage in any business ventures without discussing the matter with her husband. Of course, not all wives follow these suggestions. Lady Anne Clifford calendars in her diary that many times her husband puts great pressure on her to do his bidding in financial matters, but she usually stands firm. [24]

The provident wife, however, seems to be less in evidence than her prodigal sister; according to a large number of Elizabethan writers, many if not most wives are inclined to have what they want even if they ruin their husbands by their reckless spending. According to Bishop Pilkington, 'it is to be feared, that many desire rather to be like dallying Dinah than sober Sara. And if the husband will not maintain it, though he sell a piece of land, break up house, borrow on interest, raise rents, or make like hard

128

shifts, little obedience will be shewed.' Swetnam tells us of wives who must have their houses stored with expensive material, even though the servants may starve for lack of meat; he says they give a new turn to the Biblical account that woman was made to be a helper to man, 'for she helpeth to spend & consume that which Man painefully getteth.' And when she cannot get what she wants, she behaves childishly, as Accutus tells Graccus in an anonymous play, *Everie Woman in Her Humor*:

> *Another powtes and scoules, and hangs the lip,*
> *Euen as the banckrout credit of her husband,*
> *Cannot equall her with honors liuerie,*
> *What doth she care, if for to decke her braue,*
> *Hee's carryed from a Gate-house to his graue.*

If her husband cannot afford to give in to her whims, Brathwait pictures such a woman as going to bed and claiming she is at death's door. Similarly, in *Epicoene*, True-Wit tells Morose of such an evil wife: 'Shee feeles not how the land drops away; nor the acres melt; nor forsees the change, when the mercer has your woods for her veluets; neuer weighes what her pride costs.' [25]

Perhaps we may wonder what all of this money is spent on. It is nothing unusual – clothes of course, new coaches, new houses, tapestries, hunting horses, silver plate, jewels, rings, beads, girdles, many servants, exotic food, music lessons, French lessons, and so on without end. It may be informative to see what kind of system an Elizabethan wife uses in order to get some of these desirables from her husband. Thomas Dekker tells us. He pictures the wife as moping around the house until her husband finally notices her and asks what is the trouble; then she replies:

Well husband, if you will needs, you shal: you know on Thursday last, I was sent for, and you willed me to goe to Mistress M. Churching, and when I came thither I found great cheare, & no smal companie of wiues, but the meanest of them all was not so ill attired as I, and surely I was neuer so ashamed of my selfe in my life, yet I speak it not to praise my selfe: but it is well knowne, ... that the best woman there came of no better stocke then I. But alas I speake not this for my selfe, for God wot I passe not how meanely I am apparelled, but I speake it for your credit & my friends... The meanest that was there, being but of my degree, was in her gowne with trunck sleeues, her vardingale, her turkie grograin kirtle, her taffety hat with a gold band, and these with ye rest of her attire, made of ye newest fashiō. [26]

It should seem unnecessary to point out that a wife will continue to be chaste after marriage, but the Elizabethan writers feel that it is incumbent upon them to say so; 'a wyfe ought to be dyscrete, chaste, ... shamefaste, good, meke, pacyent and sober,' writes Herman V, the archbishop of Cologne, while *The Flower of Friendshippe* puts the matter thus: 'And if so be that there were but one onely vertue in a woman, it might well be shamefastnesse.' The good wife will, further, give no cause to her husband for jealousy: 'Shee leaves the neat youth, telling his *lushious* tales, and puts backe the *Serving-mans* putting forward, with a frowne.' She will also refuse to consort with any woman who has an ill name or who deserves to be so suspected. Nor will the good wife be too easily suspicious of her husband: 'Neyther ought she to be Iealous of him without great cause of desert, shewing also that it is better for her to couer his faults then to disclose them.' [27]

Elizabethan writers have little reticence in discussing the matter of sex in marriage. They feel, furthermore, that it is the province of the wife to make certain that sexual conduct is modest; in *The Womans Prize*, for example, Maria says:

> *By the faith I have*
> *In mine own noble Will, that childish woman*
> *That lives a prisoner to her husbands pleasure,*
> *Has lost her making, and becomes a beast,*
> *Created for his use, not fellowship.*

The Reverend William Whately, moreover, says that it is just as necessary to know the duties of the marriage-bed as to know other duties of marriage, because offenses here are not so public but are even more capital and dangerous. According to him, the matrimonial meetings must have three properties. First the meetings must be cheerful; the couple must willingly and familiarly unite, since this is the best way to 'nourish their mutuall [and] naturall loue, and by which the true and proper ends of matrimony shall bee attained in best manner.' Next, the meetings must be sanctified by prayer; this in itself 'will make it moderate, and keepe them from growing wearie each of other.' Last, the meetings must be at seasonable and lawful times; 'there is a season when God and Nature seioynes man and wife in this respect. The woman is made to be fruitfull; and therefore also more moist and cold of constitution; but a quantity redounding is set apart in a conuenient place to chearish and nourish the conception, when they shall conceiue. Now this redundant humour (called their flowers or termes) hath (if no conception bee) it monethly issue or euacuation, (and in some oftner) vnlesse there bee extraordinary stoppings and obstructions, lasting for sixe or seuen dayes in the most: Sometimes also this issue, through weakenes and infirmitie of nature, doth continue many more dayes.' In a work printed at the instance of the Archdeacon of Wells (Polydore Virgil), William Harrington states that there are certain times when the marriage bed should be avoided: during Lent, during Rogation days, during Holy days, during menstruation, and during pregnancy.

Further, a wife should, in a manner of speaking, let her duties correspond to the periods of her husband's life. Without mentioning Francis Bacon's name, Alexander Niccholes quotes from 'Of Marriage and Single Life' that 'wiues are yong mens Mistresses, companions for middle age, and old mens Nurses,' but adds that since the apostle said to rejoice in the wife of thy youth, this age is the fittest time in which to begin marriage. A wife should be all things to her husband:

> *Each Woman is a* briefe *of Womankind,*
> *And doth in little even as much containe,*
> *As, in one Day and Night, all life we find,*
> *Of either, More, is but the same againe:*
> *God fram'd Her so, that to her* Husband *She,*
> *As* Eve, *should all the* world of woman be. [28]

To summarize the various duties of the woman to her husband, we may turn to John Ley's work entitled *A patterne of pietie. or The religious life and death of that graue and gracious matron, Mrs. Jane Ratcliffe widow and citizen*

THE NEEDLES EXCELLENCY
A New Booke wherin are diuers Admirable
*Workes wrought with the Needle . Newly inuented and
cut in Copper for the pleasure and profit of the Industrious.*

WISDOME   INDVSTRIE   FOLLIE

Printed for Iames Boler and are to be sold at the Signe of the Marigold in Paules Church yard.
The 10th Edition inlarged wth diuers newe workes as needle-workes purses & others neuer before printed.

Engraved title page showing a garden

of Chester. Chapter headings in this work praise Mrs. Ratcliffe for her knowledge of the Bible, her prudence in speech and her avoidance of intemperate prattling, her discreet behavior, her faith, her piety, her precise walking in the precepts of God, her charity, patience, modesty, humility, sincerity, and constancy.

Besides these duties to her husband, the wife naturally has duties to the household, or, to put it differently, she has duties to the husband through her management of the household. She is a fellow-helper with her husband; she will take the best care of her husband's property, will see that his orders are obeyed, and will help him to spy out any evils that are breeding in the household so that his wisdom may prevent or cure them. If the office of the husband be to provide the necessaries, it is her duty to keep them; if he must go outside the home for matters of profit, she must stay at home to see that all be well there. Whatever the man procures through his work in the field or in the town,

> *The wyfe with her wysdom, must kepe from decay*
> *And suffer no proffyte in losse to fall downe.*

She must be economical and make sure that there is no wastage in the house; she will use the kitchen leavings (presumably in a stew) and will save the drippings of candles that they may make more candles. She will repair or have repaired anything in the house which may become worn or broken, and will inform her husband of anything which is needed in the house. Patrick Hannay would have her not only victual the household, but be able to tell good from shoddy merchandise, be able to buy, sell, and exchange at a profit, and even to survey and buy a field. The *Mulierum Pean* makes some additions to this list, putting it all down in verse:

> *Estates comenly where I go*
> *Trust theyr wyues to ouerloke*
> *Baker, brewer, butler, and coke*
> *Wyth other all, man medleth no whytte*
> *Bycause the woman hathe quycker wytte.*
>
> *My lady must receyue and paye*
> *And euery man in hys offyce controll*
> *And to eche cause gyue ye and nay*
> *Bargayne and bye and set all sole*
> *By indenture other by court roll*
> *My lady must ordre thus all thynge*
> *Or small shall be the mannes wynnynge.*

Apparently, the man provides the money, and the woman does everything else. [29]

The governing and instructing of the maids lie entirely in the wife's hands. She must serve as an example to them in keeping busy, remembering that she stands *in loco parentis* to her maids. She must never permit them to be idle, for idleness breeds trouble, and she must bring them up to value honor and chastity. It is her duty to instruct them in their occupations and trades, to assign them to their work and then to oversee it. She will discharge any servant guilty of 'swearing, vncleannes, drunkennes or riot.' She will instruct the servants in religion, giving over at least two hours a week to this instruction; she will keep a diligent eye upon the behavior of her maids, particularly 'what meetings and greetings, what tickings and toyings, and what words and countenances there be betweene men and maides; least such matters being neglected, there follow wantonesse.' If there be any maids in the household who cannot read, the good wife will instruct them until they can read the ten commandments. She is to provide her servants with three important particulars: 'worke, meate, and correction.' [30]

The mother of the Elizabethan time was a stern one by our standards. Small allowance was made for individuality among children; set rules were followed, and obedience exacted as a matter of course. It would seem that the girl-child was the especial subject of harsh correction; society reinforced the authority of the parents to the point where youthful rebellion was almost unheard of. The precepts concerning the training of children in religion and deportment make clear the position of children. They were supposed to be, in effect, miniature adults – even to their clothes. Just how far parental responsibility extended to their behavior in later life is a matter for conjecture. Once away from the family roof, or given in marriage, apparently the young people were received as mature adults, and the training they had undergone as children was not taken into account by society in explaining their development as citizens, as we do today.

The parents thus have many duties toward their children, but since the mother is chiefly responsible for their early education and training, and for rearing the daughters to become good wives, this care becomes another duty of the housewife. First of all, she must nurse her children herself. She must remember that children are not given to her for her pleasure, but rather for the glory of God, for the benefit of the church, and for the profit of the commonwealth. Then she must take care of them in all possible ways: teaching them, taking heed for them, ministering to them when they are ill, watching over them, covering them, washing them, and doing whatsoever needs to be done. The mother must particularly instruct her children in religion; she must bring them up in the fear of the Lord, in shamefastness, in hatred of vice, and in love of virtue; she must make them examples of Godliness and virtuousness. She must also teach her children good manners and civil behavior. They need to learn that silence is golden, that they must let their elders and betters speak first, and that they must never interrupt. When they speak, they must use fair speech to all and greet lovingly all Christians; they must express thankfulness for all kindnesses shown them; they must always speak humbly of themselves. The children must learn how to meet those approaching, to rise in the presence of their elders or betters and stand uncovered, and to make a proper bending of the knee or proper curtsy. They must never be idle, and must be taught some employment, so that 'they may get their liuing with honestie and trueth.' [31]

The good wife has the health of her household under her care. It is she who must treat the illnesses and even perform minor surgery. *The Good Huswifes Iewell* serves as an aid to her medical requirements by including many medical formulas. The housewife's interest in such matters accounts for the popularity of many works of medical recipes; Girolamo Ruscelli's *The Secrets of Alexis*, for example, was issued in four parts and ran to a total of some nineteen editions. This work contains recipes for salves and ointments for all sorts of diseases; on folio thirteen appears a treatment 'to heale Ringwormes, or the Morphew.' John Pattridge's *The Good Huswiues Closet of Prouision for the Health of Hir Houshold* goes so far as to present a short course in urinalysis. If the housewife consults Sir Hugh Platt's *A Closet for Ladies and Gentlewomen*, she will find the following suggestions:

For a Teter

Take Oates and seeth them in water, and where the Teter is, hold ouer the reeke thereof as hot as may be, laying a cloth ouer it to keepe in the recke, so that the cloth doe not touch the Teter, vse this fiue times morning and evening.

For a pinne and web

Take the oyle compacted of the bone of the Gooses wing, & rub it in the palme of your hand that no shiuers do sticke in it and put it in with the poynt of a pinne, for the bignesse of a pinnes head is ynough at once.

If one of the youngsters has eaten too many green apples, the wife may wish to try Lupton's recipe, since it is 'prooued, and a secrete': 'if you giue to them that haue the Hickop, euerye morning three howers before meate, one roote of greene Ginger, and immediatlye after drinking two draughtes of Malmesey, you shall see that he will be soon cured. *Empirici benedicti victorij.*' Of course many women were famous over a countryside for their success in treating ailments, such as Robert Burton's mother; he tells of her as follows: 'Being in the country in the vacation time not many years since, at Lindley in Leicestershire, my father's house, I first observed this amulet of a spider in a nut-shell lapped in silk, &c., so applied for an ague by my mother; whom, although I knew to have excellent skill in chirurgery, sore eyes, aches, &c., and such experimental medicines, as all the country where she dwelt can witness, to have done many famous and good cures upon diverse poor folks, that were otherwise destitute of help: yet among all other experiments, this methought was most absurd and ridiculous, I could see no warrant for it.' [32]

The good wife is also to be a kind of Lady Bountiful, taking care of the poor and needy. In a sermon of commemoration, John Donne speaks with reverence of the deceased wife of Sir John Danvers:

As shee receiv'd her *daily bread* from God, so *daily*, she distributed, and imparted it, to others. In which office, though she never turn'd her face from those, who in a strict inquisition, might be call'd idle, and vagrant Beggers, yet shee ever look't first, upon them, who *labour'd*, and whose *labours* could not overcome the *difficulties*, nor bring in the *necessities* of this life; and to the *sweat* of their *browes*, she contributed, even hir *wine*, and her *oyle*, and any thing that was, and any thing, that might be, if it were not, prepar'd for her owne table. And as her house was a *Court*, in the conversation of the best, and an *Almes-house*, in feeding the poore, so was it also an *Hospitall*, in ministring releefe to the *sicke*. [33]

In addition to the ordinary household duties, the housewife is supposed to be skilled in many arts which lie outside the running of her home. As an example, she is responsible for the growing of food and the preparation

136

of drink. Gervase Markham says that in turning to 'the outward and active knowledges which belong to the English Housewife, I hold the first and most principall to be a perfect skill and knowledge in Cookery, together with all the secrets belonging to the same, because it is a dutie rarely [*i.e.,* excellently] belonging to the woman.' He goes on to say that if a woman be ignorant of these matters she can keep only half her marriage vow: 'she may loue and obey, but shee cannot serue and keepe him with that true dutie which is euer expected.' We learn from Vives that the woman reigns alone in the kitchen, 'but yet in such wise & maner, that she put to her hande to dresse her husbādes meate, and not to cōmaunde it to be drest being absent. . . .' Even ladies, as we have earlier seen, should not disdain to know how to cook; Tasso, however, although he says that the good housewife will not scorn to set her hands to some work, is in the minority when he states that she should not work in the kitchen: 'I meane not in the Kitchin, or other soyled places, which may spoile or ray her garments, because such busines are not to be manedged and handled by noble Matrons . . . but in those onely that without noysomnes or filthines she may be bolde to touch.' We can only lift our eyes at this revelation of the cooking conditions; sometimes we feel that we are practically contemporaneous with the Elizabethans; but in matters of sanitation, no. Tasso does find it within the province of such a matron to see that some of her household corn be ground for bread while the rest is brewed for drink; and he thinks that she should especially have extra provisions on hand in case a stranger should turn up for dinner when the markets are unable to furnish food fit for her master's table. Estifania, in *Rule a Wife and Have a Wife*, says that she considers it as much her duty to be her husband's maid or cook in the kitchen, as to be his mistress in the hall. The good wife will of course know the various dishes she wants to appear on the table, and she at least knows the recipes, so that she may be able to tell the cook what to prepare. She can learn from *The Good Huswiues Closet of Prouision* how to gild a marchpane or any other kind of tart, how to make vinegar of roses, or a fine rice porridge, or hippocras. When the gossips meet in *The Gossips Greeting*, a good bit of their conversation has to do with the preparation of capons, rabbits, partridge, woodcocks, geese, plover, quail, fruit, cheese, marchpane, sweet suckets, marmalade, biscuits, caraways, comfits, and so on. Our Elizabethan ancestors surely loved the table, and seem capable of eating enormous amounts of food. We have no record that the following dinner was ever served, but at any rate we have here J. Murrell's suggestion for a summer feast for fifty guests, as recorded in his *Two Books of Cookerie and Carving:*

First Course

1. A Grand Sallet.
2. A boyld Capon.
3. A boyld Pike.
4. A dish of boyld Pea-chickens, or Partridges, or young Turky-chicks.
5. A boyld Breame.
6. A dish of young Wild-ducks.
7. A dish of boyld Quatles.
8. A Florentine of Puft-paste.
9. A forced boyld meate.
10. A hansh of Venison roasted.
11. A Lomber Pye.
12. A Swan.
13. A Fawne or Kid, with a pudding in his belly, or for want of a Fawne you may take a Pigge and fley it.
14. A Pastry of Venison.
15. A Bustard.
16. A Chicken Pye.
17. A Phesant or Powtes.
18. A Potato Pye.
19. A Couple of Caponets.
20. A set Custard.

The second Course

1. A Quarter of a Kid.
2. A boyld Carpe.
3. A Heron or Bitter.
4. A Congers head broyled, or Troute.

5. A Hartichoake Pie.
6. A dish of Ruffes or Godwits.
7. A cold baked meate.
8. A sowst Pigge.
9. A Gull.
10. A cold bakte meat.
11. A sowst Pike, Breame, or Carpe.
12. A dish of Partriges.
13. An Orengado Pye.
14. A dish of Quailes.
15. A cold baked meat.
16. A fresh Salmon, Pearch, or Mullet.
17. A Quodling Tart, Cherry, or Gooseberry Tart.
18. A dryed Neates-tongue.
19. A Jale of Sturgeon.
20. A sucket Tart of puffe-paste.

A third cou[r]se for the same Messe

1. A Dish of Pewets.
2. A dish of Pearches.
3. A dish of green pease, if they be dainty.
4. A dish of Dotrels.
5. A dish of Hartichoakes.
6. A dish of buttered Crabs.
7. A dish of Prawnes.
8. A dish of Lobstars.
9. A dish of Anchoues.
10. A dish of pickled Oysters.

Like the Queen in *Cymbeline*, a woman should know all about confections, conserves, distillations, etc., preserving fruits, making gingerbread, sweetmeats, and about baking. If she is sufficiently wealthy, she may possibly hire a woman to manage this part of the household, but this housekeeper will still receive her orders from the mistress. [34]

In a large household, the wife will know the duties and oversee the offices of the butler, pantler, and yeoman of cellar and ewry, as well as the offices of all the maids. The office of the butler is particularly important; he must have on hand at all times butter, cheese, apples, pears, nuts, plums, grapes, dates, figs, raisins, compote, green ginger, chard, and quince. For in-between-meals he provides butter, plums, damsons, cherries, and grapes; for 'after meate' he provides pears, nuts, strawberries, whortleberries, hard cheese, and pippins with caraways in 'confects'; for 'after supper' he provides apples and pears with blanched powder, and hard cheese. Similarly, the housewife must know the offices of the maltster, the brewmaster, etc. [35]

Besides taking care of affairs within the house, the housewife must 'see her Garden weeded, her Vines cut, and in her Orcharde her fruite Trees pruned.' She must know when her flowers and herbs should be planted and gathered. If she turns to William Lawson's *A New Orchard and Garden:... with the Country Houswifes Garden for herbes of Common Vse*, she will find many elaborate designs for the plot of her gardens, discussions of various sites and soils, the size of the garden, whether or not it should be fenced, and other problems of gardening. According to Lawson, there are two types of gardens: the flower garden or summer garden, and the kitchen garden or winter garden. The summer garden may contain roses, rose-mary, lavender, bee-flowers, hyssop, sage, thyme, cowslips, peonies, daisies, cloves, gilliflowers, pinks, southernwood, and lilies; the winter garden may contain onions, parsnips, fennel, saffron, strawberries, lettuce, and so forth. The herbs and vegetables of both gardens are used to make salads, as is shown by the following passage from Gervase Markham's *Country Contentments, or The English Huswife*: 'Your compound Sallats, are first the young Buds and Knots of all manner of wholsome hearbes at their first Springing, as Red-sage, Mints, Lettice, Violets, Marigolds, Spinage, and many other mixed together, and then serued vp to the table with Vinegar, Sallet Oyle and Sugar.'

The good housewife will have the dairy under her charge. She will know enough about animal husbandry to be a judge of milch cows, and will know how to make and market butter and cheese, even if she be of the gentry. Richard Brathwait writes that he has often seen his wife come from the dairy and then hurry in to entertain her important guests. [36]

It is the further province of the housewife to oversee the making of cloth from its beginning. She should be a good needlewoman both in making and in mending. Even if she is too lady-like to be seen in the kitchen, yet it is quite proper for her to handle 'the wheeles, lombes, & other instruments that appertaine to weauing.' Margaret Hoby writes in her diary that she and her maids dye wool, wind yarn, make wax lights and sweetmeats, and that on long winter evenings they spin and embroider while one of their number reads from books of devotion. First the wool and flax must be raised or purchased; then come the beating of the flax and hemp, the carding and spinning of the wool. The wife clearly knows the use of the rocke or distaff and the spindle; in fact: 'Women through their subtill inuention founde out the meanes to spinne and carde Woll.' She knows how to weave on looms and to make the cloth into clothes. She often makes fine needlework, bone-lace, and so forth. Like Gallathea, in Lyly's play of that name, she sews on her sampler; in a poem, Lyly gives the sort of sampler which a forsaken young gentlewoman might work:

> *Come, giue me needle, stitch cloth, silke & chaire*
> *y' I may sitt and sigh, and sow & singe*
> *For perfect coollo's to describe y' aire*
> *a subtile persinge changinge constant thinge*
> *No false stitch will I make, my hart is true*
> *plaine stitche my Sampler is for to c̄oplaine*
> *How men haue tongues of hony, harts of rue.*
> *true tongues & harts are one, men makes them twaine.*
> *Giue me black silk y' sable suites my hart*
> *& yet som white though white words do deceiue*
> *No green at all for youth & I must part*
> *Purple & blew, fast loue & faith to weaue.*
> *Mayden no more sleepeless ile goe to bedd*
> *Take all away, y' work works in my hedd.*

Campaspe, in another play by Lyly, reminds herself that 'a needle will become thy fingers better then a Lute, and a distaffe is fitter for thy hand then a Scepter.' Women are able to embroider on silk, as does Emilia's maid in *The Two Noble Kinsmen*, and we also remember the embroidered design on Desdemona's handkerchief, which both Emilia and Cassio intend to have 'taken out' or copied, and which Bianca is apparently capable of copying, although she refuses to do so. And in one of Greene's anecdotes, Margaret 'beautified the house with Cusheons, Carpets, stools and other deuises of needle worke, as at such times diuers will doo, to haue the better report made of their credite amongst their seruants friends in the Countrey.' Thomas Nashe, however, seems to think that women are not much given to the use of the needle anymore:

In *Rome* the bride was wont to come in with her spyndle and her distaffe at her side, at the day of her marriage, and her husband crowned and copassed the Gates with her yarne, but now adaies Towe is either too deere or too daintie, so that if hee will maintaine the custome, hee must crowne his Gates with their Scarfes, Periwigs, Bracelets, and Ouches; which imports thus much vnto us, that Maides and Matrons now adaies be more charie of their store, so that they will be sure they will not spend too much spittle with spynning, yea theyr needles are nettles, for they lay the aside as needlesse, for feare of pricking their fingers, when they are painting theyr faces.

In taking care of the clothes, the housewife will also be the complete laundress, and will know how to remove spots of grease, oil, or anything else from any kind or color of cloth; how to wash, beat, and wring clothes; how to heat and use the pressing tool; and how to use the 'sleeke-stone to smooth hir linnen.' [37]

As another part of her care of the clothing, the housewife has to know about mothproofing – how to make a 'fumigation for presse and clothes that no Moth shall breede therein.' In this connection, also, she will be able to make sachets, and will know how to compound 'a Violet powder for wollen Clothes and Furres,' and 'a sweete powder for Napery, & all linnen clothes.' Related to her duties with food, she should know how to set a correct table, as well as how to serve the meals. She must not stop at the merely practical arts, but must know how to 'dress a house with flowers,' and to 'set all her plate on the Cubboorde for shewe.' Like the Queen in *Cymbeline*, she will be able to make perfumes and cologne, and be competent in the making of cosmetics. [38]

Perhaps the following passages may seem to exaggerate the industry of the housewife, but they present stirring pictures of the country housewife's day. First we have an early morning routine of the wealthy country matron, as set forth by Thomas Tusser in *The Points of Huswifery* appended to his *Five Hundred Points of Good Husbandry:* she gets up at cock-crow to oversee the servants and set their tasks for them – some to peel hemp, some to peel rushes for candlewicks, some to spin and card, some to boil saltwater to get salt, some to take care of the cattle, some to grind malt for brewing. She serves breakfast for the men and the maids, supervises the making of bread, and does her own brewing. She makes her own candles, and saves feathers for beds and pillows. She locks and guards the dairy from cats and vagabonds. The farmer's wife is perhaps even busier, or so John Fitzherbert presents her around the clock:

And whan thou arte vp and redy, than first swepe thy house, dresse vp thy dyssheborde, and sette all thynges in good order within thy house: milke thy kye, secle thy calues, sye vp thy mylke, take vppe thy chyldren, araye theym, prouyde for thy husbandes brekefaste, dynner, souper, and for thy chyldren, and seruauntes, and take thy parte with theym. And to ordeyne corne and malte to the myll, to bake and brue withall when nede is. And mette it to the myll, and fro the myll, and se that thou haue thy measure agayne desyde the tolle, or elles the myller dealeth not truly with the, or els thy corne is not drye as it shoulde be. Thou must make butter, and chese whan thou maist, serue thy swyne bothe mornynge and euenyng geue thy poleyn meate in the mornynge, and whan tyme of the yere cometh, thou muste take hede howe thy hennes, duckes and geese dooe ley, and gather vp theyr egges, and whan they waxe broodye, sette them there as no beastes, swyne, nor, other vermyn hurte them. And thou muste knowe, that all hole footed fowles wyll sytte a moneth, and all, clouen footed fowles wyll sytte but three weekes, excepte a peyhenne, and greatte fowles, as cranes, bus-tardes, and suche other. And whan they haue broughte forthe theyr byrdes, so see, that they be well kepte from the gleyd, crowes, fullymartes, and other vermyne. And in the begynnynge of Marche, or a lyttell afore, is time for a wyfe to make hir garden, and to gette as many good seedes and herbes, as shee can, specyally suche as be good for the potte, and to eate: and as oft as nede shall requyre, it muste be weded, for els the wedes wyll ouergrowe the herbes. And also in Marche is tyme to sowe flaxe and hempe. for I haue hearde olde houswyues saye, that better is Marche hurdes, than Apryll flaxe, the reason appereth: But howe it shoulde be sowen, weded, pulled, repeyled, watred, wasshen, dryed, beaten, braked, tawed, hecheled, spon, wounden, wraped, and wouen, it nedeth not for me to shewe, for they bee wise enough, and therof maie they make shetes, bordeclothes, towels, shertes, smockes and suche other necessaries, and ther fore let thy dystaffe be alwaye redye for a pastyme, that thou bee not ydle. And vndoubted a woman can not gette hir lyuynge honestily with spynnynge on the dystaffe, but it stoppeth a gap, and muste nedes he had. The bolles of flaxe, whan they be ripiled of, must be rideled from the wiedes, and made drye with the son, to get out the sedes. Howe be it one maner of lynsede, called loken sede, wyll not open by the sonne: and therfore whan they be drye, they muste be sore brused and broken, the wyues knowe howe, and than winowed and kepte drye, tyll yere tyme came agayn . . . It may fortune sometime, that thou shalt haue so many thinges to dooe, that thou shalt not well knowe, where is best to begyn. Than take hede, whiche thing shulde be the greattest losse, if it were not done, and in what space it wold be done: than thinke what is the greatest losse, & there begyn. But in case that thynge, that is of greattest losse, wyll be longe in doynge, and thou myghtest do three or foure other thynges in the meane whyle, than loke well, if all these thynges were sette together, whiche of theim were the greattest losse, and if all these thynges be of greatter losse, and maie be all done in a morte space, as the other, than dooe thy many thynges fyrste. It is conuenyente for a housbande to haue shepe of his owne for many causes, and than maye his wife haue part of the woll, to make hir husbande and hir selfe some clothes. And at the leaste waye, she maie haue the lockes of the shepe, ether to make clothes, or blankettes and couer lettes, or bothe, and if she haue no woll of hir owne, she maie take woll to spynne of clothe makers, and by that meanes she maye haue a conuenyent liuynge, and many tymes to do other warkes. It is a wyues occupacion, to wynowe all maner of cornes, to make malte, to wasshe and wrynge, to make heye, shere corne, and in tyme of nede to helpe hir housbande to fyll the mucke wayne or dounge carte, dryue the ploughe, to lode hey, corne, and suche other. And to go or ride to the market, to sel butter, chese, mylke, egges, chekyns, capons, hennes, pygges, gese and all maner of cornes. And also to bye all maner of necessarye thynges belongynge to housholde, and to make a trewe rekenynge and a compte to hir housbande, what she hath receyued, and what shee hathe payed. And yf the housbande go to the market, to bye or sell, as they ofte do, he than to shewe his wife in lyke maner. For if one of theim shoulde vse to deceyue the other, he deceyueth hym selfe, and he is not lyke to thryue. And therfore they muste be trewe eyther to other. [39]

Some women, of course, found it necessary to obtain work outside the home. It is rather needless to go into this subject at length because of the excellent account given by Miss Alice Clark in her *Working Life of*

¶The spider to his sonne and twelue spiders giueth his best
aduise for most quiet and best gouernance. His tale standinge
most vpon these three terms, first a decleracion of him selfe,
second an exhortacion to them, the third a submission for him
self, wherunto he desireth licēce to take his child in his armes:
now at their departing, which the maide graunteth. Cap.92.

Pp   My

A housemaid

Women in the Seventeenth Century. We know that a large number of girls found employment as household maids, and from an assessment for the East Riding of Yorkshire we learn that a special rate of wages was provided for women who hired out as overseers of brewing, baking, cooking, and making of dairy products, or as housekeepers. And wives would often have the management of the entire estate during the absence of the husband; Lady Brilliana, the wife of Sir Robert Harley, is an example. But there were other women who were engaged in work quite outside the home. Around 1610 Dorothy Selkane, for instance, wrote to Salisbury reminding him that she had been promised a patent to mine coal on a royal manor. It is not clear why the coal business should have appealed to women, but Mary Hall, Barbara Riddell, and Barbara Milburne were listed in 1622 as among the owners of collieries; since widows often continued the enterprises of their husbands, perhaps we have the explanation here. Indeed, the statutes of the Carpenters' Company for November 10, 1607, clearly indicate that widows could retain the husband's apprentices upon his death. Trade guilds seem to have been open to girls who had to earn their livelihood; not many availed themselves of the opportunity, however, although in 1622 women were members of the Bakers' Company. On the other hand, marriage to a member of a guild conferred rights upon the wife, and she could retain these after his death. A printer's widow, for example, was a very eligible woman, for the following reasons: the Stationers' Company included stationers, booksellers, binders, and printers; apprenticeship to any of these eventually conferred the right of freedom of the company; but the position of printer could not be obtained in this fashion by an apprentice, and was considered quite a prize since the privilege of printing was limited to twenty-two firms; further, a vacancy seldom occurred, because on a printer's death the rights were retained by his wife, who could pass 'them on to her next husband. Many books, for instance, were printed by the widow of R. Wolfe and by Elizabeth Alde. Another example of the widow's continuing her husband's enterprise is Margaret Greeneway, who in 1630 begged leave to finish carrying out the contract made by her husband to supply biscuit to the

East India Company, notwithstanding the restraint on the bringing of corn to London.

The keeping of inns and the management of alehouses might seem legitimate occupations for women; Ben Jonson, in *the Masque of Augures*, writes of such an alehouse ('the three dancing Beares in Saint *Katherines*') which is kept by a 'distressed Lady' and her two gentlewomen. It is rather curious, however, to find that in 1614 Anne is included with Roger and James Wright in a grant for life to keep a tennis court in Suffolk. And what are we to think of Lady Roxburgh, who petitioned in 1624 for a license to assay all gold and silver wire before it is worked; or Anne Hodsall, who petitioned in 1628 for permission to make pipe staves in Ireland to be sent to her estate in the Canaries, so that she might import her wine into England; or Elizabeth Bennett, who, with Thomas Berry, contracted to furnish one hundred suits for the soldiers at Plymouth?

Women also worked as upholsterers, milliners, mantua-makers, and so forth; and remembering that women made their own candles at home, it is not surprising that Alice Fox was a wax-chandler in 1619. We are all familiar, also, with fishwives and orangewomen; one of Ben Jonson's characters in *Epicoene* seems to indicate that these women added to their income by serving as go-betweens or panderesses. If we are to believe Heywood's *The Wise Woman of Hogsdon*, women also posed as fortunetellers, astrologers, and medical quacks. Here are mentioned Mother Nittingham, who is expert in diagnosis by urinalysis, Mistress Mary on the Bankside, who is proficient in erecting an astrological figure, Mother Sturton and another practitioner in Westminster, who are adept at divination, and Mother Phillips, who is known for her success in treating weakness of the back. Familiar, too, are the women who were paid for being wet, dry, and sick nurses, not to speak of the women who practiced the profession of midwifery, which must really have been woman's oldest profession. Jonson, again, in *An Entertainment at the Blackfriars*, lists the proverbial characteristics of the midwife: 'Manye a good thinge, passes through the Midwifes hand, manye a merrye tale by her mouth, manye a Gladd cup through her lippes, shee is a leader of wiues, the lady of light harts, and the queene of Gossipps.'

It may be interesting to go back a few centuries and find what trades were followed by women in 1380. The poll-tax returns for Oxford in this year indicate that there were thirty-seven spinsters, eleven shapesters or tailors, nine tapsters or inn-keepers (Chaucer's 'tapesterres'), three sutrices or shoemakers, three hucksters, five washerwomen, and that others were employed as butchers, brewers, chandlers, ironmongers, netmakers, and kempsters or wool-combers. [40]

Thus we see that women were beginning to emerge as legal entities, as a concomitant of the rise of the middle-class in England. Their progress toward freedom in the business world seems to have been steady; and in the home, as helpmeets in that enterprise, women were advancing to a state of full partnership with their husbands. No doubt it was here that women first had to win their way and prove themselves capable of being good managers, or no woman would ever have been given the chance to run any business.

In the home we find that the Elizabethan woman has now become a curious mixture of the slave and the companion – the necessary evil and the valued lieutenant. Not yet has the Elizabethan woman achieved the basis of the equality of today. But we have definitely moved away from the medieval conception of woman as a chattel. Sometimes, as we have seen, a writer will list virtues expected in a wife (including submission to the husband, having moods corresponding to those of the husband, being silent like the child of yesterday – seen, but not heard), but will then argue that only a tyrannous husband would require such a wife.

As we read of the housewife's duties, we become rather exhausted ourselves; if a good wife must accomplish all of these tasks, was there ever a good wife? And yet it is perhaps in the home that the Elizabethan woman seems most like her twentieth century sister; conversation on the subject of housekeeping could easily bridge the four hundred years. Moreover, until the twentieth century housekeeping problems were almost identical with those of the time we are discussing. It is quite true, however, that the going has not always been smooth. Under the aegis of Puritanism, in both Old and New England, women lost ground as regards freedom and recognition, and only slowly was the ground regained. But clearly recognizable here are the efforts of Elizabethan women to improve their status.

CHAPTER VI

Pastimes and Amusements

Sweet recreation barr'd, what doth ensue
But moody and dull melancholy,
Kinsman to grim and comfortless despair,
And at her heels a huge infectious troop
Of pale distemperatures and foes to life?

The Comedy of Errors

Gaming in a brothel

Not all of an Elizabethan woman's time was taken up with household duties and religious meditation. The ladies of the court, at least, found a need to fill in some boring hours, to entertain their guests, to increase their knowledge, or simply to avoid any semblance of idleness. Orlanio, in Greene's *The Card of Fancie*, gives particular direction on this last point to the woman who is put in charge of his daughter: 'Suffer not my Daughter to passe her time in idlenesse, least happilie . . . discouert, shee become a carelesse captiue to securitie, for when the minde once floateth in the surging seas of idle conceites, then the puffes of voluptuous pleasures, and the stiffeling stormes of vnbrideled fancie, the raging blastes of alluring beautie, and the sturdie gale of glozing vanitie, so shake the shippe of recklesse youth, that it is dailie in doubt to suffer most daungerous shipwracke.' He urges, therefore, that the governess 'let her spend her time in reading such auncient authors as may sharpen her wit by their pithie sayings, and learne her wisedome by their perfect sentences. . . . And *Melytta*, for recreation sake, let her vse such honest sportes as may driue awaie dumpes, least shee bee too pensiue, and free her minde from foolish conceites, that shee bee not too wanton.'[1] We remember, however, that Vives objects to many of these ancient works, such as those by Ovid, Lucian, Apuleius, Aristeides, and others, as well as the romances and English stories of war and love. On the other hand, Vives approves of Plato, Homer, Hesiod, Propertius, Anacreon, Sappho, Callimachus, Cato, Publilius Syrus, Plutarch, Lucan, some of Horace, some of St. Jerome, St. Augustine, St. Ambrose, and others. Certainly the Elizabethan women do read rather widely. Lady Politic Would-be apparently is familiar with Montaigne, Petrarch, Dante, and even Aretino. Princess Mary certainly read works in Latin, French, and Spanish, since she knew these languages well; and being interested in botany and dialing, she may well have read works on these subjects. Lady Hoby, who was successively the wife of Walter Devereux (Essex's younger brother), Thomas Sidney (Philip's younger brother), and Thomas Posthumous Hoby (the younger son of

Sir Thomas) read religious works almost entirely: the Bible, sermons, Foxe's *Book of Martyrs*, and sometimes a herbal. She followed Vives' suggestion in starting the day with reading the Scriptures, and offering prayers both night and morning. Lady Mary Grey similarly restricted her reading to the Bible and religious works. Other ladies read romances, particularly in French, such as *Poleander* and *L'illustre Bassa*. *Cleopâtre* and *La Reine Marguerite* were also favorites. Dorothy Osborne read books of travel and such poetry as Cowley's. Anne Clifford records in her diary that 'the 26th [of April, 1617] I spent the evening working and going down to my Lord's Closet where I sat and read much in Turkish History and Chaucer.' She also read the Bible regularly, alone or with Mr. Rand (or Ran), her spiritual guide. She finished reading Leviticus on March 13, 1617, and by the twenty-seventh of the same month she had finished Deuteronomy. At that point her husband stopped her from reading with Rand, saying that Rand's study was being interfered with. Whether or not the ladies could read, they liked to have their maids read to them; indeed, this reading was often a part of the duty of a lady's maid. Gertrude, in *Eastward Hoe*, tells her newly employed maid that she needs her to 'tell me tales, and put me riddles, and read on a book sometimes when I am busy,' and Quicksilver later supports this information about Gertrude. Similarly, in *The Womans Prize*, Petruchio complains that it costs too much money to keep a wife, ending the list of items he must provide thus: 'then for Musick, and women to read French.' And in Massinger's *The Guardian*, Calipso says that her lady has no parallel

> *In all the books of* Amadis de Gaul,
> *The* Palmerins, *and that true Spanish story*,
> *The* Mirror of Knighthood, *which I have read often.*

At any rate, the ladies had to know enough about the stories to talk of them, whether they read them themselves or were read to. [2]

Many of the more literary ladies tried their hands at poetry. Queen Elizabeth's 'When I was fair and young' and 'The doubt of future foes exiles my present joy' are well known, the latter appearing in *The Art of*

Huntsman reporting to the Queen by showing evidence of a hart

English Poesy, where the author of the collection wrote of her as follows: 'But last in recital and first in degree is the Queen, our sovereign lady, whose learned, delicate, noble muse easily surmounteth all the rest that have written before her time or since, for sense, sweetness, and subtility, be it ode, elegy, epigram, or any other kind of poem heroic or lyric wherein it shall please her Majesty to employ her pen, even by as much odds as her own excellent estate and degree exceedeth all the rest of her most humble vassals.' Mary Herbert, the Countess of Pembroke ('Sidney's sister, Pembroke's mother'), translated into verse Robert Garnier's French tragedy, *Antonius*, while her *The doleful lay of Clorinda* appeared in 1595 with Spenser's *Astrophel*. During the second quarter of the seventeenth century, Katherine Philips was writing such delicate pieces as ''Tis true our life is but a long disease' and 'I did not live, until this time.' Although these poems sound very much like many of those by well-known poets of the time, one of Ben Jonson's characters makes a distinction between the sort of verse written for men and that written for women: 'Your Mans Poet may break out strong and deep i' th' mouth as he said of *Pindar, Monte decurrens velut amnis*. But your Womans Poet must flow, and stroak the eare, and (as one of them sayd of himselfe sweetly)

> *Must write a Verse as smooth, and calm as Creame,*
> *In which there is no torrent, nor scarce streame.'* [3]

Some ladies spent a good deal of time carrying on extended correspondence with friends. To help them in their composition of such letters, Jerome Hainhofer translated from the French of Jacques Du Bosc a helpful work entitled *The secretary of ladies or a new collection of letters and answers, composed by moderne ladies and gentlewomen. Collected by Mr. Du Bosq*. The book consists of letters between two ladies (sometimes more) on various groups of subjects; thus is created a manual of letters for all occasions. William Averell has a peculiar objection to letter-writing for women, however, since he includes it among such other 'lewde and vnseemely pastimes' as fixing the hair, playing the lute, singing sonnets, and dancing. [4]

Elizabethans loved their gardens, which were at first of the strictly formal Italian style, introduced into England early in the Renaissance; later gardens became a mixture of the formal and the medieval monastic garden, with emphasis still on the formal. Francis Bacon, in one of his most delightful essays ('Of Gardens'), charmingly describes an ideal formal garden, which must not, however, contain 'knots or figures,' since they are 'but toys.' In their gardens the ladies spent many pleasant hours escaping from the world, talking, and admiring the sweetbrier, roses, camomile, eglantine, daisies, and the other flowers and herbs which grew in abundance. Giovanni Michele Bruto writes in his *The Necessarie, Fit, and Convenient Education of a Yong Gentlewoman* that walking in the garden is one of the very best pastimes for the young lady of England: 'She shall for her recreation vse to passe her time in her gardens & cuntry houses, which in this cuntry are so delightfull & pleasant, recreatiue & beautifull, that neither in Italie nor in any other part of Europe, ther are any to be foūd that may surpasse thē: yet she shall not stay there so long, that therby she shold forget the customes and maners of the cities, although our villages are so full of houses and pleasant buildings, that nothing is wanting wherby they may not seeme to deserue the names of populous towns.' After meals, the ladies often retire to the garden while the men engage in philosophic conversation, as happens in *Euphues His Censure to Philautus*. In Greene's *Orpharion*, when Philomenes passes into the privy-garden of the court, he finds 'all the Ladies sparseled about in sundry borders, som gathering flowers, others in discourses of the excellency of the place, some in prattle with the birds, all busie, none idle.' Similarly, in *The Woman Hater*, the Count tells Oriana: 'Faith the Lady Honoria cares for you as she does for all other young Ladies, she's glad to see you and will show you the Privy Garden, and tell you how many Gowns the Duchess had.' Sometimes the ladies are able to entice their husbands into the gardens; some young gentlemen in *Greenes Farewell to Folly*, being ashamed to have slept so late, 'passing into the garden, found the olde Countie, his wife and foure daughters walking for health and pleasure in a fresh and greene arbour.' [5]

The ladies of the Elizabethan court circles had various kinds of pets, the most popular of which was the dog; although the breed is generally nameless, pictures of the time, showing ladies with their dogs, portray a creature which resembles a Maltese. In the preface to Lyly's *Euphues and His England*, the author writes 'To the Ladies and Gentlewoemen of England,' urging them to read his book if only in their spare time: 'It resteth Ladies, that you take the paines to read it, but at such times, as you spend in playing with your little Dogges, and yet I will not pinch you of that pastime, for I am content that your Dogges lye in ycur laps, so *Euphues* may be in your hands, that when you shall be wearie in reading of the one, you may be ready to sport with the other.' Later in the same work, Euphues speaks of bringing little dogs from Malta. Barnaby Rich relates that a courtier can make no progress with his lady fair unless, among other attentions, he play with her 'little Puppie,' while Thomas Nashe complains that the woman of his time would rather play cards or drink wine than spin or weave, and delights 'more in a daunce then in Dauids Psalmes, to play with her dogge then to pray to her God.' In *Eastward Hoe*, further, is pictured the utter sadness of the mother who cannot bear to see her poor daughter without the proper accoutrements of her condition in life: 'I haue not dole inough to see her in this miserable case, I? without her Veluet gownes, without Ribbands, without Iewels, without French-wires, or Cheat bread, or Quailes, or a little Dog, or a Gentleman Vsher, or anything indeed, that's fit for a lady.' Though dogs were the usual pets, more exotic animals were chosen by some ladies, since we have references to monkeys and even to parakeets. [6]

The Elizabethan age was a musical age. Individual and group singing was very much in favor, as was the playing of various instruments. From 1560 to 1640 (mostly after 1590) there were over one hundred and twenty-five editions of works on how and what to sing and play, together with the principles of music. The names of many of the composers and collectors of song books have come down to us and are quite familiar; Thomas Morley, William Byrd, and Thomas Campion are probably the best known, but there were also John Dowland, Orlando Gibbons, Michael East, Robert Jones, Thomas Weelkes, and others, who had many books of music to their credit. These works contained music for the virginals, the lute, the orpharion, the bandore, the cittern, and the various viols. The types of music written covered both vocal and instrumental music – canzonets, airs, madrigals, anthems, plain songs, fantasies, motets, hymns, ballads, pastorals, and just songs. Special music was written and published for dances like the pavan, the galliard, the almain, and others. Isabell, in

Greenes Never Too Late, 'tooke her Cittern in her hand' and sang a verse from Ariosto; and Insidia, another of Francesco's mistresses in the same work, 'tooke a Lute in her hand, and in an angelicall harmonie warbled out this conceited dittie.' Greene must have loved music, for his carefully drawn women are usually practiced performers. Philomela, the countess in the work of that name, is a good example, as we find her 'sitting al alone in hir Garden, plaieng vpon a Lute many pretie Roundelaies, Borginets, Madrigals, and such pleasant Lessons, as it were amorous loue vowed in honour of *Venus*, singing to hir Lute many pretie and merie ditties, some of hir owne composing, and some written by some wittie Gentlemen of *Venice*.' Theodora, too, in *Greenes Vision*, when her jealous husband has locked her in her room, has recourse to prayer and to singing sad songs, accompanied by her lute. Oddly enough, in one of Greene's cony-catching pamphlets a woman remarks that it is better to listen to nothing at all than to listen to 'vnreuerent Musicke.' Nicholas Breton, a prolific Elizabethan author, thinks that no matter what sort of mind or body a girl may have, she can be successful with men,

> *If she can play vpon an Instrument,*
> *And sing, and turne the white vp of the eye:*
> *And tell a tale of wantons merriment,*
> *And fleere and flatter, laugh, and looke awry,*
> *And make a shewe for very loue to die.*

As we might expect, Lady Politic Would-be, in *Volpone*, knows all of this, and has been making a study of the art: 'I'm all for music, save, i' the forenoons, . . . your music . . . is your true rapture.' A complaint of Robert Burton, however, is that once the ladies have got their men, they leave their music behind them: 'We see this daily verified in our young women and wives, they that being maids took so much pains to sing, play, and dance, with such cost and charge to their parents, to get those graceful qualities, now being married will scarce touch an instrument, they care not for it.' Giovanni Bruto, the apparent misogynist, naturally agrees with writers of the Puritan stamp in opposing women's 'vsing musicke,' although he believes that music is quite correct as recreation for men, since he adds: 'Let vs grant the vse of singing, and of this curious harmonie, to such as being wearied with great and important affaires, haue need of recreation.' His work was published in 1598, and as his reference to 'curious harmonie' shows, the singing of four, five, and six part music was becoming very popular. [7]

The more sophisticated lady indulged in many card games, much to her husband's sorrow. Anne Clifford, in her diary, chronicles her losses, chiefly, and it may be presumed from her account that she lost pretty regularly. At least 1616 seems to have been a bad year for her: on the fifteenth of February she lost fifteen pounds playing 'glecko' (probably a form of gleek) with three or four women, and on the twenty-eighth of December she lost twenty-seven pounds to 'my Lady Gray.' Twenty-seven pounds must have been between fifteen hundred and two thousand dollars in purchasing power of today's money. Princess Mary, too, played cards. Naturally most of the men objected to their wives' playing at cards, as did the hero of *Perimedes the Black-Smith*. In *Euphues*, Lyly lets the ladies down more easily when he says: '*Philautus* and *Euphues* repaired to the house of *Ferardo*, where they found Mistres *Lucilla* and *Livia* accompanied with other gentlewomen neither beeing idle, nor well employed, but playing at cardes.' Some of the more popular card games were gleek, primero, noddy, post-and-pair, and God-make-them-rich.

Group games, other than cards, were another source of amusement. *Purposes*, a game of questions and answers, was frequently played, as was *draw-gloves*, a game based on a race at drawing off gloves when certain words were spoken. At the turn of the century, shuttlecock was all the rage, as is witnessed by Manningham, who put the following note in his diary for February 12, 1602: 'I heard that about this last Christmas the Lady Effingham, as shee was playing shuttlecocke, upon a suddein felt hir selfe somewhatt, and presently retiring hir selfe into a chamber was brought to bed of a child without a midwife, shee never suspecting that shee had bin with child. The play at shuttlecocke is become soe muche in request at Court, that the making shuttlecockes is almost growne a trade in London.' Manningham does not make it clear, however, whether or

Queen Elizabeth on sidesaddle, hunting with falcons

not the Lady Effingham's experience was responsible for the vogue. We learn from *Epicoene* that the gentlemen often make anagrams of the ladies' names, but know not if this became a parlor game. Two lovers may engage in a game at chess as do Lutesio and the countess in *Philomela*, and Ferdinand and Miranda in that surprising scene in *The Tempest*. Often a group will gather for telling stories; in *The Flower of Friendshippe*, Pedro suggests that they all tell stories in the fashion of *The Decameron*, saying that formerly this custom prevailed only in Italy, but that now it is in favor at the English court as well. Sometimes various members of the group pose riddles for each other, or interpret each other's dreams. In *Sapho and Phao* the heroine and her ladies recount their dreams to one another, while Meleta interprets them. A somewhat similar scene occurs in *Antony and Cleopatra*. The ladies of *Euphues* and of *Euphues and His England* indulge in many conversational evenings, hearing discourses on love and on learning, or simply talking about the men.

It would seem needless to mention just plain gossiping – the sort of thing to which Burton refers when he says: 'Their merry meetings and frequent visitations, mutual invitations in good towns, I voluntarily omit, which are so much in use, gossipping among the meaner sort, &c., old folks have their beads; an excellent invention to keep them from idleness, that are by nature melancholy, and past all affairs . . .' And yet Van Meteren finds this mode of entertainment a notable characteristic of Elizabethan women. In speaking of the women of England, this Dutch traveler relates that 'all the rest of their time they employ in walking and riding, in playing at cards or otherwise, in visiting their friends and keeping company, conversing with their equals (whom they term *gosseps*) and their neighbors, and making merry with them at child-births, christenings, churchings, and funerals; all this with the permission and knowledge of their husbands, as such is the custom.' Note, too, that Van Meteren mentions riding as being in favor. Because of the many pictures of women at the hunt to be found in George Turberville's works and elsewhere, it is quite evident that hunting is a sport much enjoyed by the women; and yet references to it in the literature seem rather scarce. [8]

Perhaps the most popular group entertainment in which the Elizabethan women participated was dancing. In John Lyly's plays, ladies dance upon many occasions. In *Midas*, for example, when Sophronia asks for suggestions as to what the ladies can do to spend time without losing it, Amerula recommends telling tales, Caelia favors singing, but Camilla argues for

The hunt picnic

dancing. Dancing produces the desirable quality of grace in the young
ladies, and is thus an aid in providing them with husbands. We remember
Burton's lament that all too often the grace is lost after marriage. But

dancing does seem to be especially for the young; at least nothing amiss is seen in the suggestion of the king, in Greene's *Euphues His Censure to Philautus*, that the ladies under the age of twenty perform the dancing steps. [9]

Dancing, however, was thought by many writers, especially the Puritans, to be a particularly vicious mode of amusement. Besides the numerous antagonistic passages in works dealing with all sorts of moral questions, there were some books dealing wholly or almost wholly with the evils of dancing. Christopher Fetherstone's *A Dialogue against light, lewde, and lasciuious dauncing* was published in two editions of 1582 and 1595; Pietro Martire Vermigli's *A briefe Treatise Concerning the Vse and Abuse of Dauncing* was probably published in 1580; the two editions of John Lowin's *Conclusions vpon Dances* appeared in 1607 and 1609; and John Northbrooke's important and well-known *A Treatise wherein Dicing, Dauncing, Vaine Playes or Enterluds with other idle pastimes &c. commonly vsed on the Sabboth day, are reproued by the Authoritie of the word of God and Auntient writers* was issued in two editions of 1577(?) and 1579. By means of a dialogue between Youth and Age, Northbrooke's treatise tells us that there are several kinds of dancing: the dance of joy, or *Chorea*; the warlike dance, consisting of leaps and gestures, called *Saltatio Pyrrhica;* and the modern dance, which is instituted only for pleasure and wantonness. He calls this last type 'vaine, foolish, fleshly, filthie, and diuelishe.' It consists of dances, like the saraband, where men and women dance together, and it is the kind to which most writers are opposed. John Downame writes that this 'light, wanton and lasciuious dancing betweene men and women,' is 'too too common in these times, wherein they vse one towards another, all manner of inticing gestures, and sometimes wanton and obscene behauiour, seruing as the bellowes to inflame lust.' In a work which seems to have been written for the general public, not the courtly group, Fetherstone insists that this type of dancing is morally bad, and that men like it simply because they may use it to set traps for unwary women. Thomas Nashe, too, as he wanders around London and sees the evil lives led by its inhabitants, includes dancing among such other evils as 'wiues cockolding

164

their husbandes, vnder pretence of going to their next neighbors labour.' And numbered by William Averell among the improper recreations of the age is the custom of dancing with lovers. Northbrooke admits that many marriages are the result of dancing, but he is likely speaking of the shotgun type. In his work on the education of Christian women, Ludovicus Vives particularly castigates dancing, calling it the extreme of all vices. His description of dancing at this period is remarkably vivid:

So moche the pagās were better and more sadde than we be: nor they neuer knewe this newe fasshion of daunsyinge of ours, so vnreasonable, and fulle of shakynge and braggyng, and vnclenly handlynges, gropynges, and kyssyngis: and a very kēdlyng of leachery. Wherto serueth all that bassynge, as hit were pydgyns the byrdes of Venus. In olde tyme kyssyng was not vsed, but amonge kynsfolke: nowe is hit a cōmon thynge in Englande and France. . . . What good doth all that daunsynge of yonge women, holden vp on mennes armes, that they maye hoppe the hygher? What meaneth that shakyng vnto mydnyght, & neuer wery, which if they were desyred to go but to the nexte churche, they were nat able.

The practice of kissing your dancing partner, to which he refers, was apparently used as a means of embarrassing the pedantic Gabriel Harvey. According to Thomas Nashe, 'at one Master *Bradburies*, . . . after supper they fell to dansing, euery one choosing his mate as the custome is; in a trice so they shuffled the cards of purpose (as it wer to plague him for his presumption) that, will he nill, he must tread the measures about with the foulest vgly gentlewoman or fury that might be, . . . thrice more deformed than the woman with the horne in her head. A turne or two hee mincingly pac't with her about the roome, & solemnly kist her at the parting.' But this custom, even among kissing cousins, seems to have begun to die out during the time of the Stuarts. [10]

During the earlier reign of Elizabeth, the dances became far less stately than they had been. The young folk seem to have paid little heed to what Northbrooke and the others had said, and went their own joyful, leaping way. In a rather general attack on the dance, Gascoigne refers to 'oure tossings and oure turnes, owre frysks, oure flyngs'; he continues with the description of contemporary dances:

the movings wth we make,
As forward, backward, lefte hande turne, and right|
Upwards, and downewards, tyll owre hartes do quake|
And last of all, (to shew owre selves owtright)
A turne on toe, must grace owre giddy spright,
Untyll sometymes, we stoomble in the same,
And fall downeright, to geve the gazers game.|

If we are to believe Philip Stubbes, this new type of dance was pretty dangerous, since 'some haue broke their legs with skipping, leaping, turning, and vawting.' A contemporary painting of Queen Elizabeth dancing with the Earl of Leicester makes this statement quite understandable, since the Earl is on the tips of his toes, and Queen Elizabeth must be a foot or two up in the air. Slow, stately dances like the base dances, pavans, and almains were still performed by the older devotees, and are indeed included in the usual suite of dances. But far more popular, at least among the young, were the galliards, tordions, brawls, capers, courants, voltes, lavoltas, canaries, and other vigorous steps. Thomas Lodge cautions his older readers against such active entertainment by relating the story of Lewis, Archbishop of Magdeburg, 'who in treading his lauolas and corrantos with his mistresse, in trying the horsetrick broke his necke.' As an illustration of the activity required, Professor Baskervill relates a French description of the volte as being 'a species of galliard in which the leap is preceded by two steps instead of four. With each movement the dancers turn their bodies sharply so that they whirl round and round. The man encircles his partner with one arm and holds her so that, as she springs for the leap, he lifts her high in the air. Arbeau strongly disapproves of this dance on the ground that it is unseemly for young girls, and produces a vertigo as well. A woman often shows her bare knees, says the old dancing master, unless she holds her dress down with her hands.' The braggart Armado's boy, Moth, in *Love's Labour's Lost*, thinks that a girl may be wooed more easily by the dance accompanied by song than by a song alone, recommending the French brawl, which he describes thus: 'to jig off a tune at the tongue's end, canary to it with your feet, humour it with turning up your eyelids; sigh a note and sing a note, sometime through

166

The honors of the chase

the throat, as if you swallowed love with singing love, sometime through the nose, as if you snuff'd up love by smelling love, with your hat penthouse-like o'er the shop of your eyes, with your arms cross'd on your thin-belly doublet, like a rabbit on a spit, or your hands in your pocket, like a man after the old painting; and keep not too long in one tune, but a snip and away. These are complements; these are humours; these betray nice wenches that would be betrayed without these, and make them men of note – do you note me? men – that most are affected to these.'

While the lords and ladies and courtly hangers-on were busily engaged in agile, virile, and even acrobatic dances, the English folk were matching them in their country dances. Baskervill follows Playford in picturing the country dance as being marked 'not only by variety but by spontaneity and dramatic quality. The dances call for kissing, shaking hands, clapping, stamping, snapping the fingers, peeping, wiping the eyes.' Longways dances for four, six, or eight, square dances for eight, and round dances for six, eight, or more, were well liked, with the round being a favorite. At the May dances, the sword dance, morris dance, and country dance all appeared on the program, some of the dances being single, and some for groups. Jigs and hornpipes are often alluded to as folk steps. [11]

Of course the most impressive of the dance spectacles of the time was the masque. It was a combination of the dance, drama, music, and pageant, much akin to light opera. It was chiefly a dramatic dance, which was introduced by a song, accompanied by the many disguisings beloved by the Elizabethans. The formal masque of the Stuart age was a sumptuous extravaganza, with plot and dialogue by the king's poet (Jonson), music by the King's musician (Ferrabosco), and scenery and costumes by the king's architect (Inigo Jones). Originally, the masque seems to have been introduced into England from France or Italy around the time of Henry VIII, and in its beginnings was merely a novel and dramatic method of introducing the dancers into the hall. In the masque there were five formal dances, separated by periods of general dancing (called revels), songs, and dramatic interludes. These last were usually of a humorous nature and in the later period were performed by professional actors. The masked dancers were always of the nobility. In the *Masque of Beautie*, for example, one dance in the masque had for its maskers the Queen, Lady Arabella, Arundel, Derby, Bedford, Montgomery, Lady Elizabeth Gilford, and others. Princess Mary not only appeared in court masques, but danced in ballets, and even acted in Terence. Although the impetus for the masque during the early sixteenth century seems to have come from the continent, there is evidence that as early as 1377 disguised mummers entertained Prince Richard in a dramatic device ending in a dance.

According to H. A. Evans (*English Masques*, 1897), the first masque was presented in January, 1604, being Samuel Daniel's *Vision of the Twelve Goddesses*. He is speaking, however, of the height of the formal dramatic entertainment from the pens of such writers as Jonson, Beaumont, Middleton, Campion, and the like. Our particular interest, on the other hand, is with the chief feature of the masque, which was the dances of gorgeously costumed lords and ladies. The expense of these productions was stupendous. When the gentlemen of Gray's Inn in 1613 presented the *Masque of Flowers* for the wedding of the Earl of Somerset, the performance cost Francis Bacon some £2,000, while Jonson's *Hue and Cry after Cupid* is supposed to have cost £3,600. If the commodity index for this period be considered as ten (it may be as high as twelve or fifteen), the purchasing power of that sum in today's money would be well over $150,000. The Puritans, of course, objected to these heedlessly wasteful productions. When Robin-Goodfellow, in *Love Restored*, tries to be admitted to the masque by announcing that he is a masker and a Puritan, the doorkeeper immediately challenges the contradiction; Robin then argues against the extravagance of masques and suggests that they play parlor games instead. Typical dances of the folk often were introduced into the masque. In Jonson's *Masque of Owles*, the ghost of Captain Coxe introduces the third owl, apparently once a weaver, saying:

> *For since the wise towne*
> *Has let the sports downe*
> *Of May-games, and Morris*
> *For which he right sorry is:*
> *Where their Maides, and their Makes,*
> *At dancings, and Wakes,*
> *Had their Napkins, and poses,*
> *And the wipers for their noses,*
> *And their smocks all-be-wrought*
> *With this thred which they bought.* [12]

Amusements of the spectator type were favorites in employing the idle hours of the ladies. Tourneys and tiltings were still in popularity, but were becoming somewhat rare. Puppet plays entertained the villagers, while the cock-pit often served as a place to which the young Elizabethan blade could take his lady of the moment. When Dauphine, in *Epicoene*, expresses a wish to know more about women, True-Wit, who represents himself as an authority, advises him to go to more gatherings: 'You must leave to live i' your chamber, then, a month together upon *Amadis de Gaul*, or *Don Quixote*, as you are wont; and come abroad where the matter is frequent, to court, to tiltings, public shows and feasts, to plays, and church sometimes: thither they come to show their new tires too, to see, and to be seen. In these places a man shall find whom to love, whom to play with, whom to touch once, whom to hold ever. The variety arrests his judgment. A wench to please a man comes not down dropping from the ceiling, as he lies on his back droning a tobacco-pipe. He must go where she is.' As we may see from this passage, too, one of the chief sources of entertainment for women, just as for men, was the theater. In *The Staple of News*, Gossip Mirth asks the Prologue to help them to stools on the stage; when the Prologue expresses surprise, Gossip Mirth explains: 'Yes, o' the *Stage;* wee are persons of *quality*, I assure you, and women of *fashion;* and come to see, and to be seene.' When, in *The Devil is an Ass*, Mrs. Fitz-dottrell is confined by her husband, Pug comforts her by saying:

> *I will contriue it so, that you shall goe*
> *To* Playes, *to* Masques, *to* Meetings, *and to* Feasts.

Continuing in this same vein, Richard Brathwait declares that the theater is the 'chiefest place of repose' of women, and that they attend each new presentation, each day bestowing 'the afternoone on a Play.' The moralists, who vociferously objected to any resort to the theater, thought entertainment of this sort was particularly deplorable for women. In the words of John Downame, who has just finished warning women from lascivious books, paintings, and other wanton spectacles: 'but especially it behooueth those who haue any care of preseruing their chastitie, that they turne away their eies from beholding stage plaies, which are vsually fraughted with scurrilous iests, and ribauld filthines.' John Northbrooke is even more emphatic as he urges the utter degeneracy of the theater: 'If you will learne howe to bee false and deceyue your husbandes, . . . to obtayne ones loue, . . . to flatter, lye, sweare, . . . to bee idle, to blaspheme, to sing filthie songs of loue . . . shall not you learne them, then, at such enterludes howe to practise them.' He believes that theaters make adulterers out of women as well as out of men, and William Perkins calls the 'Theatre' and the 'Curtain' bawdy houses. Another moralist, Stephen Gosson, pictures the importunate attempts of men to sit by women, saying: 'You shall see suche heauing, and shoouing, suche ytching and shouldering, too sitte by women.' On December 6, 1575, the Common Council felt that corrections should be made for the good of the people, and they offered some recommendations for the improvement of the situation. Remembering the rather Puritanical leanings of this group, we are not surprised that the preamble to the Act should state that 'sundry great disorders and inconveniences have been found to ensue to this city by the inordinate haunting of great multitudes of people, specially youth, to plays, interludes, and shows . . . inveigling and alluring of maids, specially orphans, and good Citizens' children under age, to privy and unmeet contracts.' A sad picture, no doubt! particularly the orphans. Perhaps it is in the nature of a reply to the Puritan divines who had so attacked the theater, that Ben Jonson includes their sermons in the following list of current entertainments, as True-Wit, in *Epicoene*, says to Moroso: 'Alas sir, doe you euer thinke to find a chaste wife, in these times? now? when there are so many masques, plaies, puritane preachings, mad-folkes, and other strange sights to be seene daily, priuate and publique?' [13]

CHAPTER VII

Gilding the lily

Painting, sir, I have heard say, is a mystery.

Measure for Measure

The devil applying cosmetics

In Elizabethan days, women had much recourse to cosmetic aids. Indeed, the practice became so common that a character in Chapman's *Humourous Day's Mirth* could say, when he spied a beautiful creature approaching: 'She is very faire, I thinke that she be painted.' Writing in the same idiom, Thomas Overbury describes the typical woman of the period thus: 'Shee reads over her face every morning, and sometime blots out pale, and writes red. Shee thinks she is faire, though many times her opinion goes alone, and she loves her glasse and the Knight of the Sunne for lying. She is hid away all but her face, and that is hang'd about with toyes and devices, like the signe of a Taverne, to draw *Strangers*.' There is particular reference made to this drugstore type of beauty with 'box complexions.' In *A Wife for a Month*, Frederick tells Podrama to 'look in that Box, methinks that should hold secrets,' and receives the reply: ''Tis Paint, and curls of Haire.' The prolific Richard Brathwait makes several references in his writings to 'complexion inclosed in a box,' and asks: 'How base is her *shape*, which must borrow complexion from the *shop*? How can shee weepe for her sinnes ... when her teares will make furrowes in her face?' And Ben Jonson has his character Moria say to Phantaste, in *Cynthia's Revels:* 'I would wish to ... know all the secrets of court, citie, and countrie ... which ladie had her owne face to lie with her a-nights, & which not; who put off her teeth with their clothes in court, who their haire, who their complexion; and in which boxe they put it.' The dramatist becomes so enamoured of this passage that he repeats it almost word for word in *Sejanus*, scarcely blotting a line, while Shakespeare joins in speaking of beauty which is 'purchas'd by the weight.' According to Nashe, the aids to beauty are so lavishly applied that 'if a Painter were to drawe any of their counterfets on a Table, he needes no more but wet his pencill, and dab it on their cheekes, and he shall have vermillion and white enough to furnish out his worke, though he leaue his tar-box at home behinde him.' It seems to have been the custom for the ladies to repair their complexions after eating, even though an extensive preparation had been made just before. At least such an occurrence takes place in Francesco Colonna's *Hypnerotomachia: The Strife of Loue in a Dreame*, as a lady describes the custom: 'Afterward when we had made our selues redy, which was somwhat long after the manner of other women, by reason of many gewgawes and gimmerie whatchets, they did open their vesselles of daintie confections, and refreshed themselues, and I amongst them, and with precious drinke. When they had eaten sufficiently, they returned againe to their looking Glasses, with a scrupulous examination, about their bodies, and the attire of their heades, and dressing of their yealow curling haires depending and hemicirculately instrophiated about their diuine faces.' Apparently, too, the age even finds need for the professional beauty expert, since in Marston's *The Malcontent* Maquerelle asks Bianca: 'Do you know Doctor Plaster-face? by this curd, he is the most exquisite in forging of veins, spright'ning of eyes, dying of hair, sleeking of skins, blushing of cheeks, surphling of breasts, blanching and bleaching of teeth, that ever made an old lady gracious by torchlight.' Furthermore, women from all levels of society indulge in the use of aids to beauty, if we are to believe John Downame, 'Bacheler in Diuinitie, and Preacher of Gods word.' According to him, 'Neither hath this corruption of manners entred into the court alone, where wantonesse and immodesty chellenge vnto themselues a place by the right of prescription and long custome; but it is crept also into City and Country, amongst those that should be modest virgins and graue matrons, and examples of sobriety vnto others. Euen here naturall beauty is hid with a painted vizard, and naked breasts are laid out to the view; if at least they may be called naked which are commonly couered with false colours, or vncouered when as they are masked in a net.' [1]

One Elizabethan version of the source of beauty aids has its inevitable roots in classical Greek fable. As the story goes, Venus was the first to use paints and perfumes, and men learned this knowledge when Oenone, one of Venus' nymphs, indiscreetly conveyed the information to her lover, Paris; he in turn passed it on to Helen of Troy, who used the information to retain and enhance that marvelous beauty which launched a thousand ships. Elizabethans, however, had other ideas concerning the origin of

Queen Jane Seymour: gown with train; little dog

May Day scene

Private theatrical performance before Queen Elizabeth

this art; writing in 1616, *Thomas Tuke has this to say: 'Holinshed* in his description of Scotland, tells how the *Picts* vsed to paint ouer their bodies: and some write, that *Medea* a notable Sorceresse deuised these arts: and sure it is, that the Heathen and Infidels did first and most vsurp them: seeing therefore we haue cast off their Barbarisme & Infidelity, let vs also lay aside their other vanities and adulterous deuises.' This same idea is expressed later in the seventeenth century by Samuel Butler in his *Hudibras:*

> *As Pyrates all false Colours wear,*
> *T'intrap th'unwary Mariner:*
> *So Women, to surprize us, spread*
> *Their borrowed Flags, of White and Red.*
> *Display 'em thicker on their Cheeks,*
> *Than their old Grandmothers, the Picts.*

But according to Richard Brathwait, who could never resist freely commenting on feminine affairs, the contemporary ladies have made an essential change in the use of paints, since the ancient Britons painted 'not to make their faces more amiable, but to appear more terrible to the enemie.' [2]

As to why women indulge in the art of beautifying, the answer is obvious: 'For take away their painted cloathes, and then they looke like ragged walls; take away their ruffes, and they looke ruggedly; their coyfes and stomachers, and they are simple to behold; their hayre vntrust, and they looke wildely.' Authors of the period frequently enjoy asking dramatic questions and then supplying the expected answer. In reply to the question: 'But why is all this labour, all this cost, preparation, riding, running, far-fetched, and dear bought stuff?' Burton quotes from Ovid: 'Because forsooth they would be fair and fine, and where nature is defective, supply it by art.' And Thomas Draiton gives his conclusion concerning the subject in a quatrain entitled: 'Of the originall of painting the face':

> *Describe what is faire painting of the face,*
> *It is a thing proceedes from want of grace:*
> *Which thing deformitie did first beget,*
> *And is on the earth the greatest counterfet.*

No new ideas are here, however; of course women beautify themselves to supply the defects of nature. Naturally, too, writers of the Puritan leaning believe that the only reason these defects need to be remedied is so that men may more easily be enticed to sin. Such authors are represented by Alexander Niccholes, who argues:

There is a Text in woman, that I would faine haue woman to expound, or man either; to what end is the laying out of the embrodred haire, embared breasts, virmilioned cheekes, alluring lookes, fashion gates, and Artfull countenances, effeminate, intangling, and insnaring gestures, their curles and purles of proclaiming petulancies, boulstred, and layed out with such example and authority in these our daies, as with allowance and beseeming conueniency, such apish fashions and follies, that the more seuerer out-worne ages of the world, deceased and gone, should they haue but lifted vp their head and in their times would haue hyssed out of countenance to death. [3]

Since the ideal of feminine beauty in the Elizabethan age expressed itself in extremes of white and red, the women lavished most of their attention upon the face and neck, employing whatever gave the best results, was easy to acquire, and was in fashion at the time. As early as 1519 William Horman wrote in his *Vulgaria* that women 'whyte theyr face, necke and pappis with cerusse,' and authors throughout the period under discussion make reference to this cosmetic. Ceruse is just another name for white lead, and although it would whiten the face nicely, its use would produce many skin and other disorders. We may probably say that the general public were ignorant of those dangers, and indifferent to them. Indeed, in a time when general health failed at an early age, and youth in women was ephemeral in the extreme, why should one be concerned with possible ill effects in later life? Yet some Elizabethans knew of the danger of using white lead, since we find that by 1598 Giovanni Paolo Lomazzo could write: 'The *Ceruse* or *white lead* which women vse to better their complexion, is made of lead and vinegar; which mixture is naturally a great drier; and is vsed by *Chirurgions* to drie vp moiste sores. So that those women who vse it about their faces, doe quickly become withered and gray headed, because this doth so mightely drie vp the naturall moysture of their flesh.'

The application of ceruse was also objected to by Thomas Tuke, but for another reason:

The ceruse or white Lead, wherewith women vse to paint themselues was, without doubt, brought in vse by the diuell, the capitall enemie of nature, therwith to transforme humane creatures, of faire, making them ugly, enormious and abominable. For certainly it is not to be beleeued, that any simple women without a great inducement and instigation of the diuel, would euer leaue their natural and gracefull countenances, to seeke others that are suppositions and counterfeits, and should goe vp and downe whited and sised ouer with paintings laïed one vpon another, in such sort: that a man might easily cut off a curd or cheese-cake from either of their cheekes.

Borax was also used to give this necessary whiteness of the skin, as were other chemicals, such as sulphur ('surphling of breasts'). Almost any bleaching substance might be put on the face. An interesting prescription for whitening or bleaching is given by one Girolamo Ruscelli: take talcum and burned tin, heat them together in a glassmaker's furnace for three or four days, and mix the resulting ashes with green figs or distilled vinegar. Only ceruse, however, was able to produce the effective degree of whiteness, and consequently was used to the exclusion of even the typical recondite prescriptions as that illustrated above. [4]

Apparently the ceruse was somewhat lavishly applied to the face, neck, and upper part of the chest, and afterwards a red color was added to the cheeks and lips. The use of red coloring was thus the next step in accomplishing the ideal of beauty. We hear of women 'paynting theyr faces ruddie' and remember Hamlet's words to Ophelia: 'I have heard of your paintings too, well enough.' The generic term for any paint thus applied is properly *fucus*, although the term came to be used for any kind of cosmetic. In the play *Westward Ho*, for example, a character speaks of 'an excellent *Fucus* to kill the *Morphew*, weede out Freckles, and a most excellent groundworke for painting.' Ben Jonson frequently employs the word in its more exact usage; thus, in *The Devil is an Ass*, a character speaks as follows of Lady Tail-bush:

> *She, and I now,*
> *Are on a proiect, for the fact, and venting*
> *Of a new kinde of* fucus *(paint, for* Ladies*)*
> *To serue the kingdome.*

And in *Sejanus*, Eudemus tells Livia:

> *I'le haue an excellent new* fucus *made,*
> *Resistiue 'gainst the sunne, the raine, or wind,*
> *Which you shall lay on with a breath, or oyle,*
> *As you best like, and last some fourteene houres.*

A number of different dyes are used for the desired red coloring, such as 'purpurice'; it seems to have been a red dye, possibly from madder, although around 1569 C. Pyrrye speaks of the application of 'purple culler on her chekes' if nature has not provided enough color. Red ocher was also used, as was red crystalline mercuric sulphide, commonly called vermilion. Nicholas Breton refers to 'motley cheekes with pure Vermilion wet'; and Brathwait moralizes on the use of cosmetics, saying that 'when vermillion has laid so deepe a colour on an impudent skinne, ... it cannot blush with sense of her owne shame.' Brasil, the product of a red East Indian tree, used in cloth dyeing, was also applied to the face, as was 'coccum' or cochineal—originally a berry, but now a dye from crushed cactus insects. These could be used alone, although they were more often made into preparations which were easily applied. Cochineal was mixed with the white of hard-boiled eggs, the milk of green figs, plume alum, and gum Arabic; brasil was steeped well in water and then mixed with two ounces of fish glue that had itself been steeped in white wine for five or six days. Red sandal (or sanders) is another red dye, which Ruscelli makes use of in the following prescription: 'To make a redde colour for the face. Take red Sandall finely stamped, and strong Vineger twice distilled, then put into it as much Sandal as you wil, and let it boile faire and softely, and put to it also a litle Rock Alume stamped, and you shal haue a very perfect red.' Lomazzo is quite frank in telling the ladies what may be expected from the use of such minerals as plume alum and rock alum:

Of scaling or Plume-alume. This alume is a kinde of stone, which seemeth as if it were made of tow; and is so hot and drie by nature, that if you make the weeke of a candle therewith, it is thought it will burne continually without going out: ... With this some vse to rubbe the skinne off their face, to make it seeme red, by reason of the inflammation it procureth, but questionlesse it hath divers inconveniences, and therfore to be auoyded .... Rocke alume doth likewise hurt the face, in so much as it is a very pearcing and drying *minerall*, and is vsed in strong water for the dissoluing of mettals ... one droppe thereof being put vpon the skinne, burneth, shriueleth, and parcheth it, with diuers other inconveniences, as loosing the teeth, &c.

Apparently the use of alum is for a double purpose, that of astringent and of abrasive. Perhaps the ingredient was used to scrape the skin so that the coloring matter could penetrate better; more probably it was used simply to heighten the natural color of the cheeks, as Victorian ladies used to give their cheeks a brisk rub with a handkerchief before joining the gentlemen. If the Elizabethan ladies are somewhat taken aback with the prospect of using these preparations, perhaps they will be more interested in another method of beautification advanced by Lomazzo: 'This Arte consisteth of a twoofold method; either by way of a preparation and abstertion, of some naturall or aduentitious imperfections of the skinne, which is done with *fomentations, waters, ointments, plaisters,* and other matters, which I meane not to prescribe; or by a more grosse illiture and laying on of materiall colours; whereby such vnpleasing defectes are rather couered then abolished and taken away.' [5]

In order to protect what we should like to call the peaches and cream complexion, the ladies wore masks when going out of doors; perhaps, too, these masks were used as a method of covering defects and adding a little mystery. Queen Elinor, in Peele's *Edward I,* descends from her litter and gives her servant her mask, cautioning that it must not be rumpled. Masks are mentioned by Shakespeare, as well; it is said of Julia, in *The Two Gentlemen of Verona:*

> *She, in my judgement, was as fair as you*
> *But since she did neglect her looking-glass*

And threw her sun-expelling mask away,
The air hath starv'd the roses in her cheeks
And pinch'd the lily-tincture of her face.

Lyly points up in verse this need for protection of the face:

Behold, likewise, dame Beautie's gyrles,
  Whose daintie mindes are such,
As not the sun-shine, nor the wind,
  Must their faire faces touch:
Theyr maskes, their fannes, and all the toyes,
  That wanton heads can crave,
To maintaine beautie in her pride,
  These prancking dames must have.

Since fairness of the skin was greatly admired, it is readily understandable that the condition of the skin was a source of anxiety to all ladies; they must emulate their queen, who was a type of the blonde, and whose pale, fair skin set the standard of beauty. It was the country maids who were nut-brown, and the sun-tanned beauty was quite out of place. [6]

Rose-water, cherry-water, and roseberry-water were used as general improvements of the complexion, as were oils and fats. According to True-Wit in *Epicoene*, ass's milk was much in favor as a wash for the face, and buttermilk was used as well. If the face became unsightly, however, perhaps from using ceruse and other cosmetics too frequently, there was a natural feeling that some immediate steps were necessary. Sun-masks and complexion waters might do well enough for the daily ritual, but if the looking glass suddenly disclosed a new and unsightly blemish, something had to be done right away. Freckles were a minor tragedy; if the mask should be forgotten or prove inadequate, the following recipe is offered: 'For the Freckles which one getteth by the heat of the Sun: Take a little Allom beaten small, temper amonst it a well brayed white of an egg, put it on a milde fire, stirring it alwayes about that it wax not hard, and when it casteth up the scum, then it is enough, wherewith anoint the Freckles the space of three dayes: if you will defend your self that you get no Freckles

on the face, then anoint your face with the whites of eggs.' One sovereign
remedy for more serious troubles was *lac virginis*, or 'maiden's milk'; it was
good for 'stains in the face' and similar diseases. Acne caused much natural
anguish; to correct this condition a character in *Westward Ho* suggests
'*Ginimony* likewise burnt, and puluerized, to be mingled with the iuyce of
Lymmons, sublimate Mercury, and two spoonefuls of the flowers of Brimstone, a most excellent receite to cure the flushing in the face.' Dr. Wirtzung,
on his part, thinks that a better remedy is to anoint the face with the
whites of two eggs mixed well with rose-water, plantain juice, and dock
juice. This treatment should be followed by the application of the following:
eight ounces of vinegar and rose-water, one ounce of brimstone, one
quarter of an ounce of alum – boiled softly until one-third has evaporated.
This physician gives several other remedies, and then concludes: 'I suppose
inward medicines purging the peccant humour, by the advise of a discreet
Physitian prevaileth more for clearing of the face from rednesse and spots,
then any outward medicine can do. Yet with purging use outward means.'
Spots, pushes, or pimples were treated by Dr. Ambroise Paré with a
preparation made from cantharides. But Wirtzung suggests turpentine
rosin, beeswax, hog lard, and honey, applied to the face warm and then
covered with clean white paper; this mixture is to be changed every three
days, and requires two or three three-day periods for healing. Sometimes
drying agents were used on these blemishes, camphor and salnitrum being
popular. But it must be remembered that 'Camphire is so hott and drie,
that . . . being applied to the face scaldeth exceedingly, causing a great
alteration by parching of the skinne, and procuring a flushing in the face,'
while 'Salnitrum is so drie and cold, that being vsed about the face, it
mortifieth and drieth the naturall moysture, leauing the flesh insensible;
and is a greater enemy to the flesh, then any of the other minerals, dimming
the complexion, dulling the hearing, and offending the stomacke.' Thus
the users of camphor were worse off than if they had not started, and must
now begin treatment for red-face. If a scaly condition is noticed, called
scurfs, it can be treated with a two-part solution: first mix half a pound of
litharge of gold in half a pint of vinegar; then mix a handful of salt in four

ounces of water and boil it until half has evaporated; when you wish to treat the face, take three parts of the salt water to one part of the vinegar mixture, add a little rose-water and sal ammoniac, and apply. [7]

If the face needs extensive renovation, bleaches and skin-peelers are used. The skin can be peeled with ceruse or with sublimate of mercury. In *Cynthia's Revels*, Cupid says to Mercury: 'Alas, your palmes... they are as tender as the foot of a foundred nagge, or a ladies face new *mercuried*,' and in *Epicoene* True-Wit indicates that a different custom is to apply oil and birdlime at night, and rinse with ass's milk in the morning. Thomas Tuke quotes Galen as saying that the ladies of his native Spain have no need for cosmetics and use only a little 'Soliman' or sublimate of mercury. Lemon juice is applied as a skin bleach, although Lomazzo argues against its use saying that since it will dissolve the hardest stones to water, and since there is nothing which will dissolve a pearl faster, it is obvious what will happen to the face of a woman who uses it. The application of canthar-ides as a skin bleach is reported by Pedro Mexia. An almost complete pharmacopoeia is given in *The Devil is an Ass*, as Wittipol tells Lady Tail-bush that the ladies in Spain have, for cosmetics,

> *Water of* Gourdes, *of* Radish, *the white* Beanes,
> *Flowers of* Glasse, *of* Thistles, Rose-marine,
> *Raw* Honey, Mustard-seed, *and Bread dough-bak'd,*
> *The crums o' bread,* Goats-milke, *and whites of* Egges,
> Campheere, *and* Lilly-roots, *the fat of* Swannes,
> *Marrow of* Veale, *white* Pidgeons, *and pine*-kernells,
> *The seedes of* Nettles, perseline, *and* hares gall,
> *Limons, thin-skind* . . . .
> *No, the true rarities, are th'* Aluagada,
> *And* Argentata *of Queene* Isabella!

Lady Tail-bush now asks the ingredients of Isabella's cosmetics, receives the reply:

> *Your* Allum Scagliola, *or* Pol di pedra;
> *And* Zuccarino; Turpentine *of* Abezzo,
> *Wash'd in nine waters:* Soda di leuante,

As the poet pictures his sweetheart

Or your Ferne *ashes;* Beniamin di gotta;
Grasso di serpe; Porcelletto marino;
Oyles of Lentisco; Zucche Mugia; *make*
The admirable Vernish *for the face,*
Giues the right luster; but two drops rub'd on
With a piece of scarlet, makes a Lady *of sixty*
Looke at sixteen. But, aboue all, the water
Of the white Hen, *of the* Lady Estifanias!
. . . . *you take your* Hen,
Plume it, and skin it, cleanse it o' the inwards:
Then chop it, bones and all: adde to foure ounces
Of Carrauicins, Pipitas, Sope *of* Cyprus,
Make the decoction, streine it. Then distill it,
And keepe it in your galley-pot well glidder'd:
Three drops preserues from wrinkles, warts, spots, moles,
Blemish, or Sun-burnings, and keepes the skin
In decimo sexto, euer bright, and smooth,
As any looking-glasse; and indeed, is call'd
The Virgins milke for the face, Oglio reale;
A Ceruse, *neyther cold or heat, will hurt;*
And mixt with oyle of myrrhe, *and the red* Gilli-flower
Call'd Cataputia; *and flowers of* Rouistico;
Makes the best muta, *or dye of the whole world.*

The ingredients seem pretty fantastic to our ears, and of course one expects satire from Jonson, but since most of them have been found in actual cosmetic preparations of the time, no doubt the others were in use as well. Cataputia, or catapuce, was an herb; myrrh was a common medicine; etc. A substance almost as popular and universally used as ceruse was whites of eggs, mentioned above. A preparation of egg whites was frequently used successfully as a wrinkle remover to eradicate 'the worm-eaten records in her face,' and for 'renewing old riueld faces.' But egg whites were also in use as a foundation for all cosmetics, to 'glaze' the features. To the boy playing Ganymede in *Poetaster*, Tucca says: 'You should haue rub'd your face, with whites of egges, you rascall; till your browes had shone like our sooty brothers here, as sleeke as a hornbooke: or ha' steept your lips in wine, till you made 'hem so plump, that IVNO might haue beene iealous of 'hem.' Exotic washes and baths were at times in favor, as we learn from John Taylor's verse:

> *Some I haue heard of, that haue beene so fine,*
> *To wash and bathe themselues in milke or wine,*
> *Or else with whites of egges, their faces garnish,*
> *Which makes th̄e looke like visors, or new varnish.*
> *Good bread, and oatmeale hath bin spilt like trash,*
> *My Lady Polecats dainty hands to wash.*

Thomas Nashe speaks of Sabina as being a possible mirror for Elizabethan ladies in that she 'vsually bathed herself in the milke of fiue hundred Asses, to preserue her beauty,' while William Averell tells the story of a woman who would not use plain conduit water on her delicate skin, but insisted that her servants gather dew for her. But it was Mary Queen of Scots who applied for an additional allowance of wine for her bath. The truth is, indeed, that not many baths were taken; Anne Clifford thought a bath an occasion of sufficient importance to be noted in her diary for June 3, 1617: 'This night I went into a bath.' As a final touch to beautification of the face, Elizabethan women placed on their faces beauty-spots, Venus moles, or love-spots. As a character in the anonymous comedy, *Swetnam, the Woman-hater, arraigned by Women*, explains:

> *Nay, by Art they know*
> *How to forme all their gesture, how to adde*
> *A* Venus *Mole on euery wanton cheeke,*
> *To make a gracefull dimple when she laughs.* [8]

In addition to all the beauty preparations for external use, many medicines were recommended as aids to youth and loveliness. Thomas Lupton comes to the aid of the ladies with a preparation which 'wil make you soeme young a great while.' It consists of powdered elder flowers ('gathered on Midsomer day') mixed in borage-water, and a teaspoonful should be taken night and morning for a month. Dr. Christopher Wirtzung suggests the drinking of wine steeped in coarse marjoram, or partaking of 'Tristrams

Water.' This latter is made as follows: 'Take twelve ounces of Nutmegs, Mace, Ginger, Grains, Cloves, of each half an ounce, Rubarb one ounce, Bevercod, Spikenard, of each half an ounce, oyl of Bay two ounces, leave the spices unbeaten, pour to it four quarts of wine, cover it close, and let it stand so the space of four weeks, afterwards pour away the wine, pownd all the spices to pap, and put it again to the foresaid wine, let it stand well stopped three dayes, stir it well about: then distill it in hot water without seething, and preserve it well. Besides that this water doth take away all spots of the face and of the body, there is ascribed more unto it these wonderful vertues, to wit, some holden in the mouth taketh away the tooth-ach ... if any drink the same, or annoint the head therewith, it taketh away a stinking breath; also it keepeth one long youthfull if one drink a little of it in the morning, as many times hath been proved.' Maquerelle, a character in *The Malcontent*, has an even better recipe, which with tongue in cheek she describes, saying that it 'purifieth the blood, smootheth the skin, enliveneth the eye, strengtheneth the veins, mundifieth the teeth, comforteth the stomach, fortifieth the back, and quickeneth the wit; that's all.' According to her, this panacea is made as follows: 'Seven and thirty yolks of Barbary hens' eggs; eighteen spoonfuls and a half of the juice of cock-sparro bones; one ounce, three drams, four scruples, and one quarter of the syrup of Ethiopian dates; sweetened with three quarters of a pound of pure candied Indian eringoes; strewed over with the powder of pearl of America, amber of Cataia, and lamb-stones of Muscovia.' On this basis, any lack of female beauty in England could easily be explained.

In describing the beauty of women, Elizabethan writers emphasize especially the eyes and eyebrows. The ideal of beauty required that the eyes be set wide apart ('well divided,' 'large ... space goyng from eye to eye'), sparkling 'like two planets, in a twinckling frostie night,' and graceful ('traytys'). Women should display 'small pensild eye browes,' which are to be 'well ranged, thin and subtile.' Obviously not every woman can be born with these definite attributes, and those who are not have to remedy the defect with cosmetics. The eyebrows are plucked to make them 'thin' and to make the eyes seem far apart. They are also treated with kohl to make them black, and the eyelids are probably treated with the same substance. The quack referred to in *The Malcontent* was good at 'sprightn'ing of eyes,' we remember, which must have meant to make them sparkling. Belladonna was used to produce this illusion by making the eyes appear large and glistening. Thus the lady 'tempereth her eyes by arte,' as Pyrrye says, and paints 'the black of eyes,' in the words of Vives. [9]

The lips, of course, were painted red, and the same colors were seemingly employed for the lips as for the cheeks; the use of 'purpurice,' for example, will be recalled. The lip-rouge was far from being permanent, however. Shakespeare was as usual writing for the ages when Leontes, in *The Winter's Tale*, says: 'Let no man mock me for I will kiss her,' and receives the reply:

> *Good my lord, forbear.*
> *The ruddiness upon her lip is wet;*
> *You'll mar it if you kiss it, stain your own*
> *With oily painting.*

The teeth which came into view when the lips were opened, however, were scarcely to be the focus of attention. The English seem proverbially to have had poor teeth, though not because they have not known how to care for them. In Ben Jonson's *Sejanus*, Eudemus says to Livia: 'You should use of the dentifrice I prescrib'd you too, to clear your teeth.' It is also recommended that general care of the teeth should include rubbing them often with the bark of an evergreen shrub called tamarisk, with the peels of pomegranates, or with the red blossoms of the peach tree—all of which would not only cleanse the teeth but strengthen the gums as well. Other preparations for similar use were sugar and honey; honey and salt burned to ashes; the powder of a burned rabbit's head; or a mixture of myrrh, plume alum, burned alum, and vinegar. If the teeth have become rather stained, a somewhat more drastic treatment must be used; a powder made of the following will invariably whiten the teeth, probably by removing the enamel: cuttle bone, pumice, red brick, egg shells, prepared red and white coral, pellitory, burned alum, mastic, sandarac resin, and myrrh. The teeth should always be kept clean and pure;

they should never be picked with an iron toothpick, however, but always with one made from the lentiscus or mastic tree. 'Remember also,' cautions one medical man, 'to wash the teeth after each meal.' And if the teeth have a tendency to be somewhat loose, 'Myrrhe sodden in Wine, and the teeth washed therewith, fasteneth the teeth, and dryeth the superfluous humidity of them. Chew Mastick and rub the teeth and gums with it, it maketh them clean and strong.' If the teeth are badly eaten away, or lacking, or too large, perhaps the best plan is to lisp and simper instead of laughing 'wide and open.' There are sufficient references on all sides, in typical Elizabethan frankness, to unpleasant breath, to make us wonder if there were also remedies for this ailment. Certainly there were many prescriptions for mouthwashes extant. A simple and rather pleasant one can be made from flowers of rosemary boiled in white wine. For those who judge the efficacy of a mouthwash by its unpleasant taste, a rather nauseous remedy can be made from four ounces each of rose-water and plantain-water, an ounce of honey of roses, half an ounce of syrup of mulberries, and one dram of burned alum – all mixed together with eight ounces of white wine and boiled about as long as it takes to cook an egg. It is effective as either mouthwash or gargle, and should be used warm. [10]

Perhaps the Elizabethan lady bestows more care upon her hair than upon any other portion of her anatomy. The hair is powdered, pinned with bodkins, curled, pomaded, perfumed, dyed, and arranged in elaborate coiffures. Constantly is heard the complaint that the popular beauty spends too much time on herself and will 'all the morning learne to dresse her head.' Philip Stubbes gives us a somewhat ludicrous description of the picture presented by these women. After the painting of the face, he informs us,

then followeth the trimming and tricking of their heds in laying out their hair to shewe, which of force must be curled, frisled and crisped, laid out (a World to see!) on wreathes & borders from one eare to an other. And least it should fall down, it is vnder propped with forks, wyers, & I can not tel what, rather like grime sterne monsters, then chaste christian matrones. Then, on the edges of their bolstred heir (for it standeth crested round about their frontiers, & hanging ouer their faces like pendices with glasse windowes on euery side) there is layed great wreathes of gold and siluer, curiouslie wrought & cunninglie applied to the temples of their heads. And for feare of lacking any thing to set foorth their pride withal, at their heyre, thus wreathed and crested, are hanged bugles (I dare not say bables) ouches, rings, gold, siluer, glasses, & such other gew-gawes and trinckets besides, which, for that they be innumerable, and I vnskilfull in wemens termes, I can not easily recount.

As Stubbes has said, the hair is curled with irons, and then pinned with bodkins. If the use of the iron is feared, the hair can be curled with a secret preparation: ashes of burned sheep's horn, mixed with oil, to be applied frequently. Pomades and perfumes for use on the hair were very popular. Oil imperial and oil of ben could be used, as well as myrrh, all sorts of balm and expressed oils, used alone or mixed with other oils and waxes. Since the blonde beauty was much preferred by the Elizabethans, the ladies frequently dyed or bleached their hair to achieve the necessary color. As Apelles, in *Campaspe*, tells Alexander: 'If the haire of her eie browes be black, yet must the haire of her head be yellowe.' And there are constant references to 'faire lockes, resembling Phoebus' radiant beames.' In order to rectify any natural deficiency, Ruscelli gives the following preparation: 'To make haire as yellowe as golde. Take the rine or scrapings of Rubarbe, and stiepe it in white wine, or in cleere lie: and after you haue washed your head with it, you shall weatte your haires with a Spoonge or some other cloth, and let them drie by the fire, or in the sunne: After this weatte them and drie them againe.' An unexpected note of caution concerning the use of hair dye is struck by the author of *The Court of Good Counsell*, who gives a warning to the Elizabethan ladies: 'Yet it is the hayre that they make most adoe about, and there are no sorts of Oyntments which they will not proue, to make their hayre of the brauest cullour, in so much that many in going about to alter . . . the cullour of their hayre, by naughty medicines, haue wrought their owne deaths.' Sometimes, of course, the hair may fall out, either from natural causes or from the use of dyes and bleaches; then the ladies must supply the lack with periwigs, perukes, gregorians, or as we sometimes say, transformations. Thus, in commenting on the fact that 'all that glisters is not gold,' Bassanio illustrates his thoughts by referring to woman's beauty, so often 'purchas'd by the weight,' and continues:

> *So are those crisped snaky golden locks*
> *Which make such wanton gambols with the wind*
> *Upon supposed fairness often known*
> *To be the dowry of a second head,*
> *The skull that bred them in the sepulchre.*

Similarly, Pipenetta, Celia's maid in *Midas*, says to Petulus:

Pip. My mistresse would rise, and lacks your worshippe to fetch her haire.
Pet. Why, is it not on her head?
Pip. Me thinks it should be, but I meane the haire that she must weare to day.
Licio. Why, doth she weare any but her owne?
Pip. In faith sir no, I am sure it is her owne when she paies for it.

Of course, embarrassing situations can arise from the use of periwigs, such as the one True-Wit relates to Cleremont: 'I once followed a rude fellow into a chamber, where the poore madame, for haste, and troubled, snatch'd at her perruke, to couer her baldnesse: and put it on, the wrong way.' The chief objection to the use of wigs, however, was not that they were worn by women who had lost their own hair, but by those who were too lazy to care for it. This type of woman, continues Richard Mulcaster, is 'an idle, lasie, young *gentlewoman*, which hath a very faire heire of her owne, and for idlenesse, bycause she wil not looke to it, combe it, picke it, wash it, makes it a cluster of knottes, and a feltryd borough for white footed beastes: and therfore must needes haue an vnnaturall perug, to set forth her fauour, where her owne had been blest, if it had bene best applied.' Indeed some women are so rooted in the sin of vanity that they will not only buy the hair from the dead, or from the head of some poor wretch who needs the money, but even stoop to dastardly crimes which suggest Pope's poem. Philip Stubbes puts the case succinctly when he relates that 'if there be any poore women (as now and then, we see God

192

Elizabeth as Princess, wearing an embroidered gown with square-cut neck bordered with jewels

Mary Herbert, Countess of Pembroke

doeth blesse them with beautie, as well as the riche) that hath faire haire, these nice dames will not rest, till thei haue bought it. Or if any children haue faire haire, thei will intice them into a secrete place, and for a penie or two, thei will cut of their haire.' [11]

As we have seen, the hairdress of the age is most elaborate, Thomas Tuke mentioning 'loftie tires,' and Arthur Dent, writing in 1601, speaking of 'long locks, fore-tufts, shacke haire, and all these new fashions.' There are also many references to love-locks, or 'a loose locke erring wantonly over her shoulders,' and one author breaks out with what is surely the most absurdly libidinous attack on a lock of hair in the language when he rants about 'her wanton dangling lasciuious locke thats whirld and blowne with euerie lustfull breath.' The styles of hair dressed like coronets and topgallants were popular; the curled hair was often entwined or 'embrodered' with fine gold or silver wire; sometimes wire was used to support the hair. Anne Clifford, for example, records in her diary for May, 1617: 'the 12th I began to dress my head with a roll without a wire.' Styles of the Spanish, French, and Italian fashions were frequently copied. Women were not prone to change their elaborate coiffures very often, although when a character in *Cynthia's Revels* is asked if she has changed her 'head-tire' she satirically replies: 'Yes faith, th'other was so neere the common: it had no extraordinary grace; besides, I had worne it almost a day, in good troth.' In *Poetaster*, Crispinus speaks of a particular style of hair decorated with a silver bodkin: 'It stirres me more then all your court-curles, or your spangles, or your tricks: I affect not these high gable-ends, these *tuscane*-tops, nor your coronets, nor your arches, nor your *pyramid's;* giue me a fine sweet – little delicate dressing, with a bodkin, as you say: and a mushrome, for all your other ornatures.' Nor is the style of dressing the hair sufficient alone, but there must be added to it all kinds of decorations: jewels, ribbons, beads, and anything else available. Licio refers to the custom in *Midas*; after describing Celia's head in full, he turns to the 'purtenances': 'The purtenances! it is impossible to reckon them vp, much lesse to tell the nature of them. Hoods, frontlets, wires, caules, curling-irons, perriwigs, bodkins, fillets, hairlaces, ribbons, roles, knotstrings, glasses, combs, caps, hats, coifes, kerchers, clothes, earerings, borders, crippins, shadowes, spots, and so many other trifles, as both I want the words of arte to name them, time to vtter them, and witte to remember them: these be but a fewe notes.' Petulus then comments: 'I note one thing . . . That if euerie part require so much as the head, it wil make the richest husband in the world ake at the heart.' [12]

Intensive beauty culture is not confined to the face and hair. The fair ladies look to their shoulders, hands, and figures in general. Care is given to the hands to keep them soft and white; oatmeal is frequently used for this purpose, as is lavender water or spikenard water. For chapped hands, Dr. Wirtzung recommends the following: melt three ounces of fresh butter and three ounces of suet of hart, and cut four or five apples into it; add six ounces of white wine and boil until the apples are soft; add half a dram each of cinnamon, camphor, cloves, and nutmegs, two ounces of rose-water, and boil again until the rose-water is evaporated; finally, strain through a cloth. [13]

In *As You Like It*, a character speaks of the hands being perfumed with civet, and there appear other references to this custom. But a far more popular practice, which is said to have been introduced by the Marquis Frangipanni (known also for giving his name to a perfume), is the wearing of perfumed gloves; indeed, for this very reason the trades of perfumer and glover at this time are one. A particular odor preferred in gloves is almond. Both of these customs are referred to in Overbury's character 'Of a faire and happy Milke-maid': 'In milking a Cow, and strayning the Teats through her fingers, it seemes that so sweet a Milke-presse makes the Milke the whiter or sweeter; for never came *Almond Glove* or *Aromatique Oyntment* of her Palme to taint it.' [14]

The body beautiful was achieved by the use of a garment, worn under the upper part of the kirtle, which was stiffened with stays of whalebone or wood. It had the double purpose of flattening the stomach, and at the same time of holding the breasts high. The stays were called busks and were sometimes richly carved; after the busks were inserted in sheaths in the bodice, they were held there by ribbons or laces, which were called busk-points. Gosson says busks are used to keep the belly flat, while Nashe relates that 'theyr breasts they embuske vp on hie.' Arthur Dent complains about the use of 'starching and steeling, buskes, and whalebones, supporters, and rebaters,' and John Bulwer reports:

> *No Maid here's handsome thought unlesse shee can*
> *With her short palmes her streight lac'd body span.*
> *Thus we most foolishly our life invade,*
> *For to advance the* Body-makers *trade.*

This pinching in of the waist produced what was called a 'moncky-wast.' In Rich's *Faultes* is found a surprising reference to 'naked stomackes,' probably meaning the extremely low-cut gowns of one period. The farthingales are intended to hold the skirts of the kirtle out from the body. The Spanish farthingale was really a circular skirt, small at the waist and stiffened with hoops; the French farthingale, which came into style in the 1560's, was a roll placed about the hips. Later a half-roll was used 'like a rudder to the body,' which was called a 'bum' and produced what Rowlands called 'the breeching like a Bear.' In a somewhat indecent verse, Bansley (about 1550) exhorts against the use of such devices:

> *Downe for shame wyth these bottell arste bummes,*
> *and theyr trappynge trinkets so vayne*
> *A bounsinge packsadel for the deuyll to ride on,*
> *to spurre theym to sorowe and payne.* [15]

There is no need to speak at length here of the use and composition of perfumes. Elizabethan writing, both dramatic and non-dramatic is replete with allusions to them, even though Vives quotes Plautus that 'A woman euer smellethe best whā she smelleth of nothyng.' Be that as it may, perfumes were very popular, and a masculine complaint against their use is voiced by Robert Burton, in the *Anatomy of Melancholy*, who asks plaintively: 'Why do they... use those sweet perfumes, powders, and ointments in public?' These perfumes were compounded of musk, civet, oriental oils, spices, expressed flower oils, or aromatics. Myrrh, civet, and oil of jessamine frequently appear in the literature. Philip Stubbes thinks that perfumes should be eschewed as being another illustration of the great pride of women. 'Is not this a certen sweete Pride,' he asks,

to haue cyuet, muske, sweete powders, fragrant Pomander, odorous perfumes, & such like, wherof the smel may be felt and perceiued, not only all ouer the house, or place, where they be present, but also a stones cast of almost, yea, the bed wherin they haue layed their delicate bodies, the places where they haue sate, the clothes, and thinges which they haue touched, shall smell a weeke, a moneth, and more, after they be gon. But the Prophet *Esaias* telleth them, instead of their Pomaunders, musks, ciuets, balmes, sweet odours and perfumes, they shall haue stench and horrour in the nethermost hel. Let them take heed to it, and amend their wicked liues. And in the Sommer-time, whilst floures be greene and fragrant, yee shall not haue any Gentlewoman almost, no nor yet any droye or pussle in the Cuntrey, but they will carye in their hands nosegayes and posies of floures to smell at; and which is more, two or three Nosegayes sticked in their brests before, for what cause I cannot tel, except it be to allure their Paramours to catch at them.

Writing good advertising copy four hundred years ago, John Taylor argues that there may be some possible excuse in that the making of perfumes gives employment to a large number of people:

> *But yet though* Pride *be a most deadly sinne,*
> *What numbers by it doe their liuings vvinne?*
> *A vvorld of people daily liue thereby;*
> *Who (vvere it not for it) would starue and dye.* [16]

We have had some intimation that there was a vigorous opposition to the wholesale use of cosmetics. Such a supremely artificial type of beauty as we have seen described would be bound to stir up public opinion to a certain degree, even in an age given to rather exaggerated artifice. The Elizabethans pronounced upon the foibles of women with the same zest and venom that they evoked for all questions of public interest. Perhaps for the devout Elizabethan age the most forceful arguments against the use of cosmetics were religious in origin. The Puritan writers in particular urged that such vain practices were contrary to the teachings of the church and of God. 'I am sure,' writes Hannibal Gamon, 'the ancient Fathers declaime bitterly against her filthy heart, false haire, adulterate paintings, naked breasts, new-fangled fashions of superfluous, monstruous attire: & the holy Scriptures vilifie her to her face.' And the indomitable William Prynne states flatly that 'the *Fathers*, doe with one consent auerre, *the colouring of our owne Haire with an artificiall dye . . . to bee vtterly vnlawfull, and abominable,*' and that it is the invention and work of the devil. The writers of this type mention the views of such church fathers as Paul, Chrysostom, Cyprian, Ambrose, Jerome, Augustine, Gregory, and others. John Donne, seeking the support of authorities, makes special reference to two works of Tertullian: the *De habitu muliebri* attacking the excesses of women in their dress, and the *De cultu feminarum* opposing the use of cosmetics. Speaking of the words of the Apostle Timothy, Cleaver writes that no man has argued more against the excess of pride in clothing and hair-dressing than he. [17]

Further, the use of cosmetics is going directly against the wishes of God, who made women as He intended them to be, and they ought to be satisfied with the result. 'Neither can that face be a good one,' writes Brathwait, 'which stands in need of these helpes. For what madnesse is it to change the forme of nature, and seeke beautie from a Picture?' As the argument of the famous Elizabethan preacher, William Perkins, runs: 'Euery one must be content with their owne naturall fauour and complexion, that God hath giuen them; and account of it, as a pretious thing, be it better or be it worse.' Obviously, says Arthur Dent, if the women do not like God's 'handy-worke, they will mend it, and haue other complexion, other faces, other haire, other bones, other brests, and other bellies then God made them.' Waxing poetic as he ridicules women for their cosmetic practices, George Gascoigne versifies as follows:

> Behold, behold, they never stande content,
> With God, with kinde, with any helpe of Arte,
> But curle their locks, with bodkins & with braids,
> But dye their heare, with sundry subtill sleights,
> But paint and slicke, til fayrest face be foule,
> But bumbast, bolster, fris[l]e, and perfume:
> They marre with muske, the balme which nature made,
> And dig for death, in dellicatest dishes.

Thomas Tuke wonders how these women will be able to look up to God 'with a face, which he doth not owne? How can they begge pardon, when their sinne cleaues vnto their faces?' Enlarging upon this conception, Matthew Griffith questions the reasons why women make themselves unnatural: 'God will never be able to acknowledge you for his workmanship? To you, that with your itching glaunces proclaime the *wantonnesse* of your *mindes*, and the *loosenesse* of your *lives*? To you, that so frizle your heads with borrowed haire? To you, that lay open your nakednesse to all beholders; giving them (by this light of parts displayed) hopes to enjoy the whole bodie; for if your wares bee not vendible, why doe you open your shoppes?' And since these practices are abhorrent to God, they must clearly be the devices of the devil, the common enemy of man. Using the metaphor of the artist, several writers (Vives, Stubbes, Cawdrey, etc.) all argue that a painter would be mightily displeased if when he had finished a masterpiece he should leave his workshop and then find on his return that someone else had tried to amend it and changed colors, and urge how much more God will be offended when a woman takes upon herself the correction of the image and workmanship of Himself. [18]

Enlargements and restatements of this complaint abound in Puritanical writings of the period. It was said that this kind of beauty is really an adulterate beauty, and as such is abhorred by nature and by God. Artificiality is as far removed from reality as the shadow is from the substance. 'Away then,' urges the author of *Hic Mulier*, 'with these disguises, and foule vizards: these vnnaturall paintings, and immodest discoueries; keepe those parts concealed from the eyes, that may not bee toucht with the hands.' The 'artificiall or adulterate colours' make only the 'adulterate beauty' and will be of no aid whatsoever on judgment day. Further, the need for cosmetic help argues that there is 'somewhat *dead* within.' Brathwait wants the woman of his choice to be natural:

> *I'd haue her face and blush to be her* owne,
> *For th'*Blush *which* Art *makes is* adulterate.

And Tuke quotes Du Bartas to the effect that the rosy red on the cheeks 'is but borrowed stuffe, or stolne, or bought, plaine counterfeit in proofe.' [19]

Why is it, then, that women thus belabored continue to use cosmetics? 'Verily I wolde fayne knowe,' asks Vives, 'what the mayden meaneth that peynteth her selfe: if it be to please her selfe, it is a vayne thyng: if it be to please Christe, it is a foly: if it be to delyte men, hit is an vngratious dede.' The answer, however, is not far to seek; it is an excess of pride. Some women say that they may paint and still be honest and good at heart; others say they object to the use of cosmetics, too, but they have to follow the dictates of fashion; still others say they have no intention of provoking lust but merely like to have their beauty appreciated and praised by others. The Reverend Henry Smith points out that when a woman is 'pranked up in her bravery,' she thinks everyone is admiring her, and she 'hath as goodly an opinion of herself as the peacock hath of his feathers.' It is not pride but shamefastness which should be the goal of women, believes Tasso: 'No collour better graceth or adornes a womans cheekes, then y^t which shamefastnes depainteth, which increaseth and draweth as earnest loue and desire of others to them, as happily those other artificiall Oyles and dawbings which they vse, decreaseth & withdraweth from them, beeing in deede fitter for vizards, pageants & poppets, then wholesome, handsome or toothsome.' The same idea occurs in Greene's *Penelope's Web*, although the author assigns it to the Emperor Aurelius, and Spenser peoples his House of Pride with creatures such as we have been describing.[20]

Another argument of those opposed to the use of cosmetics is that since painted faces have proverbially been the sign of the courtesan, virtuous women who lower themselves to such practices are merely asking that they be looked upon as belonging in this category, for 'from the deuyll and the stewes, commeth youre tricksynesse that you lyke so well.' In the words of Barnaby Rich: 'I thinke my Ladie her selfe would laugh, to see an *Amorist* that is kindly besotted, how his Angels must flie to fetch new fashions from Venetian *Courtesans*, to please his demie honest mistresse. Then she must haue a *Maske*, to couer an impudent face, a *Periwigge* to hide a loathsome bush, a *Buske* to streighten a lasciuious bodie. And for painting, it is as generall amongest a number of women (that would faine be accounted honest) as it is to the most noted and common strumpet.' Robert Greene, Robert Burton, Philip Stubbes, as well as many preachers, all echo the same thought, as does Pompey, the clown in *Measure for Measure*, who says: 'Painting, sir, I have heard say, is a mystery; and your whores, sir, being members of my occupation, using painting, do prove my occupation a mystery.' An interesting turn to the argument is given by John Downame as he reasons that so-called virtuous women who paint are really evil inwardly; he speaks of how 'common this sinne of adultery and vncleannesse is in our times, wherein the signes and meanes thereof do so abound; seeing not onely those who are harlots by profession, but euen such as would be reputed pure virgins and chaste wiues shew these outward signes of their inward filthinesse, and vse these baits to catch the foolish in the nets of vncleannes, by painting their faces, & setting forth thēselues with adulterate beauty, and by laying out their breasts after a whorish manner to be seene and touched: for is it likely, that those who lay thē out to yᵉ show, would haue them only seen?' [21]

A further complaint against painting derives from the implications of this last quotation, and indeed seems to be the chief if unspoken basis for all the outcry: namely, the self-righteous language scarcely conceals the anguished concupiscence of the writers and attests the point that cosmetics are actually enticements to vice. Robert Greene points out that prostitutes use fancy hair designs, paintings, and elaborate dressing 'to betraie the eyes of the innocent nouice,' and Stubbes quotes St. Ambrose that 'from the coullouring of faces spring the inticements to vices, and that they which color their faces doo purchase to them selues the blot and stain of chastitie.' That the 'paintinge of shameles faces' and 'these inticing showes' are actually '*vauntcurrers* of adultry,' is a point which Barnaby Rich emphasizes, while Downame believes that these women clearly 'adorne themselues for the market, and set forth their beautie to the sale.' In pondering the problem of whether real beauty or artificial beauty is the more powerful allurement, Burton gives it as his opinion that 'artificial is of more force' and is to be preferred when allurement is the only object. [22]

Women who are constantly fixing their clothing and repairing their beauty, moreover, have no time left for their devotional duties. 'Shee bestowed too much time on her *Glasse*,' writes Brathwait, 'to reserue any for her Lampe.' Thomas Tuke describes this painted woman in a 'Character' which was originally issued as a broadside:

Shee's euer amending, as a begger's a peecing, yet is she for all that no good penitent. For she loues not weeping. Teares and mourning would marre her making: and she spends more time in powdring, pranking and painting, then in praying. Shee's more in her oyntments a great deale, then in her orizons. Her religion is not to liue wel, but to *die* well. Her pietie is not to pray well, but to *paint* well. She loues confections better a great deale, then confessions, and delights in *facing* and feasting more, then fasting.

What can an honest woman do, then, if she wishes to be attractive and yet does not want to paint? She must learn first of all 'not so much to decke and tricke her selfe vp to the eye, as to haue her *inner man adorned* with holy skill and discretion,' in the words of Thomas Gataker. And anyway, reasons Lomazzo, 'There is nothing in the world, which doth more beautifie & adorne a woman, then *Cheerefulnes* and *Contentment; according to the proverbe: Contentment is the chiefest beauty.' He continues that health, honesty, and wisdom should be added to cheerfulness and contentment to produce the most attractive of womankind. [23]

Arguments of a religious nature, however, were not the only ones drawn up to warn women against the practice of painting the lily. These were bolstered by warnings that the use of poisons and unrefined minerals would soon bring ruin to whatever natural beauty a woman may have had. Even Francis Bacon stated that the use of such cosmetics was not safe or wholesome for the health, while Vives, in his well-known work on the education of women, gives a pretty terrifying account of what will happen to many women:

The tender skynne wyll riuyll the more soone, and all the fauour of the face waxeth old and the breath stynketh, and the tethe rusten, and an yuel aire all the bodye ouer, bothe by the reason of the ceruse, & quicke siluer, and specially by the reason of the sopis, wher with they ppare the body, as it were a table, ayenst the peyntyng on yᵉ nexte day. Wherfore Ouide called these doynges venomes, & not without a cause. Also Iuuenall asketh a question properly: She that is with so many oyntementes slubbered and starched, is hit to be called a face or a sore?

Warnings against cosmetics are also made by Thomas Tuke. At first he quotes from Du Bartas to the effect that husbands are 'lothe to kisse' such poisons, and that they are particularly anxious when they consider that

> *in a yeere and lesse,*
> *Or two at most, my louely, liuely bride,*
> *Is turn'd a hagge, a fury by my side,*
> *With hollow yellow teeth, or none perhaps,*
> *With stinking breath, swart cheeks, & hanging chaps,*
> *With wrinkled neck, and stooping, as she goes,*
> *With driueling mouth, and with a sniueling nose.*

Tuke continues by referring to Andreas de Laguna (as translated by Mistress Elizabeth Arnold), who relates that many women have used cosmetics so long that their faces have changed color and are now yellow, or dark green, or 'blunket' color, or red. Other women, he goes on, have used ceruse so long that their teeth are rotten; while still others have found that sublimate of mercury (soliman) makes them old before their time, with 'wrinkeled faces like an Ape,' and makes them tremble 'as if they were sicke of the staggers.' He admits that soliman will remove 'spots and staines' of the face, but warns that in doing so it consumes the flesh underneath. [24]

Perhaps the most vigorous and graphic picture of what women who indulge in the excessive use of cosmetics may expect is portrayed by Giovanni Paolo Lomazzo in his work *A Tracte Containing the Artes of Curious Paintinge Caruinge & Buildinge,* as Englished by Richard Haydocke, student in medicine. Lomazzo states first that he is basing this section of his treatise upon the work of a physician named John Madonese, entitled *The Ornaments of Woemen.* He goes on to say that it is his intention only to put forth the nature of certain cosmetics which are in daily use, since women are ignorant of the nature of the ingredients and the effect they will have on the users. His work is very inclusive in its portrayal of the harmful effects of cosmetics, and he gives one very obvious clue to an understanding of why youth and beauty fade so early for the ladies of Queen Elizabeth's court. Since his work is not only generally informative but also gives us definitions of many terms, it will be well to quote from it at length. He begins by speaking of the very bad effects of sublimate of mercury, and his picture is quite horrifying:

Diverse women vse *Sublimate* diuersely prepared for increase of their beauty. Some bray it with *quicksilver* in a marble morter with a woden pestle; and this they call *argentatum.* Others boile it in water & therwith wash their face. Some grinde it with *Pomatum,* and sundry other waies. But this is sure, that which way so euer it be vsed, it is very offensiue to mans flesh. . . . *Sublimate* is called *dead fier;* because of his malignant, and biting nature. The composition whereof is of *salte, quicksilver,* and *vitrioll,* distilled together in a glassen vessell.

This the Chirurgions call a *corrosiue.* Because if it bee put vpon mans flesh it burneth in a short space, mortifying the place, not without great paine to the patient. Wherfore such women as vse it about their face, haue alwaies black teeth, standing far out of their gums like a Spanish mule; an offensiue breath, with a face halfe scorched, and an vncleane complexion. All which proceede from the nature of *Sublimate.* So that simple women thinking to grow more beautifull, become disfigured, hastening olde age before the time, and giving occasion to their husbandes to seeke strangers insteede of their wiues; with diuers other inconveniences.

He next discusses 'ceruse or white lead' and says that it is made of lead and vinegar; since it is such a great drier, physicians use it to dry up moist sores. Women who use it about their faces 'doe quickly become withered and gray headed.' He argues, too, against the use of lemon juice. Of oil of Tartary he says that there is nothing which is a greater 'fretter and eater,' and that 'in a very short time, [it] mortifieth a wound as well as any other causticke or corrosiue: and being so strong a fretter, it will take any spotte or staine out of linnen, or wollen cloth.' He points out next the dangers of using the two alums, salnitrum, and camphor, as we have seen earlier in the chapter, and concludes by saying: 'For it is certaine, that all Paintings and colourings made of minerals or halfe minerals, as iron, brasse, lead, tinne, sublimate, cerusse, camphire, iuyce of lymons, plume-alume, salt-peeter, vitrioll, and all manner of saltes, and sortes of alumes ... are very offensiue to the complexion of the face.' [25] If more women had read the work of Lomazzo, surely there would have been fewer of these cosmetics used, with the resulting improvement in the general health of the ladies.

Having seen the effect that the employment of harmful cosmetics could have upon women, we are naturally curious as to what effect all this artificial beauty had on the men and how they responded to these pretensions. It is not at all difficult to find references to this aspect of the subject, for the men of the age, at least the writers, are eager to express their views. And they seem to rise to unexpected heights when speaking of women's foibles. One argument frequently met with then as now is that prospective husbands are cheated by the women's use of beauty aids. A character in an anonymous play says of women:

> *Th'are nothing of themselues,*
> *Onely patcht vp to coozen and gull men,*
> *Borrowing their haire from one, complexions from another,*
> *Nothing their own that's pleasing, all dissembled.*

Prynne reasons that the wearing of false hair is a double sin, because 'they deceiue their Husbands by their excessiue Haire; and they disgrace the Lord,' in the order of their enormity. Indeed, it is the contention of Tuke that women plainly intend to deceive men in this way and that fucus itself is a clear deceit. Perhaps Tasso is the most explicit, as he writes: 'For what woman is she that marrieth, but before her husband can come to take the *Assay* of her sower sweetnesse, hath not wearied and tired him with her cheating and cunniketching so many toyes and bables, to furnish themselues withall, as wee see now adaies in euerie one of their kinde (in a maner) to weare about them, they making their bodies to shew like a Pedlers shop of new fangled deuices.' The philosophical phase of the problem is the concern of Buoni, who ponders the question of why it is that the discovery that a woman uses cosmetics breeds 'a kinde of loathing and disdaine in the hearts of men.' Two solutions are offered by this author:

Perhaps because as the first *Faire* by created *Beauty*, inclineth our hearts to Loue; So he being the first Truth, winneth vs to folowe the truth with inuisible Loue, whereby the deceipt of such *Beauties* or abilliments, which many times tie, and entangle the mindes of vnaduised yonge men, being discouered, there ariseth a strang kinde of scorne and disdaine euen against those whome they admired. *Or Perhaps* because euery obiect being altered from his naturall *Essence*, as being out of his naturall seate, doth presently decay and corrupt.

Such an argumentative proposal brings up another point – that men do not like to know that their loved ones paint. In his sermon 'The Pride of Nebuchadnezzar,' Henry Smith asserts that although women paint in order to please the men, the result is that they are not liked but disliked for such actions. And such is the belief of Du Bosc, Rich, Vives, and many other writers. According to Bishop Pilkington, most men feel that 'filthy things need washing, painting, colouring, and trimming, and not those that be cleanly and comely of themselves: such decking and colouring maketh wise men to think, that all is not well underneath.' Cosmetic aids have an even more violent effect on certain men; a character in *Euphues* finds that the thought of them is enough to turn his stomach: 'I loathe almoste to thincke on their oyntments, and Apoticarie drugges, the sleeking of their faces, and all their slibber sawces, which bring quesinesse to the stomacke, and disquyet to the minde. . . . Looke in their closets, and there shalt thou finde an Apoticaries shoppe of sweet confections, a Surgions boxe of sundrye salues, a Pedlars packe of new fangles. Besides all this their shadows, their spottes, their lawnes, their leefekyes, their ruffes, their rings, shew thē rather Cardinals courtisans, then modest Matrones, and more carnally affected, then moued in conscience.' 26

Besides, it is almost impossible for women to approach nature in their painting, and they should stop trying; they look so unnatural that most men can easily tell the difference, as Everard Guilpin's verse well illustrates:

> *For now our Gallants are so cunning growne,*
> *That painted faces are like pippins knowne:*
> *They know your spirits, & your distillations,*
> *which make your eies turn diamōds, to charm passions,*
> *Your cerusse now growne stale, your skaine of silk,*
> *Your philterd waters, and your asses milke,*
> *They were plaine asses if they did not know.*

There is really nothing a woman can do to improve her beauty, insist Gibson and Du Bosc, since no one can add to the divine graces of a real beauty, and since 'a foule woman painted makes the heauens laugh, and the earth to weep.' A character in *The Man in the Moone* adds his bit to the argument that the deception is a failure; in describing one woman he says: 'A sweete woman, no doubt, . . . doe you not smell her? a rowling eye, she turneth it with a trice; a faire haire, if it be her owne; an high forehead, if it be not forced; a rare face, if it be not painted; a white necke, if it be not plastered; a straight backe, if it be not bolstered; a slender wast, if it be not pinched; a prettie foote, if it be not in shooemakeres laste; a faire and rare creature, if she be not dishonest.' And when Clerimont, in *Epicoene*, becomes pretty well surfeited with Lady Haughty's rather obvious recourse to the apothecary's paint pot, we have one of Jonson's beautiful lyrics, which expresses in song the idea that what men want is simplicity:

> *Still to be neat, still to be dress'd,*
> *As you were going to a feast;*
> *Still to be powder'd, still perfum'd;*

Lady, it is to be presum'd,
Though art's hid causes are not found,
All is not sweet, all is not sound.

Give me a look, give me a face,
That makes simplicity a grace;
Robes loosely flowing, hair as free:
Such sweet neglect more taketh me,
Than all th' adulteries of art;
They strike mine eyes, but not my heart.

The same conception appears in another beautiful lyric, though developed somewhat differently, by Robert Herrick:

A sweet disorder in the dress
Kindles in clothes a wantonness;
A lawn about the shoulders thrown
Into a fine distraction,
An erring lace, which here and there
Enthralls the crimson stomacher,
A cuff neglectful, and thereby
Ribands to flow confusedly,
A winning wave, deserving note,
In the tempestuous petticoat,
A careless shoe-string, in whose tie
I see a wild civility,
Do more bewitch me than when art
Is too precise in every part. [27]

One reason why evidences of painting are so clearly discernible is that the painting does not last, and the colors run. As Biron remarks, in *Love's Labour's Lost*,

Your mistresses dare never come in rain,
For fear their colours should be washed away.

A verse by Arthur Dowton suggests that under these conditions the woman's face resembles the proverbial mud fence after a rain:

A Lome wall and a painted face are one ;
For th' beauty of them both is quickly gone.
When the lome is fallen of, then lathes appeare,
So wrinkles in that face from th'eye to th'eare.

In *The Devil is an Ass*, Wittipol suggests that heat and emotion can spoil the colors, as does Vives, who says: 'What a shame is hit, if any water by chance lyght on hit, or the peyntynge fortune to melte by thoccasion of swette or heate, and shewe the very skynne.' A well-known and often repeated story on the subject is sometimes attributed to Erasmus. As the tale runs, there are a number of people gathered around and passing an idle hour playing some such game as follow-the-leader. When it comes the turn of the courtesan Phryne, she calls for a bowl of water and washes her face. But in following her the ladies are disgraced by their streaked and messy faces. Although the point of the story is clear, we are left quite in ignorance as to what Phryne is doing at the party. [28]

An extension of the effect that beauty aids and outlandish dress have on mere man is put forth by Bishop Hall, who wonders what a progenitor of the Elizabethans would think if he should come back to earth and see his female descendants walking before him in Cheapside:

What doe you thinke he would thinke it were? Here is nothing to be seene but a verdingale, a yellow ruffe, and a periwig, with perhaps some fethers waving in the top; ... if then he should run before her, to see if by the fore-side he might ghesse what it were, when his eyes should meet with a poudred frizle, a painted hide shadowed with a fan not more painted, brests displayed, and a loose locke erring wantonly over her shoulders, betwixt a painted cloth and skinne.... Is this (thinks he) the flesh and blood? is this the hayre? is this the shape of woman? or hath nature repented her work since my dayes, and begunne a new frame? [29]

The effect of the use of cosmetics upon the husbands of the women involved is somewhat different from that upon men in general. The husbands complain first of all that their rights are being infringed upon in that the exposed and painted parts of the body should be reserved 'for their husbands... delight.' It is therefore not only the husband's right but his

*High-necked gown with long hanging sleeves extending
from the shoulders to the knees, narrow ruff, fan, handkerchief, and muff*

Costume of middle-class women during Elizabeth's reign

duty, insist both Tasso and Cawdrey, to see to it that his wife dresses in a seemly fashion and avoids 'filthy spunging, proigning, painting and pollishing themselues.' In Du Bartas we find the puzzled husband asking:

> *What should I doe with such a wanton wife,*
> *Which night and day would cruciate my life*
> *With Ieloux pangs? sith euery way shee sets*
> *Her borowed snares, not her own haires, for nets,*
> *To catch her cuckows with aloof, light attires,*
> *Opens the doore vnto all leaud desires,*
> *And with vile drugs adultering her face,*
> *Closely allures the adulterers imbrace.*

One clear solution for this husband is to follow the method recommended by Agenor, the King of Thessaly in Greene's *Menaphon.* He gives his wife a long lecture, informing her that a woman of modesty ought not to 'lay open the allurements of her face to anie but her espoused pheere; in whose absence like the Marigold in the absence of the Sunne, she ought to shut vp her dores, and solemnize continuall night, till her husband, her sunne, making a happie return, vnsealeth her silence with the ioy of his sight.' [30]

Another complaint of the husbands is that women who pay too much attention to their looks are not likely to have any time left for their household duties. 'I haue often noted,' writes the author of *The Court of Good Counsell,* 'those dames, which are so curious in their attyre, to be very sluts in their houses, and those which neglect such folly, to be very good huswiues.' Such women act, writes Brathwait, as though 'they were created for no other end, then to dedicate the first fruits of the day to their Glasse,' and Nashe adds that 'they stande practising halfe a day with theyr Lookingglasses, howe to peirce and to glaunce and looke alluringly amiable.' In contradistinction to these fashionable ladies, Overbury's 'faire and happy Milk-mayd' does not lie long in bed, spoiling her complexion, because she has been taught by nature that too much sleep is 'rust to the soule.' She therefore arises with the cock and goes to bed with the lamb. [31]

Finally, the husbands deplore the expense to which they are put in order that this artificial beauty may be maintained. One author seems to despise particularly the chicken-hearted husband who puts up with such expenditures. 'I cannot choose,' he writes, 'but speake of the abuse which is committed now a dayes in our country, in the ornaments and trimming vp of women, who bestrow vpon garments all their husbands substance: and in garding and trimming of them, all the Dowry which they brought with them, which maketh me amazed at it: and that which greeueth me most is to see howe Husbands not onely consent to such excesse charge, but also are pleased well with the vanitie which their wiues shew in the Strumpet-like dressing of their heads, whereby they make men rather laugh at them, then like of them.' Robert Burton expresses the same view as he wonders 'to what use are pins, pots, glasses, ointments, irons, combs, bodkins, setting-sticks? why bestow they all their patrimonies and husbands' yearly revenues on such fooleries?' An often quoted remark, sometimes attributed to Marcus Aurelius and sometimes said to be an old Greek proverb, makes a comparison of women to ships: 'women and ships, are neuer so wel accomplished, but that alwayes they want repairing.'[32]

History seems to show that professed detractors of femininity have never won the battle; however reasonable the arguments for more nature and less art, they are masculine arguments, and therefore powerless to prevail. The ladies had their champions as they always have had, even if, as was waggishly suggested, their painted cheeks were but a counterfeit for the modest blushes of virtuous women – better some semblance than none at all. Certainly ridicule failed to change their ways; what if the men laughed? Women then as today dressed for other women. The church stood firmly opposed to bedizened and bejeweled women, but that was a traditional attitude, respected, but not adhered to. Of course the most realistic motive for all the leather-lunged attack on women was the sale of books, as we have suggested before. Engaging topics which would arouse the interest of the general public were not easy to find; nobody ever took women for granted, or if one did, the editorial policy was steadfastly to ignore any such unenterprising person and trumpet in a new edition the same old topic of the supposed wantonness of women.

Some writers insist on taking upon men's shoulders the responsibility of women as they are, and a well-known story is told of Augustus Caesar, who objected to the immodest way his married daughter was dressed on one day and then applauded the way she was dressed on the next; her reply was: 'The day before . . . I was dressed for my husband, to day for my Father.' Du Bosc's comment on the story is: 'Surely as the wiser sort are not offended, that Women bee constrayned to please many, to keepe but one, so we must confesse, if they dresse and attire themselves but to their Husbands, there would be no excesse therein.' Both Lyly and Edward More break into verse as they make this point; says Lyly:

> *Women confesse they must obey,*
> *We men will needes be seruants still:*
> *We kisse their hands and what they say,*
> *We must commend bee 't neuer so ill.*

Thus we like fooles admiring stand,
Her pretty foote and pretty hand.

We blame their pride which we increase,
By making mountaines of a mouse:
We praise because we know we please:
Poore women are too credulous
  To thinke that we admiring stand,
  Or foote, or face, or foolish hand.

More points out that it is men who make all the inventions which women use, and asks who it is that go to far countries and return with the outlandish styles. Others remind us that if a husband command his wife to paint so that she will appear more amiable, she must obey her husband. [33]

John Donne seems usually to have been a defender of women. In one of his sermons he points out that when the poor widow told Elisha that she had nothing in her house but a pot of oil, many authorities very properly believe that it was not oil for cooking to which she referred, 'but Oyle for unction, aramaticall Oyle, Oyle to make her looke better; she was but poore, but a Widow, but a Prophets Widow, (and likely to be the poorer for that) yet she left not that.' He continues with the story of Sarah, whom King Abimelech fell in love with and took from Abraham when she was over sixty years of age; and he comments that the authorities believe her preservation to have been due to nothing else but the use of those unctions which were ordinary to people of her race at that time. He then concludes that if women beautify themselves and mean no harm by it, then there is no harm. In another work, *Iuvenilia*, his Paradox II is given over to the proposition 'That Women ought to Paint.' Here he argues that cosmetics make your sweetheart more attractive to you, and that she is only painting her defects; if houses need repairing, why not faces? '*Foulenesse* is *Lothsome*,' he agrees, but

can that be so which helpes it? who forbids his beloued to gird in her wast? to mend by shooing, her uneuen lameness? to burnish her teeth? Or to perfume her breath? yet that the *Face* be more precisely regarded, it concernes more. . . . Nor doth it only draw the busy eyes, but is subiect to the diuinest touch of all, to

212

kissing, the strange and mysticall vnion of soules. . . . What thou louest in her *face* is *colour,* and *painting* giues that, but thou hatest it, not because it is, but because thou knowest it. Foole, whom Ignorance makes happy, the Starres, the Sunne, the Skye, whom thou admirest, alas, haue no *colour,* but are faire because they seeme to be coloured: if this seeming will not satisfye thee in her, thou hast good assurance of her *colour,* when thou seest her *lay* it on. If her *face* be *painted* on a Boord or Wall, thou wilt loue it, and the Boord, and the Wall: Canst thou loath it then when it speakes, smiles, and kisses, because it is *painted?* Are wee not more delighted with seeing Birds, Fruites, and Beasts *painted* than wee are with natu-ralls? . . . Wee repaire the ruines of our houses, but first cold tempests warnes vs of it, and bytes vs through it; wee mende the wracke and staines of our Ap-parell, but first our eyes, and other bodies are offended; but by this prouidence of Women, this is preuented. If in *kissing* or *breathing* vpon her, the *painting* fall off, thou art angry, wilt thou bee so, if it sticke on? Thou didst loue her, if thou beginnest to hate her, then 'tis because shee is not *painted.* If thou wilt say now, thou didst hate her before, thou didst hate her and loue her together, be constant in something, and loue her who shewes her great *loue* to thee, in taking this paines to seeme *louely* to thee. [34]

The man of the world, too, was inclined to compliment the ladies upon their endless attempts at self-improvement. In Jonson's *Epicoene,* True-Wit, a waggish character of this type, remarks that he loves 'a good dressing before any beauty o' the world. O, a woman is then like a delicate garden; nor is there one kind of it; she may vary every hour; take often counsel of her glass, and choose the best. If she have good ears, show 'em; good hair, lay it out; good legs, wear short clothes; a good hand, discover it often: practise any art to mend breath, cleanse teeth, repair eye-brows; paint, and profess it.' Only one proviso does True-Wit make: that the touching-up of beauty be confined to the privacy of the boudoir, and never be done in public. 'Many things that seem foul i' the doing,' he continues, 'do please, done. A lady should, indeed, study her face, when we think she sleeps; nor, when the doors are shut, should men be enquiring; all is sacred within, then. Is it for us to see their perukes put on, their false teeth, their complexion, their eyebrows, their nails? . . . They must not discover how little serves, with the help of art, to adorn a great deal.' Later he declaims that it is duty of women 'to repair the losses time and years have made i' their features, with dressings.' Besides, he goes on, 'an intelligent woman, if she know by herself the least defect, will be most curious to hide it: and it becomes her. If she be short, let her sit much, lest, when she stands, she be thought to sit. If she have an ill foot, let her wear her gown the longer, and her shoe the thinner. If a fat hand, and scald nails, let her carve the less, and act in gloves. If a sour breath, let her never discourse fasting, and always talk at her distance. If she have black and rugged teeth, let her offer the less at laughter, especially if she laugh wide and open.' Similarly, in George Chapman's play *Sir Giles Goosecap*, Clarence is another evident champion of the ladies. He harangues his audience with the well-worn argument that we do not complain if a lady tries to make her lame leg appear sound, or if she takes medicines to improve her health; why, then, should we object to a little improvement of the face? Or again, since the fact that a woman refuses to paint is no guarantee of her chastity, why should painting prove the opposite? [35]

An authoress named Jane Anger also speaks up for her sex and bears witness that times have not changed as she protests that you cannot trust men, and that 'when you heare one cry out against lawnes, drawn-works, Periwigs, against the attire of Curtizans, & generally of the pride of al women: then know him for a Wolfe clothed in sheepes raiment.' Madam Maquerelle, too, gives a defense of women in the popular play *The Malcontent;* she begins by remarking to Emilia that she must let beauty be her saint: 'bequeath two hours to it every morning in your closet . . . preserve and use your beauty; for youth and beauty once gone, we are like beehives without honey, out-o'-fashion apparel that no man will wear: therefore use me your beauty.' Emilia starts to object: 'Ay, but men say –' and Maquerelle now warms to her subject: 'Men say! let men say what they will: life 'o woman! they are ignorant of your wants. The more in years, the more in perfection they grow; if they lose youth and beauty, they gain wisdom and discretion; but when our beauty fades, good-night with us. There cannot be an uglier thing to see than an old woman: from which, O pruning, pinching, and painting deliver all sweet beauties!' [36]

Although the fine art of covering up nature's mistakes, instead of remedying them, reached a high peak in the Elizabethan day, one must not forget that woman was bound by the limitation of an age in which often not even good health was to be had as a basis for beauty, and no means of obtaining it was offered. And whether or not Ruskin was right when he remarked, in his essay *Traffic*, that the Greek religion was the worship of the god of wisdom, the medieval religion was the worship of the god of consolation, and the Renaissance religion was the worship of the god of pride and beauty – at any rate, here was beauty in God's plenty, properly boxed.

CHAPTER VIII

Clothing and Appurtenances

It is the lesser blot, modesty finds,
Women to change their shapes than men their minds.

The Two Gentlemen of Verona

Fashionable accessories: mask, fan, and gloves; with mirror, pomander, and purse hanging from the girdle

The wearing apparel of the Elizabethan lady is very elaborate, and of course the fashions change throughout the period. The changes, however, were of a rather minor nature, so that it is possible to describe the dress for one decade and yet pretty well approximate that for another decade. In dressing a lady from the inside out, perhaps a good start can be made by taking her as she arises from her bed in the morning. She has been sleeping in her smock, which is a garment somewhat akin to a shirt. When she arises she may put on a so-called nightgown, directly over her sleeping garment. This usage is suggested by Lady Macbeth when she says: 'Get on your nightgown, lest occasion call us, and show us to be watchers.' The nightgown is worn both by men and by women, and is designed to keep the wearer warm. This gown is probably very useful as morning dress, in view of the elaborate costumes worn by both sexes, since it serves as a cover-all, extending to the ankles. It has long sleeves, and a collar which may be wide or narrow, of fur or other material. This gown may be made of velvet, satin, grosgrain, taffeta, or similar materials. It is worn while either indoors or outdoors. Anne Clifford wore one to church on December 28, 1617. When dressing for an outing or an enter-tainment, the lady first puts on a chemise-like smock. This garment may be heavily embroidered or be edged in cut-work lace, as in *The Devil is an Ass*. It may be one of 'these Holland smockes so white as snow,' perhaps with a standing collar. The next garment to be put on will be the petticoat. Since the lower part of it may be exposed when lifted in walking, it is made of good material in attractive colors. In *The New Inn* there is a reference to a velvet petticoat, in *Greenes Vision* to 'a Russet Petticoate, with a bare hemme,' and in *Eastward Hoe* to a 'Stammell petticoate with two guardes.' Over the smock is worn a pair of 'whale-bone Bodies' (bodice), a corset-like affair stiffened with stays of whale-bone or of wood, called busks. These are inserted in sheathlike pockets in the bodice, and are tied in place by busk-points, as the laces are called. The busk-points are often used as favors which the ladies give to their sweethearts. Apparently the garment itself is at times called a busk; Stubbes speaks of the 'stiffe buske'; and Gosson speaks of the busk used over the belly to keep it flat. Obviously the busk is used to give form and support to the stomach and abdomen. Some busks are even made entirely of iron, with long projections in front. A character in *Everie Woman in Her Humor* makes slighting reference to

> *A body prisoned vp with walles of wyer,*
> *With bones of whales, somewhat allyed to fish*
> *But from the wast declining . . . .*

Corresponding after a fashion to the whale-bone bodice worn above, under the petticoat is worn a farthingale, a device used to hold out the skirts of succeeding garments so that they may resemble 'mishapen Elephantine bodies'; they are called by Dent 'strouting fardingales.' No one knows just when farthingales were introduced into England; Miss Linthicum, the author of *Costume in the Drama of Shakespeare and His Contemporaries* (Oxford, 1936), gives the earliest reference as 1519. According to an anonymous ballad of about 1595, however, entitled *A Warning-Piece to England against Pride and Wickedness*, it was Eleanor, the wife of Edward I, who was responsible:

> *No English taylor here could serve*
> *   To make her rich attire;*
> *But sent for taylors into Spain,*
> *   To feed her vain desire:*
> *They brought in fashions strange and new,*
> *   With golden garments bright;*
> *The farthingale, and mighty ruff,*
> *   With gowns of rich delight.*

The Spanish farthingale, here mentioned, is a 'Farthingale hooped' – a skirt stiffened with hoops of wire, wood, whale-bone, or anything else practicable. It is circular in shape, quite extensive at the bottom and narrowing to a very small waist. It was worn into the seventeenth century, but gave place to the 'French Verdingale.' This is more of an accessory than a garment, and is used in place of a regular farthingale; it consists of a roll stiffened with wire, cotton, etc., and is worn about the hips. These devices are called 'rolls,' or 'bumrowles,' or just 'bums,' in the frank language of the age. At times this contrivance can be merely a half-roll worn over the *derrière*, or perhaps made in the form of the arc of a wheel, in the Italian style, often having a radius of as much as forty-eight inches, in an exaggerated style. The difficulty of sitting with these 'Catherine-wheel' farthingales may well be imagined. It is not clear exactly what the 'Scot' or Scotch farthingale in *Eastward Hoe* is, but it is supposed to 'clip close,' 'beare vp round,' 'keepe your thighes so coole,' and 'make your waste so small.' [1]

Over the petticoat (or petticoats) and farthingale at the bottom, and the smock and whale-bone bodice at the top, is worn a kirtle. This garment is an outside dress consisting of two parts: the separable bodice or pair of bodies at the top, and the skirt or half-kirtle at the bottom. Morose thus addresses the disguised Epicoene: 'But heare me, faire lady, ... how will you be able, lady, with this frugalitie of speech, to giue the manifold (but necessarie) instructions, for that bodies ...?' Instead of the kirtle bodice, women often wear doublets, which are almost exactly like those of the men, except that they have long points in front. This infringement upon men's style is roundly attacked by male writers. Gascoigne and Stubbes berate the ladies for this male attire which they have assumed, and Brathwait speaks of 'manlike doublets.' In Greene's *Mamillia*, too, there is complaint that the ladies are 'vp from the wast like a man' with the 'new guise to be casde in a dublet,' while Harrison, in his *Description of England*, expostulates: 'What should I saie of their doublets with pendant codpeeses on the brest full of iags and cuts ...?' The kirtle has an opening in front, which extends from head to foot, the bodice opening being partly filled by the stomacher, and the triangular skirt opening being filled by a decorated accessory called the forepart. The stomacher, which is also called a placard, is detachable and is made over a pasteboard foundation. It serves as an appropriate gift to the chosen lady, and can be of any color and any expensive material. In *Greenes Vision* is a reference to a stomacher of 'Tuft Mockado,' and in one of Lyly's works to a 'Cuttwork stomacher.' Crimson is a favorite color. Seemingly, the size could vary as well, since in *Euphues and His England* we find that 'if a Tailour make your gowne too little, you couer his fault with a broad stomacher, if too great, with a number of plights, if too short, with a faire garde, if too long, with a false gathering.' [2]

Unless an extra garment, such as a cloak, is needed for warmth, the last garment to be donned is the gown. It extends from the shoulders to the ground and is worn open in front. Illustrations of Elizabethan ladies in full dress indicate that in general very little of the gown proper is visible from the front; it is worn to set off the costume, to judge from the pictures. A portrait of Queen Elizabeth shows her wearing a gown and sleeves, which are made of material which matches her kirtle. Being the final outer garment, the gown is even more elaborate than the kirtle or other wearing apparel. The cloth itself is of very expensive material, and is trimmed with lace, embroidered, and otherwise richly decorated. On November 2, 1617, for example, Anne Clifford sent the Queen 'the skirts of a white satin gown all pearled and embroidered with colours which cost me fourscore pounds without the satin' (perhaps equal to $5000 today). Some gowns are of grosgrain or buffin, tissue of gold, silk, taffeta, velvet, etc., and are lined as well with materials like velvet and satin. At the Earl of Hertford's entertainment for one of Elizabeth's progresses, Lyly has six of his ladies 'attired in gowns of taffata sarcenet of diuers colours, with flowrie garlands on their heads, and baskets full of sweet hearbs and flowers vppon their armes.' The sleeves of the gown are detachable, and much loving care goes into their making. They are long and elaborately decorated, and are often of a contrasting color with the gown. Green sleeves we know of from the song, and in *Bartholomew Fair* Zeal-of-the-land Busy joins them to a yellow gown. They can be large and puffed, snugly fitting, or loose, according to the style of the day and the inclination of the wearer. The trunk sleeves mentioned by Petruchio are large, tapering to the wrist, on a body of wire; hanging or pendant sleeves have an arm opening at the shoulder; side-sleeves may be of this latter type or may have an opening half-way down, somewhat resembling the sleeves on the modern gown for a master's degree. Sleeves are at times made in two parts: an upper sleeve, with an under sleeve to which is attached the lower half, called the foresleeve, which extends from the elbow to the hand. The 'puffe wings' referred to in *Poetaster* are devices used at the shoulder to disguise the buttons or points by which the detachable sleeves are attached. A cloak or mantle may be worn over the gown, or even instead of it. The cloak can be of 'tuft-taffata,' sable, velvet, etc., and may well be 'seeded with waking eyes, and a siluer fringe.' [3]

One of the most succinct pictures of the garb worn both by merchants' wives and by gentlewomen in 1617, is given by Fynes Moryson, a very observant gentleman. In his *An Itinerary*, he records that citizens' wives wear a gown which is gathered at the back and belted with a girdle. The skirt is decorated with many guards, or ornamental bands or borders, and over the front is worn an apron. A linen coif covers the head, and over it is worn a silk cap, or a small beaver hat. Some wear pearl necklaces or light French chains. The gentlewomen, on the other hand, are more elaborately dressed:

Gentlewomen virgins weare gownes close to the body, and aprons of fine linnen, and goe bareheaded, with their haire curiously knotted, and raised at the forehead, but many against the cold (as they say) weare caps of haire that is not their owne, decking their heads with buttons of gold, pearles, and flowers of silke, or knots of ribben. They weare fine linnen, and commonly falling bands, and often ruffes, both starched, and chaines of pearle about the necke, with their brests naked. The graver sort of married women used to cover their head with a Frenchhood of Velvet, set with a border of gold buttons and pearles: but this fashion is now left, and they most commonly weare a coyfe of linnen, and a little hat of beaver or felt, with their haire somewhat raised at the forehead. Young married Gentlewomen sometimes goe bare headed, as virgins, decking their haire with Jewels, and silke ribbens, but more commonly they use the foresaid linnen coyfe and hats. All in generall, weare gownes hanging loose at the backe, with a Kirtle and close upperbody, of silke or light stuffe, but have lately left the French sleeves borne out with hoopes of whalebone, and the young married Gentlewomen no lesse then the Virgins, shew their breasts naked.

The emphasis in Moryson upon naked breasts leaves us somewhat in doubt as to exactly what is intended. Throughout the period, from Vaughan-Burdet in 1542 to Griffith in 1633, and even to Thomas Hall (*The Loathsomeness of Long Haire*) in 1654, there are frequent references to breasts which are 'displayed,' 'naked,' 'open,' 'embared,' 'painted,' and 'layed forth.' It seems quite apparent that the style of fully exposed breasts was affected by courtesans. But did virtuous women dress in this fashion, or do these words refer only to an exaggerated type of decolletage? The question is somewhat difficult to answer. If we refer to ballads of the time, we find many woodcuts illustrating the style, although some of the women in the illustrations are clearly courtesans; on the other hand, some of them seem not to be of this profession. Speaking of a certain type of woman, Pyrrye (1569) writes: 'It is her common wonted vse, with naked brest to walke'; Rich (1606) speaks of women's 'open breasts, their naked stomaches'; Tuke (1616) has noticed the 'paps embossed layed forth to mens view'; while Nashe (1593) says that women 'theyr round Roseate buds immodestly lay foorth.' Spenser, in *The Faerie Queene*, the *Amoretti*, and the *Epithalamion*, uses such phrases as 'daintie paps,' 'paps lyke lyllies budded,' and 'nipples lyke yong blossomd jessemynes,' but probably we should admit the license of a poet in special cases and not consider his words as illustrative of fashion. Perhaps a lead to the correct answer may be found in John Downame (1608): after speaking of courtesans 'painting their faces, and laying out their naked breasts,' he goes on to say: 'not only those who are harlots by profession, but euen such as would be reputed pure virgins and chaste wiues shew these outward signes of their inward filthinesse,... by painting their faces, & setting forth thēselues with adulterate beauty, and by laying out their breasts after a whorish manner to be seene and touched: for is it likely that those who lay thē out to yᵉ shew, would haue them only seene?' We may conclude, then, that the style of fully exposed breasts did flourish, and that it was followed by some of the more advanced ladies of fashion, chiefly during the last of the sixteenth century and the first quarter of the seventeenth century. [4]

A distinguishing characteristic of the Elizabethan costume is the neckwear. The band which Lady Would-Be in *Volpone* says does not show enough of her neck is simply a separate collar which the bodice receives at the neck. Miss Linthicum distinguishes among the plain (worn until the ruff was introduced around 1550), the falling band worn turned down (from about 1580), and the ruff or ruff-band. The early bands are somewhat plain and simple. Later come the standing collar, the falling band, and the ruff. The French fall or falling band is a wide collar which is permitted to fall or rest on the shoulder, and sometimes extends to the outside of the shoulder. The standing collar is self-explanatory: it is supported on a frame of wire, called a rebato, mentioned by Marston: 'Her seate of sense is her rebato set.' Ursala, the pig-woman of *Bartholomew Fair*, may be referring to such a band when she says: 'you must ha' your thinne pinch'd ware, pent vp i' the compasse of a dogge-collar, (or 'twill not do) that looks like a long lac'd *Conger*, set vpright, and a greene feather, like fennell, i' the Ioll on 't.' According to Samuel Rowlands, the lady of 1604 wears both a band and a ruff. The English ruff seems to have come from Italy, through France, and is at first simply a pleated ruffle. Soon ruffs become so large and unwieldy that the Continent, according to Stowe, did not recognize its own export. The Elizabethan ruffs thus become larger and larger, and the pleating becomes more intricate, being supported either by starch or by pasteboard in the folds. The starched folds are set with 'poking-sticks' of wood or bone, and later of heated iron. The width of the pleat can be varied by the width of the poking-stick, Puritans seemingly using the narrowest. Also in use as accessories are very short bolero-like jackets, called partlets, usually worn over the bodice of the kirtle; gorgets or wimples; scarves to protect the face from the sun; chinclouts or mufflers; veils or kerchiefs, worn by such lower-class women as Mistress Ford and Mistress Page in *The Merry Wives of Windsor;* and rails, which are shawls or short capes. [5]

There are several styles of head attire worn by the Elizabethan ladies. Perhaps the most popular of these is the hood. Early in the sixteenth century, the hood was a rather ugly contrivance which hung heavily at the sides and back of the head, coming down over the neck. Soon, however, the French hood is introduced; it has a round front instead of a gabled one, and is made of more delicate materials. It covers the back of the head as far as the ears, and thus forms an interesting frame for the face. References to hoods appear in Stubbes, Rowlands, and almost any writer who has occasion to mention women's attire. Near the close of the century, hats become popular, so that by the time *The Alchemist* was written Abel Drugger can say of a certain woman: 'Mary sh'is not in fashion, yet; shee weares a hood.' Caps of several styles are also worn; small caps seem to have been in vogue at the end of the century and are often laughed at in the drama as 'velvet custard' or 'velvet dish'; they are small and fit the skull closely. Another small cap is the coif, which is worn indoors to cover the back and sides of the head; Gertrude, of *Eastward Hoe*, tells Mildred that she wants to be a lady and wear a 'Quoiffe with a London Licket.' Statute caps are those required by a law of 1571 to be worn by everyone over the age of seven years unless the head of the family has an income of twenty marks a year from the land. These caps are to be made 'of woll knitte, thicked, and dressed in Englande,' and are to be worn 'vppon the Sabbath and Holy daye,' the penalty being 'for euery day not so wearyng, the summe of .iii.s. iiii.d. of lawfull money of Englande.' In 1597 the law was repealed. It had been passed in order to provide cappers with a livelihood to keep them from begging and 'from raunging and gadding thorow the Realme, in practising and exercising sundry kindes of lewdnes.' [6]

Besides hoods and caps, women also wear hats. Early in Elizabeth's reign these are generally the tall, steeple hats, or the conical copintanks. Copped hats are popular throughout the period until the introduction of the Cavalier style of hats with low crowns. As the English court comes more under the influence of the French, there is a corresponding turn to smaller hats, with lower crowns, and with or without wider brims. In 1599 a visitor in England, Emanuel Van Meteren, writes: 'Married women only wear a hat both in the street and in the house; those unmarried go without a hat, although ladies of distinction have lately learnt to cover their faces with silken masks or vizards, and feathers.' The hats are usually made of taffeta, felt, silk, or such fur as ermine and beaver. In *The Magnetick Lady*, Mrs. Polish tells Mother Chaire, the midwife:

You shall have a new, brave, foure-pound Beaver hat,
Set with enamell'd studs, as mine is here.

Any woman would envy such an elaborate and expensive hat, the 'foure-pound' referring of course not to the weight but to the cost. According to Philip Stubbes, women of every station make use of some outrageous adornment for the head: 'On toppes of these stately turrets . . . stand their other capitall ornaments, as french hood, hat, cappe, kercher, and suche like; wherof some be of veluet, some of taffetie, some (but few) of woll, some of this fashion, some of that, and some of this color, some of that, according to the variable fantasies of their serpentine minds. And to such excesse is it growen, as euery artificers wyfe (almost) wil not stick to goe in her hat of Veluet euerye day, euery marchants wyfe and meane Gentlewoman in her french-hood, and euerye poore Cottagers Daughter in her taffatie hat.' Cloth hats are elaborately trimmed with embroidery, pinking, or jewelry, such as the kind mentioned in *Mamillia*, where we find 'hats from Fraunce thicke pearld for pride.' Other hats are decorated with hatbands and with feathers. Brathwait complains that in former times plumes and feathers 'were held light dressings for staid minds,' but that in his time styles have changed. Lyly seems not to support this contention, however, as he speaks without censure of the feathers in ladies' hats. The hatbands are made of every sort of material – gold, silver, pearls, cypress, ribbon, etc. At times buttons are sewed to the hatbands. [7]

In addition to conventional headgear, there are a number of accessories used to decorate the head. Under the hoods are worn cauls, or nets fitting very closely to the head. Unlike the staid coifs, they are made of hair or of finely woven gold or silver thread. Gosson speaks of them as 'glittering caules, of golden plate,' while Tuvil objects to them as being formerly worn by courtesans. Illustrations of the period prove their attractiveness. They are flattering to the wearer and like the hood have been in and out of fashion from that time to this. According to Stubbes, 'They haue also other ornaments besydes these to furnish foorth their ingenious heads, which they cal (as I remember) cawles, made Netwyse, to th'ende, as I thinke, that the clothe of gold, cloth of siluer, or els tinsell, (for that is the worst) wherwith their heads are couered and attyred withall vnderneath their cawles may appeare, and shewe it selfe in the brauest maner. Soe that a man that seethe them (their heads glister and shine in suche sorte) wold thinke them to haue golden heads.' While the French hoods are in style, the front of the hood is decorated with 'paste,' that is, a border or circlet of velvet or other material. Another type of border, worn similarly, is called a billiment; it is more likely to be a gold or silver circlet decorated with gems. When small caps or coifs are worn out-of-doors, women need a shade to protect their faces from the sun. Early in the century these are called bongraces, but near the end of the century they are known as shadows. Other bands for the head are called frontlets, and ribbons for binding the hair are known as fillets – a style as old as Greece. Veils are also worn, chiefly to protect the face from the sun, and Van Meteren indicates that they are popular with all ranks; unmarried girls wear white veils, like the one in *The Arraignment of Paris* worn by the nymph Eliza. [8]

Covering for the feet is also important for the Elizabethan woman, and the shoe should preferably display a little foot, for as Labé says: 'very often the curiosity of love in men seeks to find beauty in the feet.' Slippers are popular, but are suitable only for wear indoors; they are very low-cut and cover only a part of the foot; the difficulty experienced in keeping them on and the untidiness of their appearance is shown by the word *slip-shod*. Perhaps the most common covering for the feminine foot is the pump. This is a close-fitting, single-soled covering for the whole foot, made of cloth or thin leather. Footwear which covers the ankle is called a shoe, while that covering the foot and leg over the calf is called a boot. These last two types are clearly more serviceable than the others, and are consequently worn less often by the fashionable women. Since pumps are ill-suited for wear out-of-doors, overshoes are worn over them. Sometimes the overshoes are the tall chopines, which raise the wearer out of the mud and dust; more often they are pantofles or pantables, which cover the pumps and keep them comparatively clean. The pantofles have high cork soles,

Low-necked dress, with wheel farthingale

with cloth or thin leather uppers to the instep but not around the heel. As they become more and more richly decorated, they are worn indoors as well as out. Queen Elinor, in Peele's *Edward I*, calls for her pantofles as she descends from the litter; and in Lyly's *Endimion* the younger of two maids-in-waiting says to the other: 'I crye your Matronship mercy; because your Pantables bee higher with corke, therefore your feete must needs be higher in the insteppes: you will be mine elder, because you stande vppon a stoole, and I on the floore.' Stockings, of course, are drawn on the feet and legs before the footwear is put on. They can be made of silk, Jersey or worsted, crewel, or other cloth. Silk stockings were introduced during the sixteenth century and became the only fashionable wear. Garters are used to hold up the stockings; they consist of bands or ribbons tied just below the knee, with the stockings usually rolled down to them. Ornamen-- tation of all sorts is used on both stockings and garters, such as needlework gold and silver thread, pearls, and gems. [9]

Many other accessories for the costume are also worn by the Elizabethan woman. Around her waist she wears a girdle or belt, attached to which, by means of ribbons or chains of precious metal, are her fan, her pomander ball, her muff, and her mirror. The fan is made of feathers or decorated cloth and is used chiefly for coquetting, tapping gentlemen on the wrist, or for cooling the face. A woman may own several fans and change them several times a day. A pomander is a perfumed ball used to temper noxious odors and to ward off diseases; it usually contains a mixture of dried aromatic herbs which have been further treated to increase their perfume, and some fixative, such as civet. The Elizabethan muff is the usual roll, intended to keep the hands warm, but used chiefly as another ornamentation of the attire. It can be made of any usable material, such as fur, expensive cloth, or gold and silver twist; it is usually elaborately decorated. The mirror is made of metal or glass. Even the Puritan Lady Brilliana Harley can write to her son Ned, who is off at the university, to see if he can find for her in Oxford a good looking glass 'aboute the biggnes of that I use to drees me in. . . . I put it to your choys, becaus I thinke you will chuse one, that will make a true ansure to onse face.' The mirror is not only popular in use, but seems to have caught the imagination of the Elizabethans, as is indicated by the frequent use of the word in the titles of books. On the other hand, the word *mirror* probably appears no more frequently in Elizabethan titles than *speculum* does in medieval ones.

Gloves are used not only to keep the hands warm, to ward off freckles and tan, and to serve as costume accessories, but they can also be used as tokens of love, as wedding gifts, as favors, and as a source of the gentle aroma which should surround the lady of fashion. Perfume is used on gloves very early in the century, and soon all fashionable gloves are perfumed; recipes for perfuming gloves at home can be found in the usual books directed to the English housewife. Handkerchiefs, too, can serve as love tokens as well as costume pieces, and can naturally serve as gifts for all occasions; they bear the usual finely wrought embellishment of the time. Masks, too, are worn, as we have seen, to protect the complexion from sun and wind, and presumably to hide imperfections. At times they are used to conceal identity as well, and are then somewhat smaller in size. [10]

A picture of the *tout ensemble* of a lady's costume may be obtained from the following description of the outfit worn by a lady masker in Ben Jonson's *Hymenaei*:

A large white-striped . . . veil is stretched out with wires behind her, tied here and there with small bows of red. The hair auburn in small curls. A crown-shaped head-dress of pearls and rubies; in the centre three spikes of metal overarched by circlets of pearl and a large pearl above them. On the left side of her head a white egret plume, not feathered, but almost like an elongated shaving-brush. A pearl necklace with pendant of eight diamonds and a pearl below. A ruby and pearl ear-ring in her left ear. She wears a tightly fitting white jacket cut low at the neck with an open collar of point-lace; the jacket is open at the front and embroidered with conventionalized flowers, and has a fringe of gold on the lower edges. The sleeves white, fitted close to the arms and barred with alternate rings of red, the white portion embroidered, the red gold-edged and covered with lace-work puffs. On her right wrist a triangular string of pearls attached to a point-lace cuff. Her bodice strawberry-colour, showing in the triangular cut of the jacket; at the apex four rubies and a large pearl below. Her girdle studded with pearls and rubies; in the centre diamonds and pearls surmounted by three dark spikes. A short red upper skirt matching the bodice, with horizontal bands of gold, grey squares and white dots between the bands, and vertical lines of silver spangles; a gold-lace fringe below. A blue-green underdress richly braided in gold at the bottom and embellished with gold spangles and cross-embroidery. Red stockings with gold clocks. Blue shoes covered with lace of a circular pattern; red rosettes with a diamond in the centre. [11]

These fearfully elegant styles are railed against by Puritan divines and by many other Elizabethan writers. One charge leveled against them is that such attire is absolutely superfluous. A whole chapter of *The Praise and Dispraise of Women* is given over to 'the great curiositie and curious super-fluitie of womens apparell,' while Thomas Becon insists that 'clothes are ordayned of God to couer our vile nakednes, and to defend vs from the violence of tempestes, and not to garnishe & pride our selues with them.' This argument receives amplification from Richard Brathwait, who asks the fair ladies: 'Was *Apparell* first intended for keeping in naturall heat, and keeping out accidentall cold? How comes it then that you weare these thinne Cobweb attires, which can neither preserue heat, nor repell cold? Of what an incurable cold would these Butterfly-habits possesse the wearer, were pride sensible of her selfe? Sure, these attires were not made to keepe cold out, but to bring cold in.' The theme is developed further by John Taylor, who contributes the idea that this superfluity finds it necessary to ravage the whole animal world in order to be satisfied:

> Most vaine the pride of any rayment is,
> For neither Sea, land, fish, fowle, worme, or beast,
> But man's beholding to the most and least . . . .
> Fowles of the ayre doe yeeld both fans and plumes
> And a poore Ciuet-cat allowes perfumes . . . .
> If men (I say) these things considered well,
> Pride then would soone be tumbled downe to hell.
> Their golden suits that make them much renown'd,
> Is but the guts and garbage of the ground:
> Their Ciuet (that affords such dainty sents)
> Is but a poore Cats sweating Excrements.

It is interesting that this same problem of superfluity comes to Lear's troubled mind. When Goneril and Regan ask him what need he has for any personal servants, he replies with vigor as well as logic:

O, reason not the need: our basest beggars
Are in the poorest thing superfluous:
Allow not nature more than nature needs,
Man's life's as cheap as beast's: thou art a lady;
If only to go warm were gorgeous,
Why, nature needs not what thou gorgeous wear'st,
Which scarcely keeps thee warm.

Later, in the storm, Lear returns to this theme when in his delirium he meets Edgar, who is now disguised as Poor Tom. Edgar presents to Lear the perfect example of the person devoid of any superfluous attire; and Lear addresses him thus: 'Why, thou wert better in thy grave than to answer with thy uncovered body this extremity of the skies. Is man no more than this? Consider him well. Thou owest the worm no silk, the beast no hide, the sheep no wool, the cat no perfume. Ha! here's three on's are sophisticated! Thou art the thing itself: unaccommodated man is no more but such a poor, bare, forked animal as thou art.' [12]

The cause for the superfluity in women's apparel, however, is not far to seek: it stems entirely from woman's vanity and her proverbial seduction into pride. Some writers vainly assert that a woman is most appealing when her dress is modest. 'A *shippe under saile*, is the *fairest sight* in the Sea,' writes William Austin, 'And a *woman* modestly *attired* is the delightfullest sight in the earth.' According to Becon, 'It is enough for chaste and pure maids to wear clean and simple apparel,' because such is a kind of 'testimony of the uncorruption and cleanness both of their body & mind.' The truth is, argue several of the authors, that a woman's religion now is 'fine apparel deere bought.' 'Her *devotion*,' writes Overbury, 'is good clothes, they carry her to church, express their stuffe and fashion, and are silent; if shee bee more devout, shee lifts up a certain number of eyes, in stead of prayers, and takes the sermon, and measures out a nap by it, just as long.' And when she finds another in church dressed better than she, 'Than she thynketh her felowe set all full of pryde,' says *The Proude Wyues*

Stylized figure of Queen Elizabeth with scepter and ball – round farthingale

Probably Anne of Denmark, Queen of James I – wired ruff and farthingale

Pater Noster. Bruto warns women against such pride, stating that they must not envy their equals nor try to surpass them in expensive attire. Barnaby Rich paints for us the sad picture of the woman who refuses to leave the house because she has nothing to wear: 'But alas for pitty, how woe begone is that poore woman, that is out of the Taylers trim, that is out of the *Imbroiderers trim*, that is out of the *Haberdashers trim*: but shee that is out of the *Atiremakers trim*, shee is ashamed to shew her face, shee thinkes her selfe vnfit to conuerse with honest company.' It is said, further, that the women of England go far beyond those of other countries in their demands for luxury in dress. Emanuel Van Meteren, a 1614 visitor to England, comments on their elegant and costly garments, noting also that they change their styles each year and even wear their best clothes when traveling. [13]

The women of the Elizabethan age are severely critized, in addition, because they import new fabrics and styles from other countries; national pride is hurt. Brathwait regrets that the women of his country prefer 'forraine inuentions before the ornament of a *Maiden Isle*, constant modesty,' while Carter implies that their love of 'the fashions of the world' indicates that they have no fear of God. In *Euphues and His England* we learn that 'there is nothing in Englande more constant, then the inconstancie of attire, nowe vsing the French fashion, nowe the Spanish, then the Morisco gownes, then one thing, then another,' though indeed the charge is laid against the men as well as against the women. What seems particularly obnoxious to many writers is that even the chaste women (those supposed rarities) dress in these fantastic fashions. As Du Bosc reports: 'Their sexe is curious in their ornaments, and naturally given to sumptuous apparell, insomuch as even you shall see many most chast Women, who yet dresse themselves with extreame industry without other end in their designs, then their owne particular gust through I know not what complacence or innocent satisfaction.' What specifically fascinates Harrison is the infatuation with colors which attacks most women: 'I might here name a sort of hewes deuised for the nonce, wherewith to please phantasticall heads, as gooseturd greene, pease porrige tawnie, popingaie blue, lustie gallant, the deuill in the head (I should saie the hedge) and such like.' [14]

Natural concomitants of this indulgence in expensive clothes, believe Elizabethan writers, are the suffering of the family and the peculiar misery of the husband. When Frederick, Duke of Württemberg, visits England in 1602, he notes that the women of England have more liberty than those of any other country, and that they make use of it by giving all of their attention 'to their ruffs and stuffs.' He says, indeed, that he has been informed that many women do not hesitate 'to wear velvet in the streets, which is common with them, whilst at home perhaps they have not a piece of dry bread.' Of course it is the husband who pays and pays for these extravagant fashions, and Brathwait remarks that to be married to such a prodigal woman as those of whom we have been speaking, is utter misery. Harrison notes that it is especially the younger women who do not know how to make an end of this costly expenditure. Perhaps it is partly for this reason that the sumptuary laws were passed, particularly during the reign of Elizabeth; by these laws those persons who do not have land or fees over £ 200 on the subsidy books are restrained from wearing leopard skin, velvet, silk nether-stockings, or gold, silver, or silk pricking. No one under a countess can wear cloth of gold, cloth of silver tissue, or sables; no one under a baroness can wear any cloth mixed with gold or silver. [15]

How then should a proper and modest woman dress herself? According to Barnaby Rich, in *The Excellency of Good Women*, she may wear any sort of costume as long as it is decent, is not too expensive for her status, does not put her in debt, and is not a gift from some man other than her husband: 'This therefore may well be avowed by the rules of Christian sobrietie, that a woman, neither exceeding the decency of fashion, nor going beyond the limits of her owne estate, nor surpassing the boundes of her husbands calling, I do not thinke *but such a woman may weare any thinge. Provided alwayes, that shee braues it not out with other mens goodes, that shee hanges not in the *Mercers* bookes, in the *Goldsmithes* bookes, in the Taylers booke, maintaininge her pride with other mens purses....' [16]

Sociologists of today like to tell us that in times of peace women's dress becomes elaborate and formal; gay trifles and adornments are sought after; the age-old illusion of the mystery of women gets reinforcements; women's clothing represents the mood of the times. All that we know of Elizabethan England is mirrored in the dress of her women. There were some years of comparative quiet, and much prosperity—time enough to look around and see what their French and Spanish sisters were wearing. Through travel, England was becoming more cosmopolitan, and foreign styles caught the imagination. Add to this a Queen whose weakness was a vanity so extreme that she set the styles for all of her long reign, and it can be seen that feminine fashions were given unrivaled opportunity for elaboration on top of invention; courtly ladies no doubt presented awe-inspiring sights when in full panoply, and a good deal of this glory sifted down to the working classes. One doubts whether in this period much drab dress was seen on either men or women. *Fantastic* would be an easy adjective to apply to a good bit of the fashionable clothes of the time, but that adjective could be used to describe much of the social scene of Elizabethan England, too.

Part of the exuberance of the styles of the day must have been due to an aesthetic awakening. Elizabethans were truly aesthetic: their glorious literature reflects it; their love of music and their masques mirror it as well. Then too, science, invention, and exploration played their part. In the latter years of Elizabeth's reign carriages came into use; ladies could ride in elegant clothes and have no fear of the mud. And as we have seen, silk stockings were a new luxury, while forks and napkins heightened the elegance of table manners. As a direct reflection of the influence of exploration and of an expanding economy upon ladies' dress, we hear of a fanciful coiffure designed with a miniature ship in full sail upon the waves of my lady's hair.

CHAPTER IX

Certain controversies over women

Prithee, Kate, let's stand aside and see the end of this controversy.

The Taming of the Shrew

A BOVLSTER LECTVRE.

Dum loquor ista, taces?

Surdo canis.

Will: Marshall. sculpsit.

This wife a wondrous racket meanes to keepe,
While th' Husband seemes to sleepe but do'es not sleepe:
But she might full aswell her Lecture smother,
For ent'ring one Eare, it goes out at t'other.

The so-called problem of women has always been popular with males, since they seem unhappy with them or without them, and never so happy as when arguing about them. As Professor Utley points out, a large number of medieval manuscripts had taken one side or the other in the quarrel over whether women were composed of vice or virtue. Early printed books also catered to this fatal curiosity. The most extensive controversial series of the sixteenth century apparently began with the publication of *The Schole house of women*, probably in 1541.[1] Edward Gosynhill, to whom the work is usually attributed, so caught the temper of the times that four editions appeared between 1541 and 1572, while allusions to the work may be found in five or six other books. Professor Utley suggests that the popularity is due to the all-inclusive nature of the diatribe. Women are called impossible to please, untrustworthy, crabbed, talkative, shrill-voiced, loose in morals, and froward. When they are crossed or feel themselves slighted, 'They flusshe and flame, as hote as fyre and swell as a Tode' (A2). They are so malicious-minded that you will not hear a good word from them in a whole year. If a woman permits liberties, she says you promised to marry her; and no matter how many presents you give her,

> *Yet shall another man, come alofte*
> *Haue you ones tourned, your eye and backe*
> *Another she wyll haue, to smycke and smacke. (A3)*

It is not any better if you should marry her:

> *Wed them ones, and then a dewe*
> *Fare well all truste, and houswyfrye*
> *Kepe theyr chambres, and them selfe mewe*
> *For stayning, of theyr fysmye*
> *And in theyr bed, all daye do lye. (A3ᵛ)*

Once or twice a week they will pretend to be sick and you must send out for dainties, but nothing pleases them except to have their gossips come in to entertain them. They insist on having two or three maidservants, and if you demand that they do some work themselves, they weep, since they will neither wash, nor bake, nor brew, nor do anything but sit by the fire and let the servants labor. Their gossips give them bad advice about how to rule their husbands, such as:

> In case there be, no remedy
> But that ye must, haue strokes sadde
> Take vp the babe that then is nye
> Be it a wenche, or be it lad
> And byd him stryke, yf he be madde
> Smyte hardely, and kyll thy sonne
> And hange therfore, when thou hast done. (B1ᵛ)

The result is that there is an ointment to cure a man, within or without, of every disease except marriage and the gout. And there is

> No payne so feruent, hote ne colde
> As is man, to be called cockolde. (B3)

In fact, the reason women bark at their husbands is that Eve was really made from a dog's rib (B4ᵛ). [2]

What was probably the first reply to *The Schole house* is *The prayse of all women, called Mulierum Pean*, the conjectured date for which is 1542. This work is clearly by Gosynhill, since the last stanza contains his name. [3] The author relates that one night while he was sleeping, he suddenly saw before him a group who in dress and face seemed to be women. They told him to awake and consider their grief, which was due to a book lately printed,

> Whyche by reporte, by the was fyrst framed
> The scole of women, none auctour named
> In prynte it is passed, lewdely compyled
> All women wherby be sore reuyled.
> Consyder therin, thyne owue [sic] good name
> Consyder also our infamye
> Sende forth some other, contrary the same

For thyne and ours, bothe honestye
The Pean thou wrote, and lyeth the hye
Be quycke herein, prolonge not thus
As thou woldest our fauour, nowe do for vs.(A2)

He is informed that men have always been reproaching women, since the beginning, but yet men cannot do without them. Women take care of you when you are sick (A3-A4). Some of the greatest contributions in the world have been made by women: it was Ceres who invented the sowing of grain; Carmenta first found the letters of the alphabet; Minerva is responsible for wool; Sappho gave us the harp; etc. (A4-A4ᵛ). Woman works hard taking care of the children, while man strikes his children when they are annoying. The old story that woman had no tongue until man took long leaves and put them under her palate, is manifestly false, because God made everything perfect; and whoever heard of a perfect woman without a tongue (B2-B2ᵛ)? Signatures B3 to E3 are given over to stories from the Bible and from history showing that women have always been more commendable than men. The woman of the house is trusted to oversee 'baker, brewer, butler, and coke.' She has to receive and pay accounts, bargain and buy. 'My lady must ordre thus all thynge or small shall be the mannes wynnynge.' As further proof that women are more admirable than men, we hear constantly that 'the chylde is praysed for his mother wytte for the fathers condycions depraued alway' (E3).

What was probably another of the many replies to *The Schole house* definitely appeared in 1542 – *A Dyalogue defensyue for women agaynst malycyous detractoures*, printed by Robert Wyer. Formerly the author of this work was supposed to be Robert Vaughan, who wrote the prologue and the envoy. But since the stanzas of 'Robert Vaughan to the Reader' contain an acrostic of the name Robert Burdet, he may be the author. [4] In the prologue, Vaughan says that a friend read a book which accused women and then wrote these verses in reply. The work is a dialogue between a Falcon, who defends women, and a Pie, who puts in objections. After the Falcon has listed many women with learning and others with occult powers, the Pie insists that women put their husbands in debt, are lazy, and are wasters of 'money, meate, and cloth' (C2). The Falcon then replies that Aristotle believed a wife to be careful in caring for her family and in protecting her husband's goods:

> *A womans offyce, as Arystotle taught*
> *In his Econymyckes, is redy for to make*
> *Suche thynges for sustynaunce, as to her be brought*
> *Her famylye to fede, that paynes and labours take*
> *All rychesse procured, by nyght or els by day*
> *Throughe the manes trauayle, in felde or in towne*
> *The wyfe with her wysdom, must kepe from decay*
> *And suffer no proffyte in losse to fall downe. (C2ᵛ)*

The Falcon continues that a wife works when she is tired and gives up her sleep to do her duty. When a man lies ill, who feeds him with nourishing meats but his wife? who protects and comforts him at all times, in sickness or health but a wife? But the Pie then insists that women lead men into evil:

> *All gyftes of nature, they inclyne to prouoke*
> *Man vnto pleasure, and his reason to blynde*
> *And with Cupydes darte, to gyue him a stroke . . .*
> *Theyr eyes moste wantonly, euer roll and turne*
> *Upon syghtes semely, and all thynges aboue*
> *Because loue them burneth, they desyre to burne. (C3)*

Furthermore, argues the Pie, women insist upon keeping their hands white and their fingers full of precious rings, and they love to show a pretty foot. They dance, sing, and laugh in order to inflame youth with the lusts of love; they wear clothes of the French style and expose their breasts, wearing over them a chain 'that was gotten in theyr play' (C3ᵛ). The Falcon, however, replies that it is the women who are moved to vice by men, and offers proof with several stories from the Bible. Of course there are some bad women, but they are in the minority since women are naturally more virtuous than men. The envoy contains Vaughan's plea that women will forgive their detractors.

244

The vertuous scholehous of vngracious women seems to be indebted for its title to a desire on the printer's part to capitalize on the success of *The Schole house;* indeed, the *Short-title Catalogue* erroneously lists the former as the first edition of the latter, though there is no connection except for the similarity of the titles. *The vertuous scholehous,* according to C. H. Herford, is a translation of Wolfgang Resch's *Ein schöner dialogus oder gesprech, von zweien schwestern.* [5] The translator is probably Walter Lynn, who gives his name in the preface to the reader. The *Short-title Catalogue* tentatively dates the work around 1550, although a date closer to *The Schole house* might be more acceptable. According to the translator's preface, *The vertuous scholehous* is

a very godly communicatiō betwene two Systers. Justina a Godly wydowe out of the lande of meyssen. Serapia a waywarde vngodly maryed woman. This complayneth vpon her husband, and wilfull children. The other instructeth and comforteth her in pacience, to be obedient vnto her wedded husband, and to brynge vp her children in the feare of God, with fayre wordes, & decent nurtour and correction, groundyng the same in the holy scripture of God, & confirmynge the same by many goodly examples, for Justina is alwayes mynded to lyue godly, cōtrarywyse Serapia, which bylyke receyued that name at the fonte. And doutles, yf honest and vertuous huswyues or wydowes shall se, reade or heare thys dialogue, they shall strengthen theyr vertuous myndes in it. Agayne, yf rude, inapte stubborne wyues shall also heare the same, thei shall take occasion to knowe themselues and to amende their conditions. (A2–A2ᵛ)

Serapia begins to complain of her husband that he is 'stubberne and waywarde' towards her, and she does not know why. Justina says it is the wife who is the cause, since she is 'frowarde and obstinate' and always brawls with him, although he is 'an honest simple man, which is loth to fyghte and brawle with the, as other frowarde men do, And also I beleue, and am sure, that he is no dronkarde, hooremonger nor player' (A8ᵛ-B1). Serapia complains that her husband never gives her gifts; Justina points out that she deserves none (B8ᵛ-C). Before long, Serapia tells Justina that she stands reproved and will turn over a new leaf. From here on, Serapia asks leading questions and receives moral replies. Serapia inquires: 'Which is the crosse of the woman?' and Justina responds: 'God sayde vnto

Eua because thou hast herkened vnto the serpente, and haste eaten of the fruystes concerninge the whiche I commaūded the, that thou shouldest not eate of it. I wyll multiplye thy sorowe and thy conceyuing. In sorowe shalt thou brynge forth thy children, & thou shalt stoupe before thy husbande, and he shal haue the rule of the' (G2-G2ᵛ). This section of the work is concluded with signature H1ᵛ. Appended to the translation of Resch's composition, however, is Martin Luther's sermon on matrimony, based on a text in the Epistle to the Hebrews: 'Wedlocke is to be had in honour, amonge all men, and the bedde vndefyled. As for hoorekeepers and aduouterers, God shall iudge them.' Men can easily see, says Luther, that 'the yonger sorte, and the commō people falleth awaye, and abhorreth the state of matrimony as an heauy intollerable burthen. And suche wilde careles persons, wyll always more loue the dissolute and fre lyfe, then suche a paynefull, vertuous, and laudable lyfe in wedlocke.' But in these times, he goes on, such persons not only pollute themselves with sins, but they are also punished with plagues of the body, so that 'not onely money and goodes, doth waste away by suche people, but also they must paye for it in their skinnes' (H3). The Pope and his priests cannot show anywhere that God commanded them to live without wedlock (I2ᵛ). For God not only instituted matrimony, but gave his blessing to it (J3ᵛ). And even Saint Paul told men to love their wives and not be bitter toward them (K1). 'Wvhere are nowe the shamefull Papistes, whiche abhorre wedlocke as a carnall estate, as though God could not be serued in hys kynde of lyfe' (K1ᵛ). Luther insists further that it can be called defiling the marriage bed when the husband and wife are withdrawn from each other and are moved to dissension or hatred. From signature L8ᵛ to the end is affixed another translation: 'A briefe Exhortacion vnto the maryed couple, howe they shall behaue themselues in wedlocke.' The theme of this tract is the usual one that wives must be in subjection to their husbands; the wife rules the family and children, but is always to permit herself to be commanded by her husband and to follow him (M6ᵛ).

About 1550, also, Thomas Raynalde printed *A treatyse, shewing and declaring the pryde and abuse of women now a dayes*, by Charles Bansley. It contains a passage stating that 'the scole house of women is nowe well practysed' (A2), but there is little else which would remind us of *The Schole house* unless it be the general tone of the attitude toward women. It is chiefly given over to satire on the dress of women, expressed in billingsgate. Bansley tells the women that their love of fancy clothes comes from the devil and the brothels, and warns the husbands that they must beware lest 'youre wyues raymente and galante trickes, doo make youre thryfte full bare.' He chooses certain styles for his attack, if the author may be permitted a repetition:

> *Downe for shame wyth these bottell arste bummes,*
> *and theyr trappynge trinkets so vayne*
> *A bounsinge packsadel for the deuyll to ryde on,*
> *to spurre theym to sorowe and payne. (A2ᵛ)*

Bansley is careful, however, to excuse himself from any wish to abuse 'playne women, as walke in godlye wyse,' but insists that he speaks only against 'suche wanton dyssemblers, as doeth goddes truthe despyse' (A3ᵛ). [6]

Particular evidence that *The Schole house* was being widely read is contained in the long title of a work by Edward More, printed in 1560, *A Lytle and bryefe treatyse, called the defence of women, ... made agaynst the Schole howse of women.* Surprisingly enough, however, this defense contains on the title page the following verse, which is capable of two interpretations, perhaps being ambiguous on purpose:

> *If the turtle doue*
> *Be true in loue*
> *Voyde of reason, than,*
> *What shame is it,*
> *If man hath wyt,*
> *And hateth a Woman.*

Not being satisfied with a reference to *The Schole house* in the title, More addresses the author of this work in an epistle which also mentions the *Mulierum Pean* and thus possibly lends authority to the contention that Gosynhill wrote both works:

> *Though thy melancholy, thou canst not els assuage,*
> *No kynde of way, but only thus, on women for to rage.*
> *Pean to be a folysh worke, thou dost testyfye*
> *Whych lyk a learned poet, by the fygure onomatopei*
> *Trāsformed thou hast into pecock, as proude of hys longe tayle,*
> *Pean is more lyke in sounde in our mother tongue*
> *To pehen then pecock, whose tayle is not so longe,*
> *Nor set with sundry colors, nor of so pleasaunt hewe. (A3)*

More makes use of stories from history and from the Bible, usually quite lengthy, to show that the women of the past have been good and true, while men have usually been bad. It is no wonder, he argues, that women give so much attention to their hair, since they learned this care from men. As for their farthingales, we must remember who first invented them. Indeed, it is only the men who go to far countries and bring back new fashions for both men and women (C3).

Perhaps deriving directly from Gosynhill's supposed authorship of works taking both sides in the controversy over women, there appeared between 1563 and 1579 two books and a broadside ballad combining the praise and dispraise of women. [7] Probably the first of these was C. Pyrrye's *The praise and Dispraise of Women, very fruitfull to the well disposed minde, and delectable to the readers therof. And a fruitfull shorte Dialogue vppon the sentence, know before thou knitte*, printed by William How. This work contains a poem against women, one in defense of women, and the dialogue. The first poem is that in dispraise of women, which opens with the warning that the author does not intend to speak against good women, but only against the monsters of their sex. This monster woman is changeable, insincere, proud, servile, cruel, too talkative, and so on. She spends entirely too much time trying to be attractive to men:

> *She deckes and trims her selfe at ease,*
> *her face to beautifie:*
> *To frame her talke all men to please,*
> *her wittes she doth applye. (A6)*

She gossips too much, is deceitful, drunken, shrewish, and easily angered.

Even such famous men as Hercules, Samson, **David**, Lot, and Solomon, who were strong enough to conquer other monsters, were defeated by this one. Evil women from Ovid, the Bible, and other works are called forth to bolster the picture of this monster. She uses every art to deceive men:

> *Her shinning forhead by arte she sekes,*
> *with golden rule to bind;*
> *With purple culler on her chekes,*
> *and if it want by kinde.*
> *She gouerneth her steppes by art,*
> *her heare by arte doth place*
> *She tempereth her eyes by arte,*
> *her bodye and her face.*
> *She seekes by art her selfe to paint,*
> *because she would be faire:*
> *Her greisly shape she doth anoint,*
> *in hope of some repaire. (B2ᵛ–B3)*

When she leaves the house, she has further misleading tricks to practice on men:

> *And with her lips she simpereth,*
> *abrode as she doth goe:*
> *Her shoulders eke she tempereth,*
> *her fingar and her toe.*
> *It is her common wonted vse,*
> *with naked brest to walke:*
> *Which thinge (in faith) is daungerous*
> *for in fewe wordes to talke.*
> *It meaneth nought at all but this,*
> *(marke well what I rehearse:)*
> *That where her poison planted is,*
> *with greater stroke may perce. (B3–B3ᵛ)*

There are so many women of this type that admirable women are as difficult to find as coal-black swans. The second poem, *The prayse of VVomen*, is rather reminiscent of Gosynhill's *Mulierum Pean*; it begins with a statement by the author that once upon a time he came across a book which disgraced womankind and dispraised women (*The Schole house?*), and he wonderes how the author could have made his pen write in such a fashion. He decides to write against this book. Man is born of woman, and women give up much of their time in having children and taking care of them when they are small. And when the male children grow up, it is still the women who take care of them.

> *Eche thing to vewe and ouerlooke,*
> *as neede she may her constraine:*
> *The baker, bruer, and the cooke,*
> *no toyle doth she refraine. (B7ᵛ)*

As opposed to what men commonly say, lechery is really loathsome to women; and indeed they try to put all evil thoughts out of their heads. Nor is it fair to speak of woman's inordinate dress:

> *In desent order she doth weare,*
> *her garments on eche side,*
> *She goeth not sluttish in her geare,*
> *and yet she wanteth pride. (C1ᵛ)*

In support of his contention, the author offers a lengthy list of women from the Old and New Testaments, who were noble and honorable, and performed good deeds. Those men who dispraise women bring about their own disrepute. One must not blame all women just because a few women have been bad. The final poem, the dialogue on the text 'know before thou knitte,' is essentially a brief treatise in which 'C' tells 'W' how to choose a good wife from a bad. [8]

The ballad *In Praise and Dispraise of Women* is supposed to present both sides in the controversy, like Pyrrye's work, but the three stanzas of praise are not very complimentary and are spoken with tongue-in-cheek, while the four stanzas of dispraise offer the usual contemptuous criticisms. [9] The *Dispraise* insists that a woman never answers back to her husband, unless to hit him with a chair. The ballad makes little contribution to the controversy.

There is another work with the same main title as Pyrrye's book: *The Praise and Dispraise of Women: Gathered out of sundrye Authors, as wel Sacred as Prophane, with plentie of wonderfull examples, whereoff some are rare and not heard off before, as by the principall notes in the Margent may appeare. Written in the French tongue, and brought into our vulgar, by Iohn Allday*. London, for William Ponsonby, 1579. It is extant in a unique copy at the Folger Shakespeare Library and is not listed in the *Short-title Catalogue*. The author of this tract first praises women; he tells stories of the bravery of women, of the cleverness of women, and of women who first brought religion to men. Among the women who in learning and wisdom have excelled the grave and wise philosophers, he names the ten sibyls, the Queen of Sheba, Pythagoras' daughter Dama, Aristippus' mother Arreta, the poet Corinna, Scipio Africanus' wife Cornelia, and Lady Margaret Vallois, Queen of Navarre; he concludes the list, of course, with Queen Elizabeth, whom he praises for knowing seven foreign languages (fols. 29-35^v). He draws from history lists of many prudent women, chaste women, and constant women, and concludes that it is only common jesters, inventors of lies, and slanderous speakers who say that 'there was neuer but one good woman & yet ye deuil caried her away' (fol. 62). In taking up the dispraise of women, the author begins with Plato, who was unable to decide whether women should be catalogued 'amōgst reasonable creatures or amongst brute beasts.' He points out that the law does not recognize women; hence they are unable to inherit. Boccaccio is quoted to the effect that when the gods became displeased with mankind they 'sent therefore vppon the worlde three kindes of scourges, that is to wyt, sickenesse and diseases, then trauayle and paine, and then women that are always stirrers vp of debate and strife, which is the greatest scourge of all ye rest' (fol. 68^v). Women are seemingly born to nourish voluptuousness and idleness rather than to be trained in matters of importance. The author goes at length into the story of the so-called Pope Joan (fols. 70^v-71^v). Then comes chapter four, on the inability of a woman to keep a secret; and chapter five, on the 'curious superfluitie of womens apparell.' Many stories are told of the miseries brought into the world by women (fols. 65-70), the divers cruelties inflicted by women (fols. 81-87), and the numerous sorceries performed by women (fols. 96-101).

II

Another early controversy over women centered around John Knox's attack on the Catholic Mary Tudor, a very interesting account of which is contained in Robert Louis Stevenson's essay 'John Knox and His Relations to Women,' to be found in his *Familiar Studies of Men and Books*. Knox and his congregation were banished from England and proscribed from Scotland. From 1556 to 1559 he was minister in Geneva to a group of English refugees, and it was quite natural that *The First Blast of the Trumpet against the monstruous regiment of Women* should be published in that city, when it appeared in 1558. Since most of his troubles could be laid to Mary Tudor and to the Regent Mary of Guise, it was not surprising for the idea to occur to him that women in government were to be abhorred. [10] It is a wonder, Knox begins, that with so many wits and godly preachers in England not one of them has dared 'admonishe the inhabitantes of the Ile how abominable before God, is the Empire or Rule of a wicked woman, yea of a traiteresse and bastard. And what may a people or nation left destitute of a lawfull head, do by the authoritie of Goddes worde in electing and appointing common rulers and magistrates' (fol. 2). His *First Blast*, then, is clearly in the nature of an incitement to rebellion. He feels certain, he says, that God has revealed to some that are living that it is more than monstrous to have a woman reign over men (fol. 3v). If any should wonder why he has published his work anonymously, he wants to inform them that the fear of punishment is neither the only nor the chief reason. He intends to blow his trumpet three times: the first two without a name, but at the last to take all the blame upon himself (fol. 8v). With the preface disposed of, Knox now enters upon the blast. To put a woman to rule over man is against the revealed will of God, and against all equity and justice. Anyone can understand how repugnant it is to nature to have the blind lead those who can see, to have the weak and sick nourish the whole and strong, or that the 'foolishe, madde ād phrenetike shal gouerne the discrete, ād giue counsel to such as be sober of mind.' And yet that is exactly the situation with any woman in authority when compared with a man. Nature has made women 'weake, fraile, impaciēt, feble and foolishe: and experience hath declared them to be vnconstant, variable, cruell and lacking the spirit of counsel and regimēt' (fols. 9-10). After much long and learned argument, supported by Biblical passages, chiefly from Paul, Knox concludes that 'whether women be deposed from that vniust authoritie (haue they neuer vsurped it so long) or if all such honor be denied vnto them, I feare not to affirme that they are nether defrauded of right, nor inheritance' (fol. 51). Even though the force of circumstance must have called forth this blast, yet logic being what it is in the mind of a fervent minister, Knox must have seen that the hope of Protestantism was bound up in the fortune of the Princess Elizabeth. It was sheer hard luck that Elizabeth came to the throne in the same year that his *First Blast* was published. Of course there were no further blasts of the trumpet, and Knox had a difficult enough time making his peace with Elizabeth for what he had done. [11]

John·Aylmer, who wanted to be and later was made Bishop of London, had a much easier time of it. His answer to Knox was published in 1559 – *An Harborovve for Faithful and Trewe Subiectes, agaynst the Late Blowne Blaste, concerninge the Gouernmēt of Women.* [12] Since Elizabeth was already the Queen, he saw his duty and did it. And not being one to miss any opportunities, he dedicated it both to Francis, Earl of Bedford, and to Lord Robert Dudley. It is not known whether or not he recognized Knox as the author; at any rate he says: 'I seke to defend the cause, and not to deface the mā, Seing this errour rose not of malice but of zele' (B2ᵛ). The author of the *First Blast* was chiefly in error because he generalized that rule by any woman is against nature, reason, right, and law, whereas the former condition of the country was due to the fault of one member of that sex. Aylmer points out that Anne Boleyn was 'the chief, first, and only cause of banyshing the beast of Rome, vvith all his beggerly baggage'

(B4ᵛ). He then states that Knox's arguments may be reduced in number to six:

Fyrst that what so euer is agaynste nature the same in a common vvealth is not tollerable, but the gouernment of a vvomā is against nature. Ergo it is not tollerable. The second, vvhat so euer is forbidden by scripture is not lavvful. But a vvoman to rule is forbidden by scripture. Ergo it is not lavvful. The third, if a vvoman may not speke in the congregation: muche lesse she may rule. But she may not speke in the cōgregatiō, ergo she may not rule. The fourth, vvhat the ciuil lavve forbiddeth, that is not lavvful: but the rule of a vvoman the Ciuill lavv forbiddeth, ergo it is not lavvful. The fift, seing ther folovveth more inconueniēce of the rule of vvomē then of mens gouernmēt: therfore it is not to be borne in a common vvelth. The last, the Doctors and Canonistes forbidde it, ergo it can not be good. (C2–C2ᵛ)

Aylmer argues that a woman may rule in her capacity as a magistrate and yet be obedient as a wife. This matter comes not under the civil law but rather under municipal law; the Biblical arguments are really not applicable in this instance. At the same time he lists many female rulers in the Old and New Testaments and in secular history who have ruled successfully. And if God has placed a woman in the line of succession, who are we to question His workings?

Several other replies to Knox were written, as well. John Fowler translated into English the tract of Petrus Frarinus, and it was published in 1566 in Antwerp under the title *An oration against the vnlawfull insurrections of the Protestantes of our time.* David Chambers wrote a French attack, which was published in Paris in 1579. In 1569 was published an answer to Knox by John Leslie, Bishop of Ross, *A defence of the honour of the right highe, mightye and noble Princesse Marie Quene of Scotlande and dowager of France, with a declaration aswell of her right, title & intereste to the succession of the crowne of Englande, as that the regimente of women ys conformable to the lawe of God and nature.* As the title indicates, the first two books defend Queen Mary and urge her as the proper heir to the English throne if Elizabeth dies without issue, while the last book attempts to show that there are no impediments to the reign of a woman. His work may have contributed to Elizabeth's decision that it was only the part of reason to imprison Mary. There is also an unpublished manuscript by Henry Howard, Earl of Northampton, dated around 1590, entitled *A Dutifull defence of the lawfull Regiment of women diuided into three bookes.* [13]

III [14]

One of the most interesting of the controversies, as well as perhaps the most curious one, is that which began with the publication in 1615 of Joseph Swetnam's *The Arraignment of Lewd, Idle, Froward, and vnconstant Women: Or, the Vanitie of them; chuse you whether. With a Commendation of the Wise, Vertuous, and Honest Woman. Pleasant for married men, profitable for young men, and hurtfull to none.* It is not clear just what so appealed to Swetnam's public that his volume was attractive enough to call forth ten editions between 1615 and 1637, as well as editions in 1690, 1702, 1707, 1733, and 1807. [15] Four formal replies were made to the work, and the controversy was even responsible for a comedy on the theme. Professor Louis Wright believes that the popularity of the work may be accounted for by the fact that Swetnam had found the very elements of the iniquity of women which the middle-class folk considered their greatest sins. [16] Swetnam's arguments were certainly not new, but they must have caught the prevailing fancy. In an epistle Swetnam addresses himself 'neither to the best, nor yet to the worst; but to the common sort of Women.' He calls women necessary evils who still are not all given to wickedness. Many are so bad, however, that if he were to say the worst he knows of some women, his tongue would blister; but since scolding is for shrews, it would discredit a man to take the same tone. Moses said that woman was created to be man's helper, but what she really helps him do is to spend what he worked so painfully to get. You cannot get a woman to change her opinion or to believe she has any faults, either. She is jealous if you look at any other woman, but full of disdain if you love her too much. Yet young men are not dismayed by these facts; they rather 'cudgell their wits, and beat their braines, and spend all their time in the loue of Women,' and are happily paid with a smile (p. 4). A wife must have expensive household articles, even if her servants lack meat; she must have a new gown, new hat, and new jewels (p. 7). Wives are called night-crows because they nag a man so when he wants to sleep that he will grant them anything to get a little peace and quiet, for if a woman cannot get what she wants, say what she wants, and go where she wants, 'thy house will be so full of smoake, that thou canst not stand it' (pp. 11-12). Women are so artificial that a man does not know what they are really like (p. 25). Man has only one fault: drinking too much; but women have two: 'they can neyther say well, nor yet doe well' (p. 28). [17] When Socrates' wife chided and brawled, he left the house until she quieted down, but this action angered her the more; 'on a time she watched his going out, and threw a chamber-pot out of a window on his head; Ha, ha, quoth he, I thought after all this thunder there would come raine' (p. 39). If you want to choose a good wife, find out first what her reputation for behavior is, for only in this way can you discover if she be wise, virtuous, kind, 'wearing but her owne proper haire,' wearing clothes she can afford, and preferring to sit at home (pp. 46-47). Do not marry even a pretty woman if she does not have a dowry, for you will then treat her like a servant; but if she is wealthy she will 'haue alwaies somthing to be in loue with all' (p. 52). But a man, too, must treat his wife as if she were his only treasure; he must be faithful, honest, and loving to her; he must tell her his secrets and take her counsel, since grief becomes less if shared with another. A wife must be rebuked gently if at all, and then only in private (pp. 53-54). Since the government of a house belongs to the wife, the husband had better stay away from the kitchen, else he may offend his wife and wrong himself. And the husband should remember what a wife endures in bearing children (pp. 55-57). If you want to overcome love, follow Ovid and avoid excess of meat and drink, but rather eat rue and lettuce, and use such exercises as hunting, hawking, shooting, bowling, running, and wrestling. Whatever you do, be sure not to marry a widow, for she is the cause of a thousand woes (pp. 57-59). Swetnam's motives are not as clear as they might be. Partly his work is a recrudescence of an older misogyny; partly, too, it is the expression of cynical views to catch the attention of middle-class readers; there seems to be little of Puritanism involved.

In the preface to Daniel Tuvil's *Asylum Veneris, or A Sanctuary for Ladies. Iustly Protecting Them, their virtues, and sufficiencies from the foule aspersions and forged imputations of traducing Spirits* (1616), the author affirms that he wrote the book sometime earlier and is only publishing it now to prevent the issuance of an imperfect copy. In view of the popularity of Swetnam's diatribe, however, it would seem rather likely that Tuvil's opportune publication, if not an exact reply, was at least intended to capitalize on the popular interest. Even Tuvil does not praise all women. In a poem addressed 'To the looser sort of Women' he writes:

> *Stand of you foule adulterate brats of Hell,*
> *Whose lunges exhale a worse then sulph'rous smell,*
> *Do not attempt with your prophaner hands*
> *To touch the Shrine, in which chast Virtue stands. (A6)*

Tuvil was seemingly an admirer of Edmund Spenser; he quotes one stanza of the *Faerie Queene* (5.8.1) on the subject of beauty in women (p. 16), another (3.5.52) on the chastity of women (p. 24), and a final one (3.9.2) urging that the example of a bad woman should not make us forget the many excellent ones (p. 32). A woman, continues Tuvil, must be very sensible to any action which might demean or injure her reputation: 'Chastitie must haue setled Grauitie for hir Vsher; and for hir waiting-woman, bashfull Modestie; or she shall neuer procure respectiue reuerence and obseruance from those that doe behold hir' (p. 37). If some virtuous ladies should go abroad disguised in wanton manner, they would surely be considered courtesans. 'If Women haue immodest lookes, it will auaile them little for auoiding the worlds censure, to haue honest hearts. A booke is censured many times by what the title promiseth . . .' (p. 38). In the last analysis, the best women are those of whom men speak the least, either in praise or dispraise (p. 52). There are not two things which require more trimming than a woman and a ship (p. 56). A woman should never speak except to her husband (p. 60). And as for secrecy, lack of it is as common to men as to women (p. 79). Woman can usually be counted upon to love their husbands; when the women of a certain captured town were permitted to leave, taking with them the one thing they valued most, they carried their husbands out on their shoulders. Although learning in women is likened by their adversaries to a sword in the hands of a madman, yet learning for them is actually an ornament and would be valuable if only to supply the defects in man. But in addition there have been many women so proficient in letters that men have had just cause to blush at their own ignorance (pp. 87-97). Tuvil, then, was concerned with the presentation of woman with her natural vices and virtues, and with a description of woman at her best.

Whether or not Tuvil had Swetnam's storming assault in mind as he wrote, three writers of the sex which was attacked made definite and vigorous replies to *The Arraignment of Lewd . . . and vnconstant Women*. On November 14, 1616, was registered in the *Stationers' Register* Rachel Speght's [18] vindication of women: *A Mouzell for Melastomus, The Cynicall Bayter of, and foule mouthed Barker against Evahs Sex. Or an Apologetical Answere to the Irreligious and Illiterate Pamphlet made by Io. Sw. and by him Intituled, The Arraignment of Women* (1617). In case the reader has any doubts as to the identity of *Io. Sw.*, the preface removes all conjectures, since it is addressed 'Not vnto the veriest Ideot that euer set Pen to Paper, but to the Cynicall Bayter of Women, or metamorphosed Misogunes, Ioseph Swetnam' (B1ᵛ). The author then proceeds to lay about her, attacking Swetnam on all grounds; she even complains that in many places he has not observed 'so much as Grammer sense' (B2). She points out that although Swetnam proposed on the title leaf that he would arraign only the lewd, idle, and unconstant women, yet in the text he advised men to avoid six types of women: the good and the bad, the fair and the ugly, the rich and the poor; she then says she is unable to find any commendation of honest women at all. Rachel's arguments are not of the strongest; she reminds us that when God finished his creation he said that all was very good, and women are bound to be included in this statement. She argues that when the apostle said that it is good for man not to touch a woman, he spoke only of a special situation in Corinth; and Solomon must have been wrong when he enigmatically said that he had found one man among a thousand but not one woman among his seven hundred wives and three hundred concubines. Woman is more refined than man, since man was made of earth, while she was made of a part of man. Furthermore, woman was created to be a helper to man, but if she must be a *helper*, 'then are those husbands to be blamed, which lay the whole burthen of domesticall affaires and maintenance on the shoulders of their wiues' (p. 12). There must be mutual love in marriage, insists Rachel, and when there is it is a paradise, a 'merri-age' (p. 14). She admits that 'the Man is the Womans Head,' but maintains that the woman must not be considered the servant, and that the husband must protect her from injuries. And if men would only remember their duties, 'some would not stand on tip-toe as they doe, thinking themselues Lords & Rulers' (p. 17).

Apparently the women were unsatisfied with Rachel's mild rebuttal, for in 1617 (entered January 4th) another woman, using the pseudonym of Ester Sowernam, indited a much better defense: *Ester hath hang'd Haman: or An Answere to a lewd Pamphlet, entituled, The Arraignment of Women. With the arraignment of lewd, idle, froward, and vnconstant men, and Husbands. Diuided into two Parts. The first proueth the dignity and worthinesse of women, out of deuine Testimonies. The second shewing the estimation of the Foeminine Sexe, in ancient and Pagan times; all which is acknowledged by men themselues in their daily actions. Written by Ester Sowernam, neither Maide, Wife nor Widdowe, yet really all, and therefore experienced to defend all.* Ester says she was at a supper one evening when the conversation turned on the subject of women; finally someone mentioned Swetnam's book, which she had not read. The next day a gentleman brought her a copy, and in looking it over hurriedly she discovered that the author had not performed what the title promised. She immediately undertook to write a defense of women; but when she had spent a small time on her work, she heard that a minister's daughter had a defense ready for press. (We learn later, on page six, that this maid's book is Rachel Speght's.) She stopped working and waited for the reply to Swetnam, but was disappointed in it since it seemed to condemn women rather than defend them. With her expectations unfulfilled, therefore, she undertook the completion of her own work. Most of her early arguments are Biblical, and here she catches Swetnam in a blunder. Swetnam had said that God called women necessary evils, but she points out that it was the profane poet Euripides who made the statement, and Swetnam should be ashamed to have thought it was God (p. 11). She makes use of the usual list of women in history who have performed worthy deeds. Evil lies only in the thoughts of evil men, she asserts; therefore, only evil-minded men can be led astray by the way women dress; and anyway, women are never misled into love by man's apparel, so why vice versa (pp. 37-39)? Swetnam is in error in talking about bear-baiting a woman, since you cannot bear-bait anything as mild as a woman. 'The disposition of the minde is answerable to the temper of the body. A woman in the temperature of her body is tender, soft, and beautiful, so doth her disposition in minde corresponde accordingly; she is milde, yeelding, and vertuous' (p. 43). A husband should never complain about a froward wife, because it is his duty to see that she is not froward, and he should not air his grievances in public, anyway (pp. 43-44). Nor can man name a single offense of woman in which he was not the beginner (p. 46).

Another pseudonymous work presumably appeared in the same year (entered April 29, 1617). This was Constantia Munda's *The Worming of a mad Dogge: or, A Soppe for Cerberus the Ialor of Hell. No Confutation but a sharpe Redargution of the bayter of Women,* the title of which makes obvious reference to Rachel Speght's muzzle for 'black-mouth.' In a verse addressed to her mother 'Lady Prudentia Munda,' the author links her contribution to the controversy:

> *Yet lest you thinke I forfait shall my band*
> *I here present you with my writing hand.*
> *Some trifling minutes I vainely did bestow*
> *In penning of these lines that all might know*
> *The scandals of our adversarie, and*
> *I had gone forward had not* Hester *hang'd*
> Haman *before . . . .*

Although woman is the most important element of the *'lesser world,'* she continues, yet every 'pendanticall goose-quill' has taken her for his subject, and 'euery fantasticke Poetaster' has attempted to present unseemly false-hoods about women 'on the publique Theatre' (p. 3). Swetnam, she argues, has actually contributed to the delinquency of women by suggesting new fashions of lewdness of which they had never thought, and has imitated the pagan poet whose indignation over female vices 'opened the doores of vnbridled luxurie,' and gave a precedent 'of all admired wickednesse, and brutish sensualitie, to succeeding ages' (p. 9). She addresses Swetnam himself, and tells him: you should have made it clear just how at the beginning of your thirty year's travel you became addicted to prying into the peculiar actions of loose, strange, lewd, idle, obstinate, and inconstant women, and how you came to be 'so expert in their subtile qualities; how politikely you caught the daughter in the ouen, yet neuer was there your selfe' (p. 11). If in your travels you have been mistreated by some courtesan, is that any reason why honest and religious persons should come within your reproachful remarks (p. 13)? This sop for Cerberus has been provided for you, since I have heard that you foam at the mouth (p. 16). Your verses are only 'dogrill' rimes (p. 23). Of what use is it to say that the ancient philosophers had such a poor opinion of women, when we know that they were all married themselves (p. 29)?

Constantia's complaint concerning the poetasters who revile women in their plays is well founded, as we have seen in previous chapters. More to the point is an anonymous play registered for printing on October 17, 1619: *Swetnam, the Woman-hater, arraigned by women. A new comedie, Acted at the Red Bull, by the late Queenes Seruants* (1620). In the second scene of the first act (A4), Swetnam (alias Misogynos) attests the popularity of this controversy as he comes on the stage and soliloquizes:

> *By this, my thundering Booke is prest abroad,*
> *I long to heare what a report it beares,*
> *I know't will startle all our Citie Dames,*
> *Worse then the roring Lyons, or the sound*
> *Will be more terrible in womens eares,*
> *Then euer yet in Misogenysts hath beene.*

Later in the scene Scanfardo, a servant, tells Swetnam that he wishes to learn dueling, since he is about to become married and wishes to have the mastery at the start. Swetnam seizes the opportunity to tell him of the true nature of women:

> Th'are nothing of themselues,
> Onely patcht vp to coozen and gull men,
> Borrowing their haire from one, complexions from another,
> Nothing their own that's pleasing, all dissembled,
> Not so much, but their very breath
> Is sophisticated with Amber-pellets, and kissing causes . . .
> A woman! she's an Angell at ten, a Saint at fifteene,
> A Deuill at fortie, and a Witch at fourescore.
> If you will marry, marry none of these:
> Neither the faire, nor the foule; the rich, nor the poore;
> The good, nor the bad. (B1ᵛ)

The scene now changes, and it is decided to hold a public disputation on the subject 'Whether the Man or Woman in loue, stand guilty of the greatest offence' (E2ᵛ). Swetnam, as the advocate for the males, utters the usual complaints against women: they are full of pride, inordinate in dress, deceiving in the use of cosmetics, frivolous, and lustfull (F1ᵛ). Atlanta champions the women's side, and does a very good job; but the judges decide 'That women are the first and worst temptations to loue and . . . folly' (F3). The women complain, however, that there were no women among the judges, but they are overruled by the king. Swetnam now finds that he has fallen in love with Atlanta, and speaking of his former arguments, says:

> O doe not thinke of that, that's done and gone.
> Doe not recall what's past. I now recant.
> And (by this hand) I loue thee truly, Loue. (I1ᵛ)

But the women beat him and bring him to trial; he is convicted by them, the judgment being –

First he shall weare this Mouzell, to expresse
His barking humour against women-kind.
And he shall be led, and publike showne,
In euery Street i' the Citie, and be bound . . .
Then he shal be whipt quite thorow the Land,
Till he come to the Sea-Coast, and then be shipt,
And sent to liue amongst the Infidels. (K1ᵛ–K2)

IV

As though the women had decided that their best attack was to imitate men, in the same year that the play about Swetnam was published, a controversy began over women's impudence in copying men's dress. As early as 1617, [19] Fitzgeffrey had spoken of 'A *Woman* of the *Masculine Gender*'; but in 1620 King James, becoming annoyed at the presumption of women, urged the clergy to take the matter in hand; in a letter of January 25, 1620, John Chamberlain wrote that the clergy were called together by the Bishop of London and told that the king had given an express commandment to them 'to inveigh vehemently against the insolencie of our women, and theyre wearing of brode brimed hats, pointed dublets, theyre hayre cut short or shorne, and some of them stilettoes or poniards, and such other trinckets of like moment; adding withall that if pulpit admonitions will not reforme them he wold proceed by another course.' [20] The king's urging had its effect on the parsons, and upon male writers as well. Eighteen days later Chamberlain could testify that the pulpits were ringing continually with castigations of women's insolence, and that dramatists and ballad writers had also taken up cudgels against the feminine fad. Fearing lest the women follow masculine dress with masculine aggressiveness and rule, and thus spoil the homes for the lords and masters, male writers quickly entered the fray to stem the tide of feminine rebellion. Three days before Chamberlain's second letter on the subject, there was entered to John Trundle, for printing, a book entitled *Hic Mulier: Or, The Man-Woman: Being a Medicine to cure the Coltish Disease of the Staggers in the Masculine-Feminines of our Times. Exprest in a briefe Declamation. Non omnes possumus*

omnes. Mistres, will you be trim'd or truss'd? The author of this work protests
that since the time of Adam women have never been so masculine as now:
masculine in mood, in bold speech, and in impudent action. In addressing
himself to the men-women, he points up the general complaint of men:
'You haue taken the monstrousnesse of your deformitie in apparell,
exchanging the modest attire of the comely Hood, Cawle, Coyfe, handsome
Dresse or Kerchiefe, to the cloudy Ruffianly broad-brim'd Hatte, and
wanton Feather, the modest vpper parts of a concealing straight gowne,
to the loose, lasciuious ciuill embracement of a French doublet, being
all vnbutton'd to entice, all of one shape to hide deformitie, and extreme
short wasted, to giue a most easie way to euery luxurious action: the glory
of a faire large haire, to the shame of most ruffianly short lockes; the side,
thicke gather'd, and close guarding Safegards, to the short, weake, thinne,
loose, and euery hand-entertaining short basses; for Needles, Swords;
for Prayer bookes, bawdy legs; for modest gestures, gyant-like behauiours,
and for womens modestie, all Mimicke and apish inciuilitie' (A4-A4ᵛ).
Furthermore, you do not attend to your duties at home and are led into
vice by the desire for men's fashions: 'such as will not worke to get bread,
will finde time to weaue her selfe points to trusse her loose Breeches: and
shee that hath pawned her credit to get a Hat, will sell her Smocke to buy
a Feather; Shee that hath giuen kisses to haue her hayre shorne, will giue
her honestie to haue her vpper parts put into a French doublet: To conclude,
she that will giue her body to haue her bodie deformed, will not sticke to
giue her soule to haue her minde satisfied' (B2). The ornament of the sex,
states this author, is long hair; when it is cut, it resembles the hair worn
by thieves and murderers. God made women of material more pure and
refined, and they should conduct themselves in the light of such knowledge
(B3ᵛ-B4).

A week after John Trundle registered *Hic Mulier* with the Stationers'
Company, he registered the companion-piece, *Haec-Vir: Or The VVoman-
ish-Man: Being an Answere to a late Booke intituled Hic-Mulier. Exprest in
a briefe Dialogue betweene Haec-Vir the Womanish-Man, and Hic-Mulier the
Man-Woman.* The Womanish-Man, dressed in his outlandishly foppish

HIC MVLIER:
OR,
The Man-Woman:

Being a Medicine to cure the Coltifh Difeafe of
the Staggers in the *Mafculine-Feminines*
of our Times.

Expreft in a briefe Declamation.

Non omnes poffumus omnes.

Miftris, will you be trim'd or truff'd?

Loncon printed for I.T. and are to be fold at Chrift Church gate. 1620.

Masculine women at the barber's

Engraved title page showing a formal garden

garments, meets a Man-Woman, whom he condemns for 'shorne, powdered, borrowed Hayre, a naked, lasciuious, bawdy Bosome, a *Leaden-Hall* Dagger, a High-way Pistoll, and a mind and behauiour sutable or exceeding euery repeated deformitie' (A4). The Man-Woman replies with a spirited defense of her sex, in which she argues for the freedom of woman to change her fashions as she will. The world is governed by change: the seasons change, day and night change, men change from rich to poor, from sickness to health, from pleasure to anguish, from honor to contempt; then why should only women be prohibited from change? Further, the birds and beasts have freedom to choose what delights them; why must this choice be excluded from women? To ride sidesaddle was once considered evidence of pride; and indeed we may conclude that fashion is but a fool. If it is barbarous to escape the bounds of woman's confining clothes, then let her live in the country with the same freedom that simple creatures have (A4v-B3). [21]

Another printer apparently wished to profit by the popular mood, for a work soon appeared (entered April 29, 1620) entitled *Muld Sacke: or The Apologie of Hic Mulier: To the late Declamation against her. Exprest in a short Exclamation, non est mollis è terris ad astra via. Muld Sacke, Muld Sacke.* (1620). To make good the implication that we have here another installment in the controversy, the tone of the piece is seemingly set by some verses printed opposite the title page, and addressed in thankfulness to Hic Mulier, the Man-Woman:

> *In recompence, sweet Heart, of thy sweet Booke,*
> *My picture I thee send, whereon' pray looke.*
> *All maydes, and Bookes, not thus rewarded bee,*
> *Loue hath a Tongue, although no Eyes to see.*
> *Then fayrest faire, in this sweet little frame,*
> *My Heart and Selfe I prostrate to thy Name,*
> *Vowing my Sword, my yellow Band, and Feather,*
> *My smoking Pipe, Scarfe, Garters, Roses, either*
> *With my spruse Bootes, neat Hornes, and all I giue*
> *To thee, by whose sweet loue, I breathe, reigne, liue.*

Then comes a congratulatory letter to Muld Sacke, signed by Hic Mulier.

The author of this work upholds the historical antiquity of masculine women; and he objects further that the book *Hic Mulier* has labeled as deformed monsters only those women who have cut their hair, wear French doublets, and have open breasts and false bodies, whereas he calls any woman a Man-Woman who refuses to play the role she was created for: 'A woman was created to honour her Parents, and obey her Husband.' An opportunity is herewith given to castigate the womanish man: A father must exert his authority over his children and a husband must rule his wife; any man, then, who gives his authority to his daughter or wife is an effeminate man, just as she who takes upon herself the authority of her parents or the supremacy of her husband, or who conducts herself in ways removed from customary feminine modesty, is a Man-Woman (B1-B2). She who spends more time entertaining a sweetheart than helping a husband is a Hic Mulier. She who gossips until she is drunk, or who talks too much, or whose looks and gestures and words portray her pride, is a Hic Mulier. The woman who is secretly unchaste is a Hic Mulier, even though she may spend much time severely rebuking those of her sisters who wear loose breeches or indulge in cosmetic painting. *Muld Sacke* contributes very little to the controversy of the year 1620, since it is chiefly given over to a general treatise on morals.

There is evidence that the campaign waged by King James and the clergy against men-women was not as successful as they had hoped, at least from the Puritan point of view. As late as 1628 William Prynne was complaining about masculine women in *The Vnlouelinesse, of Loue-Lockes*. In the preface Prynne writes of his hope that his book 'may be great, and profitable in these Degenerous, Vnnaturall, and Vnmanly times: wherein as sundry of our Mannish, Impudent, and inconstant Female sexe, are Hermophradited, and transformed into men; not onely in their immodest, shamelesse, and audacious carriage ... but euen in the vnnaturall Tonsure, and Odious, if not Whorish Cutting, and (a) Crisping of their Haire, their Naturall vaile, their Feminine glory, and the very badge, and Character of their subiection both to God, and Man: so diuers of our Masculine, and more noble race, (b) are wholly degenerated and metamorphosed into women;

not in Manners, Gestures, Recreations, Diet, and Apparell onely, but likewise in the Womanship, Sinfull, and Vnmanly, Crispnig [*sic*], Curling, Frouncing, Powdring, and nourishing of their Lockes, and Hairie excrements, in which they place corporall Excellencie, and chiefest glory' (A3-A3ᵛ). [22] Later in his book (p. 35), he wonders why these 'Impudent, and mannish Viragoes, or audacious Men-Women' cut their hair, as if this action actually transformed and transubstantiated them into males. The work is essentially taken up, however, with other vices of women.

The title of a book by William Austin, *Haec Homo wherein the excellency of the creation of woman is described by way of an essaie* (1637), has the sound of a work intended to call to mind the *Hic Mulier* controversy. Actually, however, it is simply a plea for the acceptance of woman as the equal of man.

V

The last controversy which falls within the compass of the present study consists mainly of two pamphlets and an answer to them, all published by John Okes within a year of each other. Popular 'lectures' on domestic problems had been written by several authors – for example, Thomas Heywood's *A Curtaine Lecture* (1637); and John Taylor, who called himself the 'Water-Poet,' and who was not one to let a good thing get away from him, had two of this tracts printed in 1639. If the dates of entry have any significance, the first of these was *A Iuniper Lecture. With the description of all sorts of women, good, and bad: From the modest to the maddest, from the most Civil, to the scold Rampant, their praise and dispraise compendiously related.* [23] Taylor tells us in the preface that he uses the word *juniper* for several reasons: juniper wood is very lasting as firewood and will burn a year or more if covered with ashes – similarly, some revengeful women will harbor their malice for long periods; juniper is hot and dry, and so is the tongue of a scold; and juniper is like a good woman, too, because it is an antidote for anyone envenomed. The book itself is composed of several 'lectures,' most of which are by shrewish women to their husbands; only a few are delivered by the more commendable wives to their drunken, rowdy husbands. One wife complains that she is busy from morning to night taking care of the household and the children, getting meals, sewing, and getting everyone to bed, so that her work is never done. Her husband replies that she certainly never wants the work to be done when she gets in bed (pp. 12-14). A young widow replies to an old man who wants her love (pp. 17-21). An old, rich widow similarly replies to a young gallant (pp. 23-26). Again we are told that women talk too much; nothing could be more bitter than a woman's tongue beaten into powder and eaten in a pill (pp. 27-28). And the worst of all possible wives is a scold. Taylor concludes this work with several epigrams:

Epigram 3

Nells *Husband sayes, shee brought him naught but toyes,*
But yet (without his helpe) she brings him Boyes.

Epigram 7

Madge *by no means immodest pranks abides,*
Yet takes delight to goe exceeding gawdy,
To sport, carouse, and doe such things besides,
As to report of, would appeare too bawdy. (pp. 233–234)

Taylor's *Divers Crab-tree Lectures* is essentially more of the same: husbands lecture their wives; the women instruct the men. In a preface, Mary Makepeace addresses the women and implies that they should never act so as to deserve such cognomens as Tabitha Turbulent, Franks Froward, Bettrisse Bould-face, Ellen Ever-heard, or other descriptive names. [24]

For these satiric effusions John Taylor is thoroughly taken over the coals in a work from the same press. [25] The names of the authors are clearly pseudonyms, and anyone may have written the reply – even Taylor: *The womens sharpe revenge: Or an answer to Sir Seldome Sober that writ those railing Pamphlets called the Iuniper and Crab-tree Lectures, &c. Being a sound Reply and a full confutation of those Bookes: with an Apology in this case for the defence of*

268

us women. Performed by Mary Tattle-well, and Ioane Hit-him-home, Spinsters.
Twelve women, with such Taylor-like names as Sisley-set-him-out and
Tomasin-tickle-him, make up a jury to try Taylor for his crimes against
the feminine sex (pp. 12-13). They agree early that he is no scholar, since
he does not understand women's gender, number, or case (p. 16). They
investigate his grammar further and find that 'In the Nominative, by calling
us out of our Names, and in the stead of Maidenly Modest, Matron-like,
&c. to band us with the characters of scoulds, vixens, praters, pratlers,'
and so on, he has shown ignorance (p. 18). He clearly is no poet, since
he indites the opposite of love poems to his sweetheart (p. 21). They
suggest that his backbiting is due to a lack of love from women: 'It is
the fashion of all these calumniating Coxecombes, to bite those by the
backe, whom they know not how to catch by the belly' (p. 31). Taylor is
found guilty of lying and of heresy, and of perjury since he swore to his
marriage oaths and yet now abuses and reviles the whole female sex
without excluding his wife (pp. 31-35). Women are just as good as men,
if not better: many famous writers have written in praise of women; if
women are as bad as they are painted, why do men love them? You never
heard of a woman involved in a gunpowder plot; and many women have
performed brave deeds and have saved their countries from destruction
(pp. 47-56). It is the men who are actually responsible for women's vices,
anyway. When wives lie, they do so to protect their husbands; if women
are proud, it is the men who make them so by flattering them (pp. 60, 64-66).
Those who write against women are merely 'mungrill Rimsters, that with
an affectate over-weening conceite of themselves, doe imagine that they
can cough *Logicke*, speake *Rhetoricke*, neese *Grammer*, belch *Poetry*, pisse
Geometry, groane *Musicke*, vomit *Apothegmes*, and squirt *Oratory*' (pp. 90-91).
Several pages are now given over to replies in brief paragraphs to a number
of the lectures in *A Iuniper Lecture* (pp. 102-130). The Ladies take Taylor
to task for his assumption of the title of 'Water-Poet': 'Now concerning
your very passionate, but most pittifull Poetry, a question may be made
whether you be a Land Laureate or a Marine Muse; a Land Poet, or a
Water Poet; A Scholler, or a Sculler; of *Pernassus*, or puddle Dock....'

(pp. 110-111). Following older texts, they point out that the nine muses, the twelve sibyls, the four cardinal virtues, the three graces, the arts, the sciences, etc., are all females. At the last, they propose some twelve questions for Taylor to answer, such as – did you ever hear of a woman put in the pillory or one that had a hand in counterfeiting (pp. 142-153)?

These controversies point up the whole problem of the Elizabethan woman as both sides attempt to appraise her – her status and function in society. Some of the writers seem to have had an inability to see women as a whole, and with this lack went the immoderate language with which they assessed some of women's roles in society. Women were desired as lovers, and in this character they were considerably idealized in sonnets and elsewhere.[26] As sober and chaste wives, they were venerated and commemorated in sermons, in verse, and in private letters. But when women attempted to assume in any way the role of men, they were ordinarily met with scorn or with querulousness. Perhaps one of the reasons for Elizabeth's success as a ruler was the fact that she carefully dissociated herself from the common aspects of womanhood: i.e., submission to a lover, childbearing, and the petty annoyances of managing a household. As a virgin she could speak with untainted authority; she was in essence not a complete woman. One wonders if the man-woman fashion had its unconscious roots in this untraditional position. In this way the phenomenon of a female ruler, so new to England, yet so successful in swaying the hearts of the people, may be partly explained; it may also serve to show us that when we speak of Elizabethan women, we rarely consider in our scope the one who was the very epitome of female achievement.

The emergence of women as people first and as females second was rather disturbing to the social attitudes of the time. Reluctant surprise at feminine audacity underlies the inability of the Earl of Dorset to understand or to move his highly individualized wife, the Lady Anne. And yet here, too, much progress was being made, as we can see in William Austin's *Haec Homo*, where the main theme is the equality of women with men, as indeed it is in William Heale's *Apologie*, the *Haec-Vir*, and Daniel Tuvil's *Sanctuary for Ladies*. Too much emphasis must not be placed upon the Puritan castigations, since women's foibles and dress were simply two more items in the lengthy list of what was wrong with the world. Perhaps what is most significant of all is that in the many works concerned with women and their habits can be discerned a new way of thinking about women and a new attempt to evaluate their place in a rapidly changing world. Thus the beginnings of our concept of woman's place can be seen emerging from the older view in the vigorous literature of Elizabethan England.

Notes

When no place is given in references to books, London is to be understood. The abbreviation sig. *for signature has been omitted. To make reference easier, the first citation of an authority is bibliographically complete in each chapter. The authors of familiar plays have generally not been indicated.*

CHAPTER I

1   William B. Rye, *England as Seen by Foreigners in the Days of Elizabeth and James the First*, 1865, pp. 7, 14; see Robert Burton, *The Anatomy of Melancholy* (1628), New York, 1924, p. 631, which omits the servants and goes on to say that Italy is a paradise for horses and a hell for women.

2   Robert Greene, 'The Royal Exchange,' *Works*, ed. Grosart, 1881–83, VII, 231; see Joseph Swetnam, *The Arraignment of Lewd, Idle, Froward, and vnconstant Women*, 1622, A2ᵛ.

3   John Sadler, *The Sick Womans priuate Looking-glasse*, 1636, p. 12; William Bercher, *The Nobylytye off Wymen*, ed. Bond, 1904, p. 108; Alexander Niccholes, *A Discourse, of marriage and wiuing*, 1615, p. 26; William Austin, *Haec homo*, 1637, pp. 13–14, 28, 29. This view of woman's creation appears frequently; see William Heale, *An Apologie for Women*, Oxford, 1609, p. 61; Jane Anger, *Protection for Women*, 1589, C1, J5; Rachel Speght, *A Mouzell for Melastomus*, 1617, p. 9; Anthony Gibson, *A Womans Woorth*, 1599, fol. 61; Mary Tattle-well and Ioane Hit-him-home, *The womens sharpe revenge*, 1640, pp. 43, 96; *Hic Mulier: or The Man-Woman*, 1620, B4.

4   John Donne, *Iuvenilia*, 1633, C4ᵛ; Sadler, p. 12; Ercole Tasso, *Of Mariage and Wiuing*, 1599, C4; Ludovicus Vives, *The office and duetie of an husband*, 1553?, E1; Bercher, pp. 114–115, 122; Ercole Tasso, C4; *The Knight of Malta*, I. iii; C. L. Powell, *English Domestic Relations*, New York, 1917, p. 148; *The Faerie Queene*, III.xii.26; *The Warres of Cyrus*, l. 1650; *Tyde Taryeth No Man*, l. 865; John Donne,'Loves Alchymie,' *Complete Poetry and Selected Prose*, ed. Hillyer, New York, 1941, p. 26; Ludovicus Vives, *Instructiō of a Christen womā*, 1529?, C3ᵛ; John Knox, *The First Blast of the Trumpet against the Monstruous Regiment of Women*, Geneva, 1558, fols. 9ᵛ–10.

5   Esther Sowernam, *Ester hath hang'd Haman*, 1617, p. 43; Vives, *Office and duetie of an husband*, E1ᵛ–E2, Z6; Lodowick Lloyd, *The Choyce of Iewels*, 1607, p. 31; Ercole Tasso, C4; Swetnam, p. 57.

6   Torquato Tasso, *The Housholders Philosophie*, trans. Thomas Kyd, 1588, fol. 11; Tomaso Buoni, *Problemes of Beautie*, 1606, pp. 4, 54, 59; *The Warres of Cyrus*, ll. 366 ff.; Robert Vaughan (?), *A Dyalogue defensyue for women agaynst malycyous detractoures*, 1542, C3; Desiderius Erasmus, *A modest meane to Mariage*, 1568, B7ᵛ; Greene, *Mamillia, Works*, II, 44.

7   Speght, p. 11; Torquato Tasso, fol. 11ᵛ; Vaughan(?), C3; Pierre Charron, *Of Wisdome* (1607?), 1670, p. 19; Geoffrey Fenton, *Monophylo*, 1572, fol. 24; Burton, p. 518; William Averell, *Foure notable Histories*, 1590, C2ᵛ; *The Beaute of women*, 1525?, A2–A3; Edwin Wolf, 2nd, 'If Shadows be a Picture's Excellence,' *PMLA*, LXIII, 831–857; *The Faerie Queene*, II.iii.22–33; *Epithalamion*, ll. 171–180; *Amoretti*, lxiv; Greene, *Tullies Love, Works*, VII; Sir Philip Sidney, *Arcadia*, Cambridge, 1912, p. 81; *Monsieur Thomas* I.i., iii; *The Woman Hater*, III.i., iii; *Wit Without Money*, III.i.; *The Broken Heart*, V.ii. 20–23; *The Malcontent*, III.i. 158–164; *The Old Wives Tale*, ll. 130–137; *Soliman and Perseda*, IV.i. 75–82; *Campaspe*, II.ii. 62–67; *A New Way to Pay Old Debts*, III.ii.29–39; Richard Brathwait, *A Ladies Love-Lecture, The English Gentleman and The English Gentlewoman*, 1641, p. 451; Matthew Griffith, *Bethel: or, A Forme for Families*, 1633, p. 251; Niccholes, p. 31; Emilia Lanyer, *Salve Deus Rex Iudaeorum*, 1611, A4; Giovanni Paolo Lomazzo, *A Tracte Containing the Artes of curious Paintinge Caruinge & Buildinge*, Oxford, 1598, p. 133; Jacques Du Bosc, *The compleat woman*, 1639, p. 33; Thomas Gataker, *A Good Wife Gods Gift*, 1620, p. 19; *Rule a Wife and Have a Wife*, V (Beaumont and Fletcher, *Works*, III, 234); Ercole Tasso, H4.

8   *The Praise and Dispraise of Women*, 1579, fols. 63ᵛ, 65ᵛ–70, 81ᵛ–87ᵛ; Ercole Tasso, C3ᵛ; Powell, pp. 149–151; Donne, *Iuvenilia*, G2ᵛ; Thomas Nashe(?), *An Almond for a Parrat, Works*, ed. McKerrow, 1910, III, 348; Nashe, *The Terrors of the Night, Works*, I, 383; John Wing, *The Crowne Coniugall*, Middelburgh, 1620, p. 11; Edward Gosynhill, *The Schole house of women*, 1541?, B4ᵛ; William Whately, *A Care-cloth: Or A Treatise of the Cumbers and Troubles of Marriage*, 1624, p. 44; *Swetnam, the Woman-hater*, 1620, B1ᵛ (I.ii); see John Donne,.Sermon in Commemoration of the Lady Danvers, *Complete Poetry and Selected Prose*, New York, 1941, p. 357.

9   Barnaby Rich, *Faultes, Faults, and nothing else but Faultes*, fols. 23, 28; Swetnam, pp. 2, 28; *A discourse of the married and single life*, 1621, A6–A7ᵛ, p. 13; Bercher, pp. 128–129; Gosynhill, *Schole house*, A1ᵛ–A4; John Taylor, *A Iuniper Lecture*, 1639, 'To the reader,' and p. 27; *The Women Pleas'd*, V.i (Beaumont and Fletcher, *Works*, VII, 299); Edward Gosynhill, *The prayse of all women*, 1560?, B2–B2ᵛ; C. Pyrrye, *The praise and Dispraise of Women*, 1569?, A5; Thomas Nashe, *Summers Last Will and Testament, Works*, III, 271; *The Praise and Dispraise of Women* (1579), fols. 72ᵛ, 75ᵛ; Daniel Tuvil,

Asylum Veneris, or A Sanctuary for Ladies, 1616, p. 56; Anthony Nixon, *The Dignitie of Man*, 1612, p. 111; Pierre Boaistuau, *Theatrum Mundi*, 1566?, K4; Thomas Nashe, *The Anatomie of Absurditie*, 1589, A3; Sir Thomas Overbury, 'A Very Woman,' *His Wife*, 1632, E2–E4; Barnaby Rich, *The Excellency of good women*, 1613, p. 14; Greene, *Morando, Works*, III, 68; Henry Neville, *A Parliament of Ladies*, 1647, B1; John Brinsley, *A Looking-Glasse for Good Women*, 1645, p. 12; Ercole Tasso, D4ᵛ–E1ᵛ; Gosynhill, *Schole house*, A2ᵛ.

10 *The Faerie Queene*, III.ix.7, III.viii.8; Nicholas Ling, *Politeuphuia. Wits Common wealth*, 1598, fol. 24ᵛ; Anthony Sherley, *Witts New Dyall*, 1604, M2 (see Pyrrye, A6; Gosynhill, *Schole house*, A2–A3ᵛ; Greene, *Greenes Mourning Garment, Works*, IX, 195); Ercole Tasso, C1ᵛ, C4, D4; Burton, pp. 600, 631; *Proverbs*, xxxi.10; *Swetnam, the Woman-hater*, F1ᵛ–F3 (III.i.); Donne, 'Elegy III,' *Complete Poetry and Selected Prose*, p. 59; *The Praise and Dispraise of Women*, fol. 69; Tuvil, p. 47; Bercher, pp. 116–117; *Lear*, IV.vi.278, 120–131; *Bussy D'Ambois*, III.ii.321–329 (see Sherley, M2–M2ᵛ); *The Faerie Queene*, I.iv.24; Leonard Wright, *A Display of Duty*, 1616, fol. 18ᵛ; Folger MS. 1186.2.

11 Sir Thomas Elyot, *The Defence of Good women*, 1545, B5–B5ᵛ; Gibson, fol. 33 (see George Whetstone, *An Heptameron of Ciuill Discourses*, 1582, P1); Mary Tattle-well and Ioane Hit-him-home, p. 91; Vives, *Office and duetie of an husband*, P1ᵛ; Austin, p. 5; Tuvil, p. 110; *Henry V*, I.ii.39–51; Bercher, p. 115; Greene, *Orpharion, Works*, XII, 65; Christopher Newstead, *An Apology for Women*, 1620, pp. 42–48; Jane Anger, B3.

12 Stories of admirable women may be found in *The Praise and Dispraise of Women* (1579); Richard Ferrers, *The Worth of Women* (1622); Thomas Heywood, *Gunaikeion; or, Nine Bookes of Various History. Concerninge Women* (1624); Anthony Gibson, *A Womans Woorth* (1599); C. G., *The Ladies Vindication* (1651); Lodowick Lloyd, *The Choyce of Iewels* (1607); Gosynhill, *The prayse of all women, called Mulierum Pean* (1560?), A4–A4ᵛ; Mary Tattle-well and Ioane Hit-him-home, pp. 112–113.

13 Tattle-well, etc., pp. 60, 65–66 (see *Swetnam, the Woman-hater*, E4ᵛ); Bercher, pp. 122–127; Vives, *Office and duetie of an husband*, P1ᵛ; Jane Anger, B1–C3ᵛ; Gibson, fol. 53ᵛ.

14 Greene, *The Royal Exchange, Works*, VII, 258; Robert Snawsel, *A looking glasse for Maried Folkes*, 1610, B8; Abraham Darcie, *The Honour of Ladies*, 1622, chapter XI; Swetnam, p. 54; Lyly, *Entertainments at Sudeley, Works*, I, 481 (see *The Faerie Queene*, III.iv.3); Vives, *Instructiō*, N4ᵛ; Thomas Heywood, *A Curtaine Lecture*, pp. 3–4.

15 Gibson, fols. 30ᵛ, 35–37ᵛ; I. G., *An Apologie for Womenkinde*, 1605, C1ᵛ; Bercher, p. 146; Donne, *Iuvenilia*, C3–D1ᵛ; Richard Brathwait, *Ar't asleepe*

Husband?, 1640, p. 168; *The Faerie Queene*, V.v. 25; Thomas Carter, *Carters Christian Common Wealth*, 1627, p. 65; Giovanni Michele Bruto, *The necessarie, fit, and conuenient Education of a yong Gentlewoman*, 1598, A6ᵛ.

CHAPTER II

1   Robert Cleaver, *A Godlie Forme of Household Government*, 1598, p. 246; Robert Greene, *Perimedes the Black-Smith*, *Works*, 1881–3, VII, 65, 79; Ludovicus Vives, *Instructiō of a Christen womã*, 1529?, o4; T.E., *The Lawes Resolutions of Womens Rights*, 1632, p. 23.

2   Robert Greene, *A Disputation betweene a Hee and a Shee Conny-Catcher*, *Works*, X, 248; Giovanni Michele Bruto, *The necessarie, fit, and convenient Education of a yong Gentlewoman*, 1598, C2ᵛ; John Lyly, *Euphues and His Euphebus*, *Works*, Oxford, 1902, I, 278; Bruto, C4–C5, C6–C6ᵛ, D2ᵛ, E2ᵛ, I8; Bartholomew Batty, *The Christian mans Closet*, 1581, C1ᵛ–C2; Ruth Willard Hughey, 'Cultural Interests of Women in England from 1524 to 1640 Indicated in the Writings of the Women,' unpublished thesis for the Ph. D. degree, Cornell University, 1932, p. 256; Abraham Darcie, *The Honour of Ladies*, 1622, p. 97; Vives, *Instructiō*, L4ᵛ, G2; Bruto, A6ᵛ, D4ᵛ, D6, G8ᵛ; Batty, C1ᵛ–C2.

3   Vives, *Instructiō*, C2, Q1–R2ᵛ; Bruto, D6ᵛ, D8; Vives, *Instructiō*, C3, O1ᵛ, H1, H3, P3ᵛ; Bruto, K2ᵛ; Greene, *Disputation*, X, 238–9; Greene, *The Card of Fancy*, *Works*, IV, 31–32; R.B., *A Watch-word for Wilfull Women*, 1581, C8–D1; Batty, C1ᵛ-C2; Lyly, *Euphues*, *Works*, I, 207; Bruto, E2ᵛ, E4.

4   R. G., *A godlie exhortation*, 1584, A2; Robert Cleaver, *A godlie forme of householde government*, 1600, pp. 278–282; Matthew Griffith, *Bethel: or, A Forme for Families*, 1633, pp. 350–353; Bruto, I6–I6ᵛ; William Fiston, *The Schoole of good Manners*, 1629, B6ᵛ, *et passim;* Vives, *Instructiō*, N4ᵛ; *The Case is Altered*, II.iii. 3–8.

5   Hughey, p. 61; Lyly, *Euphues*, *Works*, I, 319–320; Thomas Becon, *The booke of Matrimony*, *Worckes*, 1560–64, CCC2ᵛ; Richard Mulcaster, *Positions*, 1581, p. 178; Bruto, F8ᵛ; Vives, *Instructiō*, D1ᵛ, C3–C3ᵛ; Griffith, p. 353; Bruto, I4–I4ᵛ. Three other works on the silkworm are Thomas Moffett's *The Silkewormes and Their Flies* (1599), William Stallenge's *Instructions for the Increasing of Mulberie Trees and breeding of Silke-wormes* (1609), and *Observations to be followed for the Making of Fit Roomes, to keepe Silkewormes in* (1620).

6   Daniel Tuvil, *Asylum Veneris, or A Sanctuary for Ladies*, 1616, p. 87; Robert Greene, *The Debate betweene Follie and Loue*, *Works*, IV, 222; Bruto, E4ᵛ–E6, E8ᵛ, F8–F8ᵛ.

7   Ludovicus Vives, *The office and duetie of an husband*, 1553?, O6ᵛ–O7ᵛ; John

Brinsley, *A Looking-Glasse for Good Women*, 1645, p. 11; Mulcaster, pp. 166–174; see Hughey, p. 64, and Mrs. C. C. Stopes, *Shakespeare's Environment*, 1918, pp. 304–306.

8   Vives, *Office and duetie*, P2v, Q2v; Mulcaster, p. 180; Tuvil, p. 97 (see William Bercher, *The Nobylytye off Wymen*, ed. Bond, 1904, p. 132, and Mulcaster, pp. 174–175); Sir Thomas Elyot, *The Defence of Good women*, 1545, D3v–D6; Mulcaster, p. 169.

9   See Charlotte Kohler, 'The Elizabethan Woman of Letters,' unpublished thesis for Ph. D. degree, University of Virginia, 1936, pp. 9–10; Stopes, p. 297; Mulcaster, p. 182; Hughey, p. 61; Kohler, p. 11; Mulcaster, p. 168; *A Disputation betweene a Hee and a Shee Conny-Catcher*, *Works*, X, 239; see *The Devil is an Ass*, II.viii. 19–20. On 'placing out' see Dorothy Gardiner, *English Girlhood at School*, London, 1929, pp. 114–129.

10   Bruto, C4–C4v; Vives, *Instructiō*, E2v–E3; Mulcaster, p. 182; Lyly, *Euphues*, *Works*, II, 129; *The Taming of the Shrew*, II.i. 56–58 (see Gamaliel Bradford, *Elizabethan Women*, pp. 30–31).

11   Mulcaster, p. 182, *et passim* (see Stopes, pp. 298–299); Jacques Du Bosc, *The compleat woman*, 1639, pp. 1–2; Bruto, G4–G4v; Vives, *Instructiō*, F1–F2 (see Stopes, p. 309); Bruto, G4v–G5; *The Magnetick Lady*, I.v. 36–40; Thomas Nashe, *Have with you to Saffron-Walden*, *Works*, ed. McKerrow, 1910, III, 111 (see pp. 67–68). See Carroll Camden, 'The Elizabethan Imogen,' *The Rice Institute Pamphlet*, XXXVIII, 1–17. For an enlightening survey of education, see Gardiner, pp. 154–168, 189–211.

12   Vives, *Instructiō*, E3–F1v; Vives, *Office and duetie*, O7–O7v.

13   Robert Burton, *The Anatomy of Melancholy*, New York, 1924, pp. 534, 577; Anthony Gibson, *A Womans Woorth*, 1599, fol. 24; Bruto, H4v–H5v, H8v. See Greene, *Morando*, *Works*, III, 90; and Mulcaster, pp. 168, 177.

14   Bruto, F4–F4v; Du Bosc, pp. 24, 27, 29; Vives, *Office and duetie*, Q3v; *Volpone*, III.iv. 67–97.

15   *The Praise and Dispraise of Women*, 1579, fols. 70v–71v; Darcie, Introduction; Nashe, *The Anatomy of Absurdity*, *Works*, I, 35.

16   Hughey, p. 258; C. L. Powell, *English Domestic Relations, 1487–1653*, New York, 1917, pp. 170–173; Mulcaster, pp. 173–174; T. W. Baldwin, *William Shakspere's Small Latine & Lesse Greeke*, Urbana, Ill., 1944, I, 185–189; Bercher, p. 154–155; *The Praise and Dispraise of Women*, fols. 29v–35v; Stopes, pp. 304–306, 311, 313, 315, 317–318, 320–325, 327; Gibson, A2–A7; Darcie, Dedication; Gardiner, pp. 172–189; Violet A. Wilson, *Society Women of Shakespeare's Time*, New York, 1925, p. 11; George Ballard, *Memoirs of Several Ladies of Great Britain*, Oxford, 1752, pp. 119–123, 152–153, 182–207, 248–270; Sybil Wragge, *The Age Revealed*, London and New York, 1929, pp. 78–79.

17   Hughey, pp. 9, 258–259; Nashe, *The Terrors of the Night*, *Works*, I, 342, IV, 198; Thomas Bentley, *The Monument of Matrones*, 1582, *passim*.

CHAPTER III

1   Sir Thomas Overbury, *His Wife*, 1632, D2; William Whately, *A Care-cloth: Or A Treatise of the Cumbers and Troubles of Marriage*, 1624, p. 80; Ercole Tasso, *Of Mariage and Wiuing*, 1599, B2ᵛ; *The payne and sorowe of euyll maryage*, 1509?, A1–A4; Overbury, G5; *The Court of good Counsell*, 1607, B1.

2   Thomas Nashe, *The Anatomie of Absurditie*, 1589, A3; Robert Burton, *The Anatomy of Melancholy* (1628), New York, 1924, p. 656; Joseph Swetnam, *The Arraignment of Lewd, Idle, Froward, and vnconstant Women*, 1622, p. 46; Thomas Heywood, *A Curtaine Lecture*, 1637, pp. 8–9; Matthew Griffith, *Bethel: Or, A Forme for Families*, 1633, p. 258; Alexander Niccholes, *A Discourse, of marriage and wiuing*, 1615, pp. 7–8.

3   Nicholas Breton, *Pasquils Mistresse: Or The Worthie and vnworthie woman*, 1600, E1ᵛ; Burton, p. 657; Stephen Geree, *The Ornament of Women*, 1639, p. 15; *The Court of good Counsell*, B3; Richard Brathwait, *The Good Wife*, 1618, B4; Greene, *Euphues His Censure to Philautus*, *Works*, 1881–3, VI, 174; Overbury, D3; Niccholes, p. 48; Richard Brathwait, *The English Gentleman*, 1630, p. 262; Swetnam, p. 52; Ercole Tasso, B2ᵛ; Burton, p. 613; Niccholes, p. 7; *A discourse of the married and single life*, 1621, pp. 19–20; Thomas Becon, *The booke of Matrimony*, *Worckes*, 1560–64, HHh1. In *Poetaster* (II.i. 26–33), however, we see the other side of the coin, as Chloe tells her husband that she was born a gentlewoman and lost all her friends by becoming a citizen's wife; and that she married him only because she thought he would spend large amounts of money on her.

4   Richard Brathwait, *The English Gentlewoman*, 1631, §3ᵛ; Niccholes, p. 9; *The Laws of Candy*, I.i.; Overbury, *His Wife*, D5–D5ᵛ; Richard Brathwait, *Ar't Asleepe Husband?*, 1640, p. 15; Greene, *A Princelie Mirrour of Peereles Modestie*, *Works*, III, 10; Greene, *Euphues His Censure to Philautus*, *Works*, VI, 174; Greene, *Alcida*, *Works*, IX, 59.

5   Niccholes, p. 15; George Whetstone, *An Heptameron of Ciuill Discourses*, 1582, E4, X4; Edmund Tilney, *A brief and pleasant discourse of duties in Mariage, called the Flower of Friendshippe*, 1568, A6; William Gouge, *Of domesticall duties*, 1622, p. 188; Burton, p. 654; Tilney, B4; Anthony Sherley, *Witts New Dyall*, 1604, D1; Torquato Tasso, *The Housholders Philosophie*, trans. Thomas Kyd, 1588, fol. 10; Burton, p. 655; *Tell-Trothes New-yeares Gift* (1593), Shakespeare Society, 1876, p. 5; Lyly, *Euphues and His England*, *Works*, ed. Bond, 1902, II, 128; *A discourse of the married and single life*, 1621, p. 18.

6   Robert Cawdrey, *A Treasurie or Storehouse of Similies*, 1600, p. 255; Burton, p. 655; Gouge, p. 188; Tilney, B2; Whetstone, E4, X4; Thomas Nashe, *Pierce Penilesse his Supplication to the Divell*, *Works*, ed. McKerrow, 1910, I, 179; Niccholes, p. 16; Geoffrey Fenton, *Monophylo*, 1572, fol. 17; Nashe, *The Returne of the renowned Caualiero Pasquill* (1589), *Works*, I, 80; Cawdrey, pp. 255, 483; Gouge, p. 188.

7   *A discourse of the married and single life*, p. 24; Ester Sowernam, *Esther hath hang'd Haman*, 1617, p. 42; Swetnam, p. 59; *The Court of good Counsell*, B4 (see Torquato Tasso, fol. 9); Niccholes, p. 24; Henry Cornelius Agrippa, *The commendation of matrimony*, 1545, C1ᵛ; *The Parlament of Women*, 1640, B4ᵛ. See Lu Emily Pearson, 'Elizabethan Widows,' *Stanford Studies in Language and Literature*, Stanford, 1941, p. 124, *et seq.*

8   Gouge, p. 196; Vives, *The office and duetie of an husband*, 1553?, K5. See Hardin Craig, *The Enchanted Glass*, New York, 1936, pp. 220–221.

9   Geree, p. 15; Brathwait, *Ar't asleepe Husband?*, p. 15 (see Richard Brathwait, *A Ladies Love-Lecture*, in *The English Gentleman and the English Gentlewoman*, 1641, p. 451); Ercole Tasso, B2ᵛ; Daniel Tuvil, *Asylum Veneris*, 1616, p. 16 (see *The Faerie Queene*, V.viii. 1); Greene, *Francescos Fortunes*, *Works*, VIII, 203; Greene, *Euphues His Censure to Philautus*, *Works*, VI, 174; Lyly, *Euphues and His England*, *Works*, II, 59; *The Laws of Candy* I.i (Beaumont and Fletcher, *Works*, III, 251–252); Elizabeth Grymeston, *Miscellanea*, 1606?, H8ᵛ; Niccholes, pp. 7, 10; *A discourse of the married and single life*, pp. 13, 17 (see Castiglione, *The Courtier*, book IV); Vives, *The office and duetie of an husband*, I1ᵛ (see Brathwait, *The Good Wife*, p. 102); Anthony Gibson, *A Womans Woorth*, 1599, fols. 56ᵛ–57ᵛ (see John Manningham, *Diary*, Camden Society, 1868, p. 102).

10   Vives, *The office and duetie of an husband*, N3; Greene, *Francescos Fortunes*, *Works*, VIII, 203 (see Swetnam, p. 46; Brathwait, *Love-Lecture*, p. 451; Sherley, D1; Niccholes, p. 9; Donne, 'The Perfume,' *The Complete Poetry and Selected Prose*, New York, 1941, p. 60; Torquato Tasso, fol. 10ᵛ; Tuvil, pp. 24, 52; Brathwait, *The English Gentlewoman*, 1631, §3ᵛ; Greene, *A Princelie Mirrour of Peereles Modestie*, *Works*, III, 10; William Heale, *An Apologie for Women*, Oxford, 1609, p. 11); Tuvil, p. 38; William Averell, *Foure notable Histories*, 1590, B1; Thomas Heywood, *A Curtaine Lecture*, 1637, pp. 46–47 (see Brathwait, *The English Gentleman*, 1630, p. 259; Greene, *Mamillia*, *Works*, II, 115; Overbury, *His Wife*, 1632, D4; Jacques Du Bosc, *The compleat woman*, 1639, p. 18; Fletcher, *The Wild-Goose Chase*, I.iii); Barnaby Rich, *Faultes, Faults, and nothing else but Faultes*, 1606, fol. 23ᵛ; Barnaby Rich, *The Excellency of good women*, 1613, p. 13; Tuvil, p. 50; Rich, *Faultes*, fol. 24.

11   Robert Cleaver, *A godlie forme of householde government*, 1600, p. 230; Rich,

Excellency, p. 9 (see Greene, *Mamillia, Works*, II, 115; Du Bosc, p. 18; Sherley, D1; *Everie Woman in her Humor*, 1609, A4; Brathwait, *The Good Wife*, B3); Thomas Carter, *Carters Christian Common Wealth*, 1627, pp. 89–90; Thomas Gataker, *A Mariage Praier*, 1624, p. 20 (see Giovanni Michele Bruto, *The necessarie, fit, and conuenient Education of a yong Gentlewoman*, 1598, D8v–E2v); John Taylor, *A Iuniper Lecture*, 1639, p. 114; Vives, *Office and duetie*, Q3v.

12   Leon B. Alberti, *Hecatonphila. The Arte of Loue*, 1598, fol. 23v; Breton, *Pasquils Mistresse*, 1600, D3v; Arthur Dent, *The Plaine Mans Path-way to Heauen*, 1601, p. 43 (see Niccholes, p. 9); Brathwait, *The English Gentlewoman*, 1631, § 4.

13   Heywood, *A Curtaine Lecture*, pp. 74–75 (see Brathwait, *The Good Wife*, B4; Niccholes, p. 9; Greene, *Mamillia, Works*, II, 115); Lyly, *The Woman in the Moone*, V.i. 20–22; Whately, p. 73 (see Geree, p. 20); Brathwait, *The English Gentlewoman*, 1631, § 3v; *Bartholomew Fair*, I.iii.91–96; Carter, pp. 79–80.

14   Robert Cleaver, *A Godlie Forme of Household Government*, 1598, pp. 103–109; Griffith, p. 255.

15   Niccholes, p. 48; *Every Man Out of His Humour*, II.ii. 34–37; Lyly, *Sapho and Phao*, II.iv. 85–89; Greene, *Planetomachia, Works*, V, 56–57; Rich, *Faultes*, fols. 21–21v.

16   Tilney, D3v; *Bartholomew Fair*, IV.iii. 15–17; Greene, *Orpharion, Works*, XII, 80; Greene, *Greenes Never Too Late, Works*, VIII, 36 (see *Tell-Trothes New-yeares Gift*, p. 7); Alberti, fols. 5v–6v, 9v–11, 13v (see Patrick Hannay, *A Happy Husband*, 1619, C1); Sowernam, p. 45.

17   Alberti, fols. 13v, 16v–17 (see Brathwait, *The English Gentlewoman*, 1631, p. 7); Erastophil, *An Apology for Lovers*, 1651, C2v; Fletcher, *Loves Pilgrimage*, IV.i; Fletcher, *The Wild-Goose Chase*, III.i.

CHAPTER IV

1   Herman V [von Wild], *A brefe and a playne declaratyon of the dewty of maried folkes*, 1553?, A2v; Thomas Gataker, *A Good Wife Gods Gift*, 1620, p. 6; Desiderius Erasmus, *A modest meane to Mariage*, 1568, B8; S. B., *Counsel to the husband: To the wife Instruction*, 1608, p. 11; Robert Cleaver, *A godlie forme of householde government*, 1600, p. 98 (see Heinrich Bullinger, *The golde boke of christen matrimonye*, 1543, C8); Pierre Charron, *Of Wisdome* (entered, 1606), 1670, p. 167; Leonard Wright, *A Display of Duty*, 1616, fol. 12v; Anthony Sherley, *Witts New Dyall*, 1604, M2v.

2   Anthony Nixon, *The Dignitie of Man*, 1612, pp. 112–113; Richard Brathwait, *The English Gentleman*, 1630, p. 262; Robert Burton, *The Anatomy of Melan-*

choly, New York, 1924, p. 613; *Tell-Trothes New-yeares Gift* (1593), Shakespeare Society, 1876, p. 7.

3   *The Order of Matrimony*, 1548, a6ᵛ; Herman V, B6ᵛ; Henry Cornelius Agrippa, *The commendation of matrimony*, 1545, Av3–Av3ᵛ, B2, B4; Bullinger, B7ᵛ; Bartholomew Batty, *The Christian mans Closet*, 1581, A4ᵛ–B1; John Donne, *Fifty Sermons*, 1649, p. 17; William Perkins, *Christian Oeconomie*, 1609, p. 13; Nixon, p. 111.

4   John Wing, *The Crowne Coniugall or, the Spouse Royall*, Middleburgh, 1620, p. 120; Thomas Becon, *The booke of Matrimony, Worckes*, 1560–1564, HHh1, OOo3; Robert Cleaver, *A Godlie Forme of Household Government*, 1598, p. 159; Brathwait, *The English Gentleman*, 1630, p. 258; Pierre Boaistuau, *Theatrum Mundi*, 1566?, K1ᵛ–K2; Burton, p. 623.

5   Antoine de La Sale, *The fyftene Joyes of maryage*, 1509, A7–A7ᵛ; Robert Greene, *Mamillia, Works*, ed. Grosart, 1881–83, II, 50; Pierre Charron, *Of Wisdome* (entered, 1606), 1670, p. 166.

6   Nixon, p. 111; William Whately, *A Care-cloth: Or A Treatise of the Cumbers and Troubles of Marriage*, 1624, p. 40; Charron, p. 165; Robert Copland, *A Complaynt of them that be to soone maryed*, 1535, B2ᵛ; Bullinger, F7; Desiderius Erasmus, *A ryght frutefull Epystle deuysed by the moste excellent clerke Erasmus in laude and prayse of matrymony*, 1530?, *passim;* Boaistuau, K4ᵛ; Nixon, p. 111; Barnaby Rich, *Faultes, Faults, and nothing else but Faultes*, 1606, fol. 26. See Copland, A1ᵛ–A3; and Greene, *Morando, Works*, III, 164.

7   Perkins, A6–A6ᵛ.

8   Perkins, p. 18; William Clerke, *The Triall of Bastardie*, 1594, p. 45; William Harrington, *The comendacions of matrymony*, 1528, A4ᵛ–A5.

9   Cleaver, *A Godlie Forme of Household Government*, 1598, p. 116; Perkins, pp. 23, 68; Charles Gibbon, *A Work worth Reading*, 1591, p. 1; Matthew Griffith, *Bethel: or, A Forme for Families*, 1633, p. 269; Bullinger, D4–D5ᵛ, D8; Becon, RRr1ᵛ; William Heale, *An Apologie for Women*, Oxford, 1609, p. 50.

10   Lyly, *Midas*, V.ii. 48–51; Peele, *Sir Clyomon and Sir Clamydes*, scene xxii, l. 238; Agrippa, Bv3ᵛ–C1ᵛ, A6ᵛ; George Whetstone, *An Heptameron of Ciuill Discourses*, 1582, F1; Thomas Heywood, *A Curtaine Lecture*, 1637, p. 100; *The Merry Wives of Windsor*, V.v. 233–243; Perkins, A5–A6.

11   Perkins, pp. 19–23; Jean Bodin, *The Six Bookes of a Commonweale*, 1606, pp. 14–15; Griffith, p. 270; T. E., *The Lawes Resolutions of Womens Rights*, pp. 52–54; Harrington, A3; John Lyly, *Euphues and His England, Works*, ed. Bond, Oxford, 1902, II, 218, 536; Henri Estienne, *A world of wonders*, 1608, pp. 151–152; Cleaver (1600), p. 140. An interesting discussion of these questions appears in C. L. Powell, *English Domestic Relations*, New York, 1917, particularly pages three and four.

12　*Twelfth Night*, IV.iii. 22–31, V.i. 159–164; *The Duchess of Malfi*, I.iii. 184–193; *Four Plays in One*, Beaumont and Fletcher, *Works*, X, 316. See especially a valuable paper by Davis P. Harding, 'Elizabethan Betrothals and "Measure for Measure",' *Journal of English and Germanic Philology*, XLIX (1950), 139–158.

13　Powell, p. 21.

14　Powell, pp. 13–15; Perkins, p. 55.

15　Powell (p. 16) indicates that public or secret marriages of children over seven, which are performed without the consent of the parents, are also called clandestine marriages, but I have found no such references.

16　Harrington, A4–A6; William Gouge, *Of domesticall duties*, 1622, p. 205; *Calendar of State Papers* ccxl.17 (G. B. Harrison, *An Elizabethan Journal*, 1928, p. 53); Powell, pp. 2, 13–17; Perkins, p. 93; Clerke, pp. 39, 47; Wing, p. 127.

17　Gouge, p. 180; Geoffrey Fenton, *Monophylo*, 1572, fol. 21; Sir Thomas Overbury, *His Wife*, 1632, E2^v; *The Magnetick Lady*, I.ii. 4–5; Alexander Niccholes, *A Discourse, of marriage and wiuing*, 1615, p. 11; Ludovicus Vives, *The office and duetie of an husband*, 1553?, I3^v; Sir Thomas Elyot, *The Defence of Good women*, 1545, D2; Gamaliel Bradford, *Elizabethan Women*, Cambridge, 1936, p. 52. See Thomas Gataker, *Marriage Duties Briefely Couched togither*, 1620, pp. 38–39, Greene, *The Card of Fancie*, *Works*, IV, 29; Lyly, *Euphues*, *Works*, I, 227.

18　Perkins, A5–A5^v, pp. 24, 54–65, 73; Harrington, B1–D1; Gouge, pp. 181–182, *Epicoene*, V.iii. 87–292.

19　Agrippa Av2–Av3^v; Perkins, pp. 81,117; Gouge, p. 182; Whately, A8.

20　John Dove, *Of Diuorcement*, 1601, pp. 8, 26–29; Perkins, A6; St. Augustine, *A woorke of the holy bishop S. Augustine concernyng adulterous mariages*, 1550, *passim;* Powell, pp. 61–100; Estienne, pp. 151–152; Heale, p. 50. Professor Powell gives a useful summary of the problem of divorce.

21　T. E., *The Lawes Resolutions*, p. 62; *A discourse of the married and single life*, p. 39; *The Magnetick Lady*, I.iv.50–54; Greene, *The Repentance of Robert Greene*, *Works*, XII, 177.

22　Powell, pp. 22–24; Whetstone, X3; Thomas Nashe, *The Prayse of the Red Herring*, *Works*, ed. McKerrow, 1910, III. 206; Harrington, A5^v; Greene, *Greenes Vision*, *Works*, XII, 227; Jonson, *The King's Entertainment at Welbeck*, ll. 243–249; J. C. Jeaffreson, *Brides and Bridals*, London, 1872, I, 88, *et seq.*

23　Gataker, *A Good Wife Gods Gift*, pp. 4–6; Nashe, *An Almond for a Parrat*, *Works*, III, 375; *Epicoene*, III.vi. 85–111; *The Faerie Queene*, Book V, Canto iii; Powell, p. 24.

24　Perkins, pp. 84, 98–99; R. G., *A godlie exhortation, and fruitfull admonition to vertuous parents and modest Matrons*, 1584, A2; Vives, *The office and duetie of an husband*, R5ᵛ-R6; Powell, p. 7; Thomas Taylor, *A Good Husband and A Good Wife*, 1625, p. 1; Griffith, p. 280; William Whately, *A Bride-Bush or A Wedding Sermon*, 1617, pp. 2–6.

25 Ludovicus Vives, *Instructiō of a Christen womā*, 1529?, Book III – 'Of the mournynge of Wydowes'; Powell, p. 158; Torquato Tasso, *The Housholders Philosophie*, 1588, fol. 9; Heale, pp. 50–51; Greene, *Morando, Works*, III, 54.

26 T. E., *The Lawes Resolutions of Womens Rights*, pp. 6–8, 117, 129–130; Bodin, pp. 14–15; Griffith, p. 331; Gouge, p. 296; *The Praise and Dispraise of Women*, 1579, fols. 64–65; Jeaffreson, I, 215.

CHAPTER V

1 C. L. Powell, *English Domestic Relations*, New York, 1917, p. 101.

2 S. B., *Counsel to the husband: To the wife Instruction*, 1608, p. 40 (see Robert Cleaver, *A godlie forme of householde government*, 1600, p. 3); George Whetstone, *An Heptameron of Ciuill Discourses*, 1582, Y1; William Perkins, *Christian Oeconomie*, 1609, p. 3; William Whately, *A Care-cloth: Or A Treatise of the Cumbers and Troubles of Marriage*, 1624, A2ᵛ; *The Court of good Counsell*, 1607, E3; Cleaver, p. 232; Pierre Viret; *The Schoole of Beastes, Intituled, the good Housholder, or the Oeconomickes*, 1585, C8ᵛ–D2ᵛ; Rachel Speght, *A Mouzell for Melastomus*, 1617, p. 14; William Harrington, *The comendacions of matrymony*, 1528, D4ᵛ; Robert Cleaver, *A Godlie Forme of Household Government*, 1598, p. 231; Greene, *Perimedes the Black-Smith, Works*, 1881–83, VII,12–13.

3 Whately, *Care-cloth*, A6–A6ᵛ.

4 William Heale, *An Apologie for Women*, Oxford, 1609, p. 44; see *Swetnam, the Woman-hater*, 1620, B1ᵛ.

5 Cleaver (1600), p. 89 (see Robert Greene, *The Royal Exchange, Works*, ed. Grosart, 1881–83, VII, 290; Cleaver, 1598, pp. 97, 118; Thomas Gataker, *Marriage Duties Briefely Couched togither*, 1620, pp. 6, 31; William Gouge, *Of domesticall duties*, 1622, p. 350); Herman V [von Wild], *A brefe and a playne declaratyon of the dewty of maried folkes*, 1553?, A6ᵛ; John Downame, *Lectures vpon the Foure First Chapters of the Prophecie of Hosea*, 1608, p. 43; Perkins, p. 123; Edmund Tilney, *A brief and pleasant discourse of duties in Mariage, called the Flower of Friendshippe*, 1568, C5; Gouge, pp. 406–407; Speght, p. 16; Tilney, B6. For interesting presentations of the Puritan view of marriage see two valuable papers: William and Malleville Haller, 'The Puritan Art of Love,' *The Huntington Library Quarterly*, V (1942), 235–272; and William Haller, 'Hail Wedded Love,' *ELH*, XIII (1946), 79–97.

6 Cleaver (1600), p. 118; Ludovicus Vives, *The office and duetie of an husband*, 1553?, P5ᵛ; Greene, *The Royal Exchange, Works*, VII, 312; Ercole Tasso,

Of Mariage and Wiuing, 1599, D3ᵛ; Speght, p. 16; Pierre Charron, *Of Wisdome* (entered, 1606), 1670, p. 434; *Epiccene*, IV.ii. 60–65; *Swetnam, the Woman-hater*, 1620, B1ᵛ.

7   Cleaver (1600), pp. 97, 166; Joseph Swetnam, *The Arraignment of Lewd, Idle, Froward, and vnconstant Women*, 1622, p. 390 (see Gataker, *Marriage Duties*, p. 31); Herman V, B2; Tilney, C2ᵛ–C4; Perkins, p. 125; Tilney, B5ᵛ, C2ᵛ; Whately, A6; S. B., *Counsel to the husband*, p. 87; *The Order of Matrimony*, 1548, b2; Gouge, p. 393; Tilney, B5ᵛ, C6 (see Anthony Sherley, *Witts New Dyall*, 1604, M2ᵛ; Robert Burton, *The Anatomy of Melancholy*, New York, 1924, p. 657).

8   Gouge, pp. 365, 389; Antoine de La Sale, *The fyftene Joyes of maryage*, 1509, E4ᵛ; John Manningham, *Diary* (1602–1603), Camden Society, p. 157; Greene, *The Royal Exchange, Works*, VII, 259; *Epicoene*, II.ii. 124–126, II.vi. 67–71, IV.iii. 27–32; Cleaver, pp. 76–77, 180; Swetnam, p. 12 (see *The Devil is an Ass*, II.vii. 30–38; *The Alchemist*, IV.iv. 396–399); Heale, pp. 25–27, 33–36, 46; Jean Bodin, *The Six Bookes of a Commonweale*, 1606, p. 19; Swetnam, p. 53; *The Court of good Counsell*, 1607, C4ᵛ; William Whately, *A Bride-Bush or A Wedding Sermon*, 1617, p. 24; Heale, pp. 7, 24, 28, 43; Tilney, B8; T. E., *The Lawes Resolutions of Womens Rights*, 1632, p. 128.

9   *Tell-Trothes New-yeares Gift* (1593), New Shakespeare Society, 1876, pp. 9–10; Gataker, *Marriage Duties*, p. 37; Thomas Becon, *The booke of Matrimony, Worckes*, 1560–1564, GGg6; Christopher Newstead, *An Apology for Women*, 1620, p. 16; Manningham, p. 60.

10   *The Court of good Counsell*, C2ᵛ (see Swetnam, p. 46); Tilney, C7–C7ᵛ; *Tell-Trothes*, pp. 5, 9–10; Tilney, C5ᵛ–C6; Heale, p. 45; *Volpone*, I.v. 118–120; de La Sale, second 'Joy'; Vives, *Office*, X6ᵛ; Greene, *The Royal Exchange, Works*, VII, 290.

11   Herman V, B4ᵛ; Vives, *Office*, R2; John Lyly, *Euphues and His England, Works*, ed. Bond, Oxford, 1902, II, 225; R. B., *A Watch-word for Wilfull Women*, 1581, F8ᵛ; Swetnam, p. 53.

12   Gataker, *Marriage Duties*, 1620, p. 41; Louise Labé, *Debate between Folly and Cupid (Oeuvres*, Lyons, 1555), ed. Cox, 1925, p. 38; Ercole Tasso, I2; Swetnam, p. 53; Herman V, B6; Vives, *Office*, Q8ᵛ; William Bercher, *The Nobylytye off Wymen* (1559), Roxburghe Club, 1904, p. 121; Speght, p. 12; John Brinsley, *A Looking-Glasse for Good Women*, 1645, p. 33; Swetnam, p. 53; *The Court of good Counsell*, C4; Greene, *Francescos Fortunes, Works*, VIII, 168; Cleaver, p. 186; Tilney, C5; Gataker, *Marriage Duties*, pp. 17–18.

13   Thomas Heywood, *Gunaikeion; or, Nine Bookes of Various History. Concerninge Women*, 1624, p. 118; Thomas Carter, *Carters Christian Common Wealth*, 1627, p. 91; Robert Cawdrey, *A Treasurie or Storehouse of Similies*, 1600, p. 827.

14 Whately, *Bride-Bush*, p. 32; Gouge, pp. 367–368; Perkins, pp. 164–170; Cleaver, 49, 57; Lyly, *Euphues and His England*, ed. Arber, 1868, p. 475 (from Gamaliel Bradford, *Elizabethan Women*, Cambridge, 1936, p. 55).

15 Cleaver, p. 186; Ercole Tasso, D4; Patrick Hannay, *A Happy Husband or Directions for a Maide to choose her Mate*, 1619, C3ᵛ; Gataker, *Marriage Duties*, p. 18; *The Court of good Counsell*, E2ᵛ (*The Court* is chiefly taken from Guazzo's *Civil Conversations*, 1581; this particular passage has been lifted by Joseph Swetnam, and appears on page 56 of his work); Vives, *Office*, U3ᵛ; Vives, *Instructiō of a Christen womā*, 1529?, i4ᵛ; Lodowick Bryskett, *A Discourse of Civill Life*, 1606, p. 58; Lyly, *Euphues, Works*, I, 259; Cleaver, p. 20; Perkins, pp. 166–171.

16 Carter, pp. 67–68; Vives, *Office*, p. 7; Greene, *Mamillia, Works*, II, 161; *The Parlament of Women*, 1640, A6; Sir Thomas Overbury, *His Wife*, 1632, D7ᵛ; Carter, pp. 66, 68–69, 74–75; Greene, *The Royal Exchange, Works*, VII, 291; Daniel Tuvil, *Asylum Veneris, or A Sanctuary for Ladies*, 1616, p. 85; Tilney, D4; Gataker, *Marriage Duties*, pp. 6, 12; Charron, p. 434; Perkins, p. 130; Cleaver, p. 218; Hannay, C1–C1ᵛ; John Donne, *Fifty Sermons*, 1649, p. 32; Whately, *Bride-Bush*, pp. 39–41; Gouge, p. 355; Matthew Griffith, *Bethel: or, A Forme for Families*, 1633, pp. 322–323.

17 References to the necessity of the wife to obey her husband are without end: Cleaver, pp. 118, 165, 239; Gouge, pp. 269, 279, 287, 315, 320, 323; Griffith, 326; Whately, p. 36; Tilney, D3, D8; *The Order of Matrimony*, b2–b2ᵛ; Brinsley, p. 37; R. B., *A Watch-word*, B5ᵛ; Herman V, A3; Becon, BBB5ᵛ; Bodin, p. 19; Charron, p. 169; Anne Clifford, *Diary*, ed. V. Sackville-West, 1923, pp. 40–41; Perkins, p. 133; Bartholomew Batty, *The Christian Mans Closet*, 1581, N4ᵛ; Greene, *Penelope's Web, Works*, V, 162–163, 192; etc.

18 John Aylmer, *An harborowe for faithful and trewe subiectes, agaynst the late blowne Blaste, concerning the gouernmēt of women*, Strassburg, 1559, G3; Cleaver, p. 227; Bodin, p. 16; Brinsley, p. 40 (see Torquato Tasso, *The Housholders Philosophie*, 1588, fol. 10ᵛ; Herman V, A5); S. B., *Counsel to the husband*, pp. 52–53, 70; Swetnam, p. 55; Gataker, *Marriage Duties*, pp. 14–15; Cleaver, pp. 219–220, 230 (see *Tell-Trothes New-yeares Gift*, p. 9); Perkins, p. 133; R. B., *A Watchword*, G1–G1ᵛ; Whetstone, P2; *A discourse of the married and single life*, 1621, p. 31; Gouge, p. 334; Thomas Heywood, *A Curtaine Lecture*, 1637, p. 143,; Becon, CCC2; Greene, *Penelope's Web, Works*, V, 192; Nashe, *The Unfortunate Traveller, Works*, ed. McKerrow, 1910, II, 263.

19 Overbury, G5ᵛ; Charron, p. 435; Greene, *Penelope's Web, Works*, V, 221; *Old Wives' Tale*, ll. 223–228 (see Leonard Wright, *A Display of Duty*, 1616, fol. 11ᵛ; Whetstone, Q3); *The Court of good Counsell*, D4ᵛ; Thomas Gataker, *A Good Wife Gods Gift*, 1620, p. 4; Philip Stubbes, *A Christal Glasse for Christian*

Women, 1592, A3; S. B., *Counsel to the husband*, pp. 84–85; Robert Snawsel, *A looking glasse for Maried Folkes*, 1610, C6ᵛ, C8ᵛ, D1ᵛ; Alexander Niccholes, *A Discourse, of marriage and wiuing*, 1615, p. 49; Sir Thomas Elyot, *The Defence of Good women*, 1545, D3; Hannay, C1–C2ᵛ; *The Knight of Malta*, I.i. (Beaumont and Fletcher, *Works*, VII, 86).

20   S. B., *Counsel to the husband*, p. 89; Tilney, E1ᵛ–E2; Lyly, *Euphues*, *Works*, I, 225; Swetnam, p. 4; John Taylor, *A Iuniper Lecture*, 1639, p. 233.

21   Cleaver, p. 96; Gouge, p. 311; Tilney, E2ᵛ; Cleaver, p. 223 (This same figure appears in Griffith, pp. 412-413); Gouge, p. 314; Vives, *Office*, U4ᵛ; Burton, p. 658; Griffith, p. 416 (See Cleaver, pp. 229, 239; Whetstone, Q3; Charlotte Kohler, 'The Elizabethan Woman of Letters,' unpublished thesis for the Ph. D. degree, University of Virginia, 1936, p. 282; Thomas Tuke, *A treatise against painting and tincturing of men and women*, 1616, p. 60; *Volpone*, II.v. 45–63); Gouge, p. 315; Bodin, p. 20; *The Noble Gentleman*, II.i (Beaumont and Fletcher, *Works*, VIII, 189).

22   Snawsel, E5; *The Court of good Counsell*, E2–E2ᵛ; Becon, CCC2; Lyly, *Euphues and His England*, *Works*, II, 11, 17; Charron, p. 435 (see Mary Bateson, 'Manners and Customs,' in Traill's *Social England*, New York, 1909, III, section II, 784; Tilney, E3ᵛ; Herman V, A5; Greene, *Menaphon*, *Works*, VI, 136).

23   Tilney, E6ᵛ; Lyly, *Works*, III, 487; *Othello*, II.i. 101–109 (see Carroll Camden, 'Iago on Women,' *JEGP*, XLVIII, 57–71); Heywood, p. 145; Swetnam, pp. 11–12; *The proude wyues Pater noster*, 1560, B1–B1ᵛ; La Sale, A8ᵛ; Nashe, *Christs Teares over Ierusalem*, *Works*, II, 144; *Othello*, III.iii. 21–24; Burton, p. 657.

24   S. B., *Counsel to the husband*, p. 46 (see Anne Clifford, p. 34; Thomas Gataker, *A Good Wife Gods Gift*, 1623, p. 9); Barnaby Rich, *The Excellency of good women*, 1613, p. 11; Swetnam, p. 47; Brinsley, p. 16; Anne Clifford, pp. 18–19, 24, *et passim*.

25   Pilkington on Nehemiah, quoted in Furnivall's notes to Stubbes' *Anatomy*, 1879, p. 273; Swetnam, pp. 1, 7; *Everie Woman in her Humor*, 1609, A3ᵛ; Richard Brathwait, *A Ladies Love-Lecture*, in *The English Gentleman and the English Gentlewoman*, 1641, pp. 281, 450; *Epicoene*, II.ii. 133–156. See *The Parlament of Women*, A7, B1ᵛ; Cleaver, pp. 218, 239, 244; Barnaby Rich, *Faultes*, 1606, fol. 28; Whetstone, Y1ᵛ; Snawsel, B8ᵛ; Charles Bansley, *A treatyse, shewing and declaring the pryde and abuse of women now a dayes*, 1540?, A2; *The proude wyues Pater noster*, 1560, A4, B3ᵛ–C2ᵛ; Burton, p. 525; *The New Inn*, IV.ii. 83–87; *The Court of good Counsell*, D3–D3ᵛ.

26   *The Womans Prize*, II.vi (Beaumont and Fletcher, *Works*, VIII, 38); Robert Copland, *A Complaynt of them that be to soone maryed*, 1535, B3; Samuel Rowlands, *Looke to it: For Ile Stabbe Ye*, 1604, E1ᵛ; Thomas Nashe, *Pierce*

Penilesse His Supplication to the Diuell (1592), *Works*, ed. Grosart, 1883–1884, II, 32; Thomas Dekker, *The Batchelars Banquet*, 1603, A3–A3ᵛ. Since fashions change, the 1631 edition of Dekker's work is brought up to date with the current style; it speaks of 'her loose gowne with hanging sleeues, her French roses, her silke grograine kirtle, her beuer hat with a gold band.'

27   Herman V, A5; Tilney, D7ᵛ; Overbury, E1ᵛ; *The Court of good Counsell*, D1 (see Cleaver, p. 239; Wright, fol. 11ᵛ; Heale, p. 13); Whetstone, Y1ᵛ; *The Court of good Counsell*, D4ᵛ.

28   *The Womans Prize*, I.i. (Beaumont and Fletcher, *Works*, VIII, 8); Batty, N4ᵛ; Whately, *Bride-Bush*, pp. 43–44; Harrington, D4; Niccholes, p. 13 (see Richard Brathwait, *The English Gentleman*, 1630, p. 256, who quotes the same passage from Bacon and also neglects to name him); Overbury, C8.

29   See chapter headings to John Ley, *A patterne of pietie*, 1640; Joseph Hall, 'Salomons Oeconomicks,' *Works*, 1634, p. 218; Griffith, p. 294; Cleaver, p. 60; Tilney, C5ᵛ; Robert Vaughan or Robert Burdet(?), *A Dyalogue defensyue for women agaynst malycyous detractoures*, 1542, C2ᵛ; Rich, *The Excellency of good women*, p. 23; Becon, CCC1ᵛ; John Donne, Satire II, *Complete Poetry and Selected Prose*, New York, 1941, p. 109; Vives, *Office*, U3ᵛ; Hannay, C4ᵛ; Edward Gosynhill, *The prayse of all women*, 1560?, E3; Torquato Tasso, fol. 20ᵛ.

30   Cleaver, p. 364; Perkins, pp. 173–174; Griffith, p. 417; S. B., *Counsel to the husband*, pp. 13–15; Becon, CCC3ᵛ–CCC4; Josias Nichols, *An order of houshold instruction*, 1596, B4ᵛ, B7ᵛ; Vives, *Instructiō*, i3ᵛ; Cleaver, p. 93; Dorothy Leigh, *The Mothers Blessing*, 1633, p. 57.

31   Gouge, p. 367; Cleaver, pp. 60–61, 231, 235, 246, 264, 278–282; Batty, O1; William Averell, *Foure notable Histories*, 1590, F1; R. B., *A Watch-word for Wilfull Women*, C8–D1, F4ᵛ; R.G., *A godlie exhortation, and fruitfull admonition to vertuous parents and modest Matrons*, 1584, *passim*; Batty, C1ᵛ–C2ᵛ, O4ᵛ; Griffith, pp. 350–353.

32   Girolamo Ruscelli, *A verye excellent and profitable Booke*, 1569, fol. 13; Thomas Dawson, *The good huswifes Iewell*, 1596, *passim*; John Partridge, *The Treasury of commodious Conceits, and hidden Secrets, commonly called The good Huswiues Closet of prouision*, 1584, F1ᵛ; Hugh Platt, *A closet for ladies and gentlewomen, or the art of preseruing, conseruing, and candying*, 1608 (apparently the third edition of *Delightes for ladies*), pp. 72, 99; Thomas Lupton, *A Thousand Notable things of sundry sortes* [1600?], pp. 100–101; Burton, p. 456. See *The Alchemist*, IV.i. 131–134, and especially Vaughan-Burdet, C2ᵛ.

33   Donne, *Complete Poetry and Selected Prose*, p. 354; Hannay, C4ᵛ.

34   Gervase Markham, *Country Contentments, or The English Huswife*, 1623, p. 57; Vives, *Office*, U3–U3ᵛ; Torquato Tasso, fols. 20–20ᵛ; C. Pyrrye, *The praise and Dispraise of Women*, 1569?, B7ᵛ; *Rule a Wife and Have a Wife*, Act I

(Beaumont and Fletcher, *Works*, III, 180); Partridge, A4v–B4; Henry Parrot, *The Gossips Greeting*, 1620, B3; J. Murrell, *Murrels two books of cookerie and carving*, 1638, pp. 3–5; Girolamo Ruscelli, *The Secretes of reuerende Maister Alexis of Piemount*, 1568, fols. 59v–63v; Burton, p. 355; Violet A. Wilson, *Society Women of Shakespeare's Time*, New York, 1925, p. 41; Alice Clark, *Working Life of Women in the Seventeenth Century*, New York, 1920, p. 50; *The Little Thief*, Act III (Beaumont and Fletcher, *Works*, VII, 350); *Friar Bacon and Friar Bungay*, ll. 330–332; Stephen Gosson, *Quippes for Vpstart Newfangled Gentlewomen*, 1595, B3.

35 Murrell, pp. 152–153; Markham, *Country Contentments*, chapters 5 and 7.

36 Whetstone, Y1v; Partridge, D4v; William Lawson, *A New Orchard and Garden*, 1623, pp. 1–8; Markham, p. 60; Hannay, C4v; *The Coxcomb*, III.i (Beaumont and Fletcher, *Works*, VIII, 439); Markham, chapter 4; Clark, pp. 53–54; *The Little Thief*, Act III (Beaumont and Fletcher, *Works*, VII, 350); Gosson, *Quippes*, B3.

37 Torquato Tasso, fol. 20v; Wilson, p. 41; Hannay, C4v; Lyly, *Mother Bombie*, III.iv. 28–31; Gosson, *Quippes*, B3; *The Praise and Dispraise of Women*, 1579, fol. 11v; Jonson, *Hymenaei*, ll. 189–195; Lyly, *Endimion*, III.iii. 23–24, 27–29; Lyly, *Gallathea*, II. iv. 9–11; Lyly (?), 'Later Love Poems,' *Works*, III, 473; Burton, p. 355; *The Coxcomb*, II.i (Beaumont and Fletcher, *Works*, VIII, 333); Peele, *Edward I*, I. 216–220; *The Maydes Metamorphosis*, II.ii. 39–40; Greene, *James IV*, ll. 834–838; Lyly, *Campaspe*, IV.ii. 12–13; *The Two Noble Kinsmen*, II.ii. 119–130; Greene, *The Third and Last Parte of Conny-Catching*, *Works*, X, 151; Nashe, *The Anatomie of Absurditie*, *Works*, ed. McKerrow, 1910, I, 18; Partridge, F1; *The Coxcomb*, II.i (Beaumont and Fletcher, *Works*, VIII, 333); *Cynthias Revels*, V.iv. 348–354; Lyly, *Euphues and His England*, *Works*, II,9.

38 Greene, *Francescos Fortunes*, *Works*, VIII, 199; *The Coxcomb*, III.i (Beaumont and Fletcher, *Works*, VIII, 349); Greene, *The Third and Last Parte of Conny-Catching*, *Works*, X, 151; *Cymbeline*, I.v. 11–13; Partridge, B7v–B8, C3, C5–C6v; Markham, chapters 1 and 2.

39 Thomas Tusser, *Five Hundred Points of Good Husbandry* (1573, etc.), ed. William Mavor, 1812, pp. 247–269 (see M. St. Clare Byrne, *Elizabethan Life in Town and Country*, 1925, pp. 128–130); John Fitzherbert, *The boke of husbandrye*, 1548, fols. 67–68.

40 Clark, pp. 15–16, 25–26, 29–31, 34, 50, 150–151, 155, 161, 173, 195, 213, *et passim;* Mrs. C. C. Stopes, 'Sixteenth Century Women Students,' *Shakespeare's Environment*, 1918, pp. 295, 299; Gamaliel Bradford, *Elizabethan Women*, Cambridge, 1936, p. 33; Jonson, *Masque of Augures*, ll. 117–124; Jonson, *An Entertainment at the Blackfriars*, ll. 137–141; *Epicoene*, I.i. 150–152; Lady Brilliana Harley, *Letters*, Camden Society, 1854, *passim.*

CHAPTER VI

1   Robert Greene, *The Card of Fancie, Works*, ed. Grosart, 1881–1883, IV, 31–32.

2   Ludovicus Vives, *the Instructiō of a Christen womā*, 1529?, E3–F1ᵛ; Ludovicus Vives, *The office and duetie of an husband*, 1553?, O7–O7ᵛ; Mrs. C. C. Stopes, 'Sixteenth Century Women Students,' *Shakespeare's Environment*, 1918, pp. 309, 311; *Volpone*, III. iv. 67–97; M. St. Clare Byrne, *Elizabethan Life in Town and Country*, 1925, pp. 256–269; Elizabeth Godfrey, *Social Life under the Stuarts*, 1904, pp. 138–140; Anne Clifford, *Diary*, ed. V. Sackville-West, 1923, pp. 57, 60, 66; John Lyly, *Euphues and His England, Works*, ed. Bond, Oxford, 1902, II, 9; *Eastward Hoe*, II.iii. 97–114, 168–181; *The Womans Prize*, II.vi (Beaumont and Fletcher, *Works*, Cambridge, 1905–1912, VIII, 38); Gamaliel Bradford, *Elizabethan Women*, Cambridge, 1936, p. 30; Greene, *Philomela, Works*, XI, 152; *The Guardian*, II. iii.

3   *News from the New World*, ll. 158–164; *The Art of English Poesy* (1589), from J. William Hebel and Hoyt H. Hudson, *Poetry of the English Renaissance*, New York, 1930, p. 922.

4   Jacques Du Bosc, *The secretary of ladies or a new collection of letters and answers, composed by moderne ladies and gentlewomen*, 1638, *passim;* William Averell, *Foure notable Histories, applyed to foure worthy examples: As, 1. A Diall for daintie darlings. 2. A spectacle for negligent Parents. 3. A glasse for Disobedient Sonnes. 4. And a myrrour for virtuous Maydes*, 1590, I4ᵛ. See Greene, *The Royall Exchange, Works*, VII, 227.

5   Edmund Tilney, *A brief and pleasant discourse of duties in Mariage, called the Flower of Friendshippe*, 1568, A6; Giovanni Michele Bruto, *The necessarie, fit, and conuenient Education of a yong Gentlewoman*, 1598, K6ᵛ–K8; Greene, *Euphues His Censure to Philautus, Works*, VI, 262–263; Greene, *Orpharion, Works*, XII, 78; *Greenes Farewell to Folly, Works*, IX, 326; *The Woman Hater*, I.iii (Beaumont and Fletcher, *Works*, X, 77). See Lyly, 'Early Autobiographical Poems,' *Works*, III, 457.

6   Lyly, *Euphues and His England, Works*, II, 8–9, 189; Barnaby Rich, *Faultes, Faults, and nothing else but Faultes*, 1606, fol. 21ᵛ; Thomas Nashe, *The Anatomie of Absurditie, Works*, ed. McKerrow, 1910, I, 18; *Eastward Hoe*, headnote to I.ii, V.i. 139–143; *Cynthias Revels*, IV.ii. 37–41. See *Poetaster*, IV.i. 3–22; *News from the New World*, ll. 239–240.

7   *Greenes Never too Late, Works*, VIII, 74–75, 96; Greene, *Philomela, Works*, XI, 122–123; Greene, *Greenes Vision, Works*, XII, 237; Greene, *A Disputation between a Hee and a Shee Conny-Catcher, Works*, X, 244; Averell, I4ᵛ; Nicholas Breton, *Pasquils Mistresse: Or The Worthie and vnworthie woman*, 1600, C3ᵛ; *Volpone*, III.iv. 67–76; Robert Burton, *The Anatomy of Melancholy* (1628), New York, 1924, p. 577; Bruto, H4ᵛ–H5ᵛ. See *The Chances*,

IV.iii (Beaumont and Fletcher, *Works*, IV, 228); *The Coxcomb*, III.i (Beaumont and Fletcher, *Works*, VIII, 346); *Poetaster*, II.i. 63–68; *The Taming of the Shrew*, II.i. 56–58.

8 Anne Clifford, pp. 18, 45; Stopes, pp. 311–312; Greene, *Perimedes the Black-Smith*, *Works*, VII, 44; Lyly, *Euphues*, *Works*, I, 201, 215; John Manningham, *Diary* (1602–1603), Camden Society, Westminster, 1868, p. 132; *Epicoene*, IV.iii. 46–50; Greene, *Philomela*, *Works*, XI, 154; Breton, C3v; Tilney, A4–A6; Jonson, *Love Restored*, ll. 151–164; *Sapho and Phao*, IV.iii; Lyly, *Euphues and His England*, *Works*, II, 85, 137; Burton, p. 355; Van Meteren in William Brenchley Rye, *England as Seen by Foreigners*, 1865, p. 72.

9 *Midas*, III.iii. 17–26; Lyly, *Euphues and His England*, *Works*, II, 103; *Euphues*, *Works*, I, 319; Burton, p. 577; Greene, *Euphues His Censure to Philautus*, *Works*, VI, 227.

10 John Northbrooke, *A Treatise wherein Dicing, Dauncing, Vaine playes or Enterluds with other idle pastimes &c. commonly vsed on the Sabboth day, are reproued by the Authoritie of the word of God and Auntient writers*, 1577?, pp. 113–114, 125; *The Devil is an Ass*, IV. iv. 164; John Lowin, *Conclusions vpon Dances*, 1607, C3–C4; John Downame, *Foure Treatises, Tending to Disswade all Christians from foure no lesse hainous then common sinnes; namely, the abuses of Swearing, Drunkennesse, Whoredome, and Briberie*, 1609, p. 200; Christopher Fetherstone, *A Dialogue against light, lewde, and lasciuious dauncing*, 1582, *passim*; Nashe, *Christs Teares over Ierusalem*, *Works*, II, 151; Averell, I4v; Greene, *A Disputation between a Hee and a Shee Conny-Catcher*, *Works*, X, 244; Vives, *Instructiō*, P3v–P4; Nashe, *Have With You to Saffron-Walden*, *Works*, III, 77; Godfrey, p. 23.

11 See the excellent discussion of the dance in Charles R. Baskervill, *The Elizabethan Jig*, Chicago, 1929, chapter X. See also *CHEL.*; *Love's Labour's Lost*, III.i. 11–26; Lodge, *Wits Miserie*, 1596, p. 34 (Baskerville). The passage from Baskerville is quoted with the kind permission of the publisher, The University of Chicago Press.

12 Stopes, p. 311; *Love Restored*, ll. 102–107, 115–116, 151–164; *The Masque of Owles*, ll. 122–131. See *Poetaster*, II.i. 63–68.

13 *Epicoene*, IV.i. 66–80, IV.iii. 46–50, II.ii. 32–36; *The Two Noble Gentlemen*, II.i (Beaumont and Fletcher, *Works*, VIII, 186); *The Staple of News*, Induction, ll. 5–10 (italics inverted); Richard Brathwait, *The English Gentlewoman*, 1641, p. 339; *The Devil is an Ass*, II.ii. 109–110; Downame, *Foure Treatises*, pp. 196–197; John Northbrooke, *Treatise against Dicing, Dancing, and Plays*, Shakespeare Society, 1843, p. 94; Stephen Gosson, *The Schoole of Abuse*, 1579, p. 35; H. S. Symmes, *Les Débuts de la Critique Dramatique*, Paris, 1903, pp. 72–73; J. A. Symonds, *Shakspere's Predecessors*, 1884, p. 271.

CHAPTER VII

1   *Humourous Day's Mirth*, I. 77; Sir Thomas Overbury, *His Wife*, 1632, E2ᵛ;
Everard Guilpin, 'Satyra Secunda,' *Skialetheia* (1598), Oxford, 1931, C 7; *A
Wife for a Month* I.i (Beaumont and Fletcher, *Works*, V, 10); Richard Brath-
wait, *The English Gentlewoman*, 1641, p. 300; Richard Brathwait, *The English
Gentleman*, 1630, pp. 259–260; Richard Brathwait, *The English Gentlewoman*,
1631, p. 9; *Cynthia's Revels*, IV.i 140–149; *Sejanus*, I. 307–313; *Merchant of
Venice*, III.ii. 88–96; Thomas Nashe, *Pierce Penilesse. His Supplication to the
Deuill* (1592), *Works*, 1883–1884, II, 43; *The Malcontent*, II.iv 33–41;
Francesco Colonna, *Hypnerotomachia. The Strife of Loue in a Dreame*, 1592,
fol. 44; John Downame, *Lectures vpon the Foure First Chapters of the Prophecie
of Hosea*, 1608, pp. 165–166. See Louise Labé, *Debate between Folly and
Cupid* (1555), 1925, p. 43; *Epicoene*, II.vi. 40–42; Thomas Dekker, *Dekker
His Dreame* (1620), *Works*, III, 1885, 51; notes to *Friar Bacon and Friar
Bungay*, ed. Grosart, Greene's *Works*, 1881–1883, XIII, 108; *Two Gentlemen
of Verona*, II.i. 59–65; George Peele, *Jests*, *Works*, 1888, II, 403; John Lyly,
Euphues and His England, *Works*, Oxford, 1902, II, 200–201; John Davies,
Microcosmos, *Works*, ed. Grosart, 1878, I, 65; Philip Sidney, *Arcadia*,
Cambridge, 1912, p. 81; *The Malcontent*, III.i; *Bartholomew Fair*, I.ii. 15–16;
Greene, *Planetomachia*, *Works*, V, 69. In view of this overwhelming evidence,
it is quite surprising that Samuel Kiechel, a visitor from the continent,
could write in 1585, concerning the women of England, 'The women there
are charming, and by nature so mighty pretty, as I have scarcely ever
beheld, for they do not falsify, paint or bedaub themselves as in Italy or
other places.' (Cited by W. B. Rye, *England as Seen by Foreigners*, 1865,
pp. 89–90.)

2   Thomas Tuke, *A Treatise against Painting and Tincturing of Men and Women*,
1616, p. 24; Samuel Butler, *Hudibras*, 'An Heroical Epistle,' ll. 177–184
(following Canto III of Book III); Brathwait, *The English Gentleman* (1630),
p. 261.

3   Joseph Swetnam, *The Arraignment of Lewd, Idle, Froward, and vnconstant
Women*, 1622, p. 25; Robert Burton, *The Anatomy of Melancholy*, New York,
1924, p. 525; Thomas Draiton's verse found in Tuke, B1ᵛ; Alexander
Niccholes, *A Discourse of Marriage and Wiving*, 1615, p. 21.

4   William Horman, *Vulgaria*, 1519, p. 169 (from *N.E.D.*); Joannes Ludovicus
Vives, *The Instructiō of a Christen Womā*, 1529?, F2; *Sejanus*, II.i. 57–103;
John Fletcher, *The Spanish Curate*, V.i.; Giovanni Paolo Lomazzo, *A Tracte
Containing the Artes of Curious Paintinge Caruinge & Buildinge*, Oxford, 1598,
p. 130; Tuke, B3–B3ᵛ; Girolamo Ruscelli (Alessio), *The Secretes of reuerende
Maister Alexis of Piemount*, 1568, fol. 72ᵛ.

5   Thomas Nashe, *Christs Teares over Ierusalem*, *Works*, 1910, II, 59; Hamlet, III.i. 148–150, V.i. 213–215; *The Devil is An Ass*, III.iv. 48–51; *Sejanus*, II. 124–136; Vives, *The Instruction of a Christian Woman*, in Foster Watson, *Vives and the Renascence Education of Women*, 1912, p. 73; C. Pyrrye, *The praise and Dispraise of Women*, 1569?, B3; Nicholas Breton, *Pasquils Mistresse: Or The Worthie and vnworthie woman*, 1600, C3ᵛ; Brathwait, *The English Gentlewoman* (1641), p. 339; Ruscelli, fols. 69, 71ᵛ, 72; Lomazzo, pp. 127, 131–132; *Westward Ho*, I.i. See the following plays in the Beaumont and Fletcher volumes: *The Tragedy of Valentinian*, II.ii; *The Faithful Shepherdess*, I.i; *The Loyal Subject*, I.ii; *The Laws of Candy*, II.i. Also see Shakespeare, Sonnet 83; *Volpone*, III.iv. 32–37; Tuke, B2–B2ᵛ (from Du bartas, 4th book, 4th day, 2nd week); anon., *Everie Woman in Her Humor*, 1609, A4. It seems somewhat peculiar that in *Epicoene*, II.ii.140, True-Wit speaks of a face 'clens'd with a new *fucus*.'

6   *The Malcontent*, II.iv. 1–27; *Edward I*, vi. 1–5; *The Two Gentlemen of Verona*, IV.iv. 156–161; Lyly, *Works*, III, 458; Furnivall, notes to Stubbes' *Anatomy of Abuses*, 1879, p. 271; John Taylor, 'A Whore,' *Works*, part II, Spenser Society, 1868, p. 111.

7   Christopher Wirtzung, *General Practise of Physick*, 4th ed., 1654, pp. 77–79; Lomazzo, pp. 129, 132; 'Lord Thomas and Fair Annet,' F. J. Child, *The English and Scottish Popular Ballads*, Boston, 1886, II, 183 (stanza 23), 186 (stanza 18), 197 (stanza 13); *Every Man in His Humour*, II.iii. 34–35; *The Devil is An Ass*, II.viii. 34–39; *Epicoene*, II.ii. 172–176; Philip Stubbes, *The Anatomy of Abuses*, ed. Furnivall, 1877, p. 65; Ambroise Paré, 'Of Poisons' (1575), *Oeuvres*, Paris, 1840, III, 328; *Westward Ho*, I.i.

8   *Cynthia's Revels*, I.i. 17–19, Palinode, 19–23; *Epicoene*, II.ii. 136–140; Tuke, B4; Lomazzo, pp. 127, 131; Ruscelli, fols. 65–68; Pedro Mexia, as translated by Thomas Milles in his compendium, *The Treasurie of Auncient and Moderne Times*, 1613, I, 169; *The Devil is An Ass*, IV.iv. 12–56; Guilpin, C5–C7; *A Wife for a Month*, II.i; Tuke, B2–B2ᵛ; *Poetaster*, IV.v. 34; *Antony and Cleopatra*, I.ii. 16–19; John Taylor, *Superbiae Flagellum, or The Whip of Pride*, *Works*, Spenser Society, 1868, Part I, II, 34; Brathwait, *The English Gentlewoman* (1641), p. 382; *Swetnam, the Woman-hater, arraigned by women*, 1620, F1ᵛ (III.i); *Midas*, V.ii. 110; Nashe, *The Anatomie of Absurditie*, *Works*, ed. McKerrow, 1910, I, 17; William Averell, *Foure notable Histories*, 1584, B1ᵛ–B2; Anne Clifford, *Diary*, 1923, p. 70.

9   Thomas Lupton, *A Thousand Notable Things*, 1600?, p. 95; Wirtzung, pp. 78–79; Pierre Charron, *Of Wisdome*, 1670, p. 19; Averell, C2ᵛ; *The Beaute of Women*, 1525?, A3; Kyd, *Solimon and Perseda*, IV.i. 79; *The Malcontent*, II.iv. 37; Pyrrye, B3; Vives, ed. Watson, p. 73; Tuke, B2ᵛ.

10   *The Winter's Tale*, V.iii. 79–83; *Sejanus*, II.i. 78–80; Wirtzung, pp. 197,

215–216; *Swetnam, The Woman-hater*, F1ᵛ (III.i.); Brathwait, *English Gentle-woman* (1641), p. 300; John Partridge, *The Treasury of commodious Conceits, and hidden Secrets, commonly called, The good Huswiues Closet of prouision*, 1584, D1.

11   Matthew Griffith, *Bethel: or, A Forme for Families*, 1633, p. 259; Breton, *Pasquils Mistresse*, D3ᵛ; John Donne, *The Complete Poetry and Selected Prose*, ed. Hillyer, N.Y., 1941, p. 97 ('Epithalamion for Robert Ker and the Countess of Essex'); Stubbes, *Anatomy* (1877), pp. 67–68; Nashe, *Anatomie of Absurditie*, p. 17; Girolamo Ruscelli, *The thyrde and last part of the Secretes of the reuerende Maister Alexis of Piemont*, 1566, fols. 34ᵛ, 42ᵛ–43, 72ᵛ–73; Ludovicus Vives, *The office and duetie of an husband*, 1553?, P2ᵛ; *Campaspe*, III.iv. 91–92; *The Court of good Counsell* (part of Guazzo's *Civil Conversations*), 1607, D3ᵛ; Stephen Gosson, *Quippes for Vpstart Newfangled Gentlewomen*, 1595, A4; *The Merchant of Venice*, III.ii. 88–96; Brathwait, *English Gentle-woman* (1641), p. 321; *Epicoene*, I.i. 13–18, 130–133; John Lane, *Tom Tel-Troths message* (1600), Shakespeare Society, 1876, p. 121; Nashe, *Christs Teares over Ierusalem*, *Works*, II, 140; *Midas*, I.ii. 114–121; Richard Mulcaster, *Positions* (1581), 1887, p. 211; Robert Cleaver, *A Godlie Forme of Household Government*, 1598, p. 244. It is interesting to note that there are also recipes for the removal of superfluous hair: see Ruscelli, *Secretes* (1568), fols. 74ᵛ–75ᵛ.

12   Arthur Dent, *The Plaine Mans Path-way to Heauen*, 1601, pp. 45–46; Joseph Hall, *The Righteous Mammon* (1618), *Works*, 1634, p. 670; *Everie Woman in her Humor*, 1609, A3ᵛ; Greene, *A Looking Glasse for London and England*, *Works*, XIV, ll. 492–508; Greene, *The Debate betweene Follie and Loue*, *Works*, IV, 212; Tuke, A3ᵛ; Clifford, p. 67; *Cynthia's Revels*, II.iv. 64–68; *Poetaster*, III.i. 49–55; *Midas*, I.ii. 76–87; Samuel Rowlands, *Looke To it: For, Ile Stabbe Ye*, 1604, D2ᵛ.

13   *Cynthia's Revels*, III.v. 39, IV.i. 98–100, IV.iii. 309; Wirtzung, pp. 149, 757.

14   *As You Like It*, III.ii. 65–66; Vives, ed. Watson, p. 199; Ruscelli, *Secretes* (1568), fol. 43; Vives, *Office and duetie of an husband* (1553?), P2ᵛ; Beaumont and Fletcher, *The Woman Hater*, III.iii; Overbury, *Wife*, L7ᵛ.

15   Gosson, *Quippes* (1595), B1; *The Maydes Metamorphosis*, II.ii. 39–40; John Taylor, *A Whore*, p. 111; Nashe, *Christs Teares*, II, pp. 137–138; Dent, p. 46; John Bulwer, *Anthropometamorphosis: Man Transform'd*, 1653, A4ᵛ; Barnaby Rich, *Faultes, Faults, and nothing else but Faultes*, 1606, fols. 23–23ᵛ; Rowlands, D2ᵛ; *Everie Woman in her Humor*, A3ᵛ; Charles Bansley, *A treatyse, shewing and declaring the pryde and abuse of women now a dayes*, 1550?, A2ᵛ; M. C. Linthicum, *Costume in Elizabethan Drama*, Oxford, 1936, pp. 178–181.

16   Vives, *Instructiō of a Christen womā*, I4–I4ᵛ; Burton, p. 526; Partridge, C1, C5–C6ᵛ; Taylor, *Svperbiae Flagellvm*, pp. 31–32; Greene, *A Looking Glasse*, ll. 503–508; *The Devil is an Ass*, IV.iv. 146–148; Stubbes, pp. 77–78.

17 Hanniball Gamon, *The praise of a godly woman*, 1627, p. 6; William Prynne, *The Vnlouelinesse of Loue-Lockes*, 1628, p. 20; John Donne, Sermon XIV (from *Fifty Sermons*, 1649), *Poetry and Selected Prose*, ed. Hillyer, pp. 434–435; Nicholas Ling, *Politeuphuia. Wits Common wealth*, 1598, fol. 28ᵛ; Griffith, p. 259; Cleaver, p. 244; Vives, ed. Watson, p. 73.

18 Brathwait, *Gentleman* (1630), p. 259; William Perkins, *The Whole Treatise of the Cases of Conscience*, 1619, pp. 338–339; Dent, pp. 46–47; Brathwait, *Gentlewoman* (1641), p. 340; George Gascoigne, *The Steele Glas, Works*, Cambridge, 1910, II, 173; Vives, ed. Watson, pp. 72–75; Tuke, A4, B3–B3ᵛ, p. 18; Griffith, p. 259; Robert Cawdrey, *A Treasurie or Storehouse of Similies*, 1600, p. 571; Stubbes, p. 64.

19 *Hic Mulier: or, The Man-Woman*, 1620, B3ᵛ; Brathwait, *Gentlewoman* (1641), pp. 307–308, 365; Brathwait, *Gentlewoman* (1631), p. 8; Griffith, pp. 261–262; Brathwait, *The Good Wife*, 1618, B8, pp. 30–31.

20 Vives, *Instructiō of a Christen womā* (1529?), H4ᵛ, F1; Downame, pp. 166–167; Henry Smith, *Works*, ed. Fuller, Edinburgh, 1866, I, 171; Torquato Tasso, *The Housholders Philosophie*, trans. Thomas Kyd, 1588, fol. 10ᵛ; Greene, *Penelope's Web, Works*, V, 200–201; *The Faerie Queene*, I.iv. 14.

21 Brathwait, *Gentleman* (1630), p. 259; Rich, *Faultes*, fol. 21; Bansley, A1ᵛ; *Measure for Measure*, IV.ii. 38–41; Greene, *Disputation betweene a Hee and a Shee Conny-Catcher, Works*, X, 243; Furnivall, notes to Stubbes, pp. 255, 439; Burton, p. 528; Downame, p. 165; John Taylor, *A Bawd, Works*, Spenser Society, XIX, 24.

22 Vives, *Instructiō of a Christen womā* (1529?), F2; Greene, *Disputation, Works*, X, 199; Beaumont and Fletcher, *The Scornful Lady*, I.i; Stubbes, pp. 66–67; Donne, Sermon XIV, *Poetry and Selected Prose*, pp. 434–435; Barnaby Rich, *The Excellency of good women*, 1613, p. 16; John Downame, *Foure Treatises, Tending to Disswade all Christians from foure no lesse hainous then common sinnes*, 1609, p. 202; Burton, pp. 521–522.

23 Brathwait, *Gentlewoman* (1631), p. 12; Tuke, pp. 57–58; Thomas Gataker, *A Good Wife Gods Gift*, 1620, p. 19; Lomazzo, p. 133; Henry Smith, *Works*, I, 206; Brathwait, *Gentlewoman* (1641), p. 277; Nashe, *The Anatomie of Absurditie, Works*, I, 18.

24 Francis Bacon, *The Advancement of Learning, Philosophical Works*, 1905, p. 491; Vives, *Instructiō*, F1ᵛ; Tuke, B3–B4ᵛ; Brathwait, *Ar't asleepe Husband?*, 1640, p. 19; Brathwait, *Gentleman* (1630), p. 260; *The Devil is an Ass*, IV.iii. 28–47.

25 Lomazzo, 129–133.

26 *Swetnam, the Woman-hater*, B1ᵛ; Prynne, p. 17; Tuke, A3ᵛ-A4ᵛ; Ercole Tasso, *Of Mariage and Wiuing*, 1599, D3ᵛ; Tomaso Buoni, *Problems of Beautie and all humane affections*, 1606, pp. 36–37; Henry Smith, 'The Pride of Nebuchadnezzar,' *Works*, I, 175; Rich, *Excellency of good women*, p. 22;

Jacques Du Bosc, *The compleat woman*, 1639, p. 55; Vivès, ed. Watson, p. 71; for Bishop Pilkington, see Furnivall's notes to Stubbes' *Anatomy*, p. 273; *Epicoene*, IV.ii. 89–100; Lyly, *Euphues*, *Works*, I, 254–255.

27   Guilpin, *Skialetheia*, C6–C6ᵛ; Tuke, B1ᵛ–B2; Donne, Satire IV, *Poetry and Selected Prose*, p. 115; Nashe, *The Terrors of the Night*, *Works*, I, 353; Du Bosc, p. 33; Anthony Gibson, *A Womans Woorth*, 1599, fol. 23; *The Man in the Moone*, ed. Halliwell, 1849, p. 35; *Epicoene*, I.i. 104–122.

28   *Love's Labour's Lost*, IV.iii. 270–271; Dowton's verse is from Tuke, A3; *The Devil is an Ass*, IV.iii. 42–47; Vives, *Instructiō of a Christen womā*, F1; Tuke, p. 34 (Erasmus).

29   Joseph Hall, *The Righteous Mammon* (1618), *Works*, 1634, p. 670.

30   Downame, *Foure Treatises*, p. 203; Cawdrey, p. 571; Torquato Tasso, fol. 11; Tuke B2ᵛ (Du Bartas); Greene, *Menaphon*, *Works*, VI, 95.

31   *The Court of good Counsell*, D4; Brathwait, *Gentlewoman* (1641), pp. 276–277, 299; Nashe, *Christs Teares*, *Works*, II, 137; Thomas Overbury, *A Very Woman*, *Miscellaneous Works*, 1856, p. 118.

32   *The Court of good Counsell*, D3–D3ᵛ; Burton, p. 525; Thomas Nashe, *The Anatomie of Absurditie*, 1589, A3; Tuke, B3; Pierre Boaistuau, *Theatrum Mundi*, 1566?, K4.

33   Buoni, pp. 33–34; Du Bosc, pp. 32–34; Burton, p. 522; Lyly, 'Later Love-Poems' no. 52, *Works*, III, 490; Edward More, *A Lytle and bryefe treatyse, called the defence of women*, 1560, C3; Robert Vaughan or Robert Burdet[?], *A Dyalogue defensyue for women agaynst malycyous detractoures*, 1542, C3ᵛ; Brathwait, *Gentleman* (1630), p. 261; Perkins, *Cases of Conscience*, p. 339.

34   John Donne, *Sermons*, ed. Smith, Oxford, 1920, pp. 87–89; Donne, *Iuvenilia: or Certaine Paradoxes, and Problemes*, 1633, B2–B3. See also Brathwait, *Gentleman* (1630), p. 261, and Boaistuau, K4ᵛ.

35   *Epicoene*, I.i. 124–146, IV.i. 39–53; *Sir Giles Goosecap*, IV.iii. 41–72.

36   Jane Anger, *Protection for Women*, 1589, D1; John Marston, *The Malcontent*, II.iv. 46–64.

CHAPTER VIII

1   *The Gypsies Metamorphos'd*, ll. 666–669; Stephen Gosson, *Quippes for Vpstart Newfangled Gentlewomen*, 1595, A4–A4ᵛ; *Everie Woman in her Humor*, 1609, A3ᵛ; John Taylor, 'A Whore,' *Works*, Spenser Society, 1868, Part II, p. 111; *The New Inn*, IV.ii. 83–87; *The Alchemist*, V.iv. 302; Thomas Tuke, *A treatise against painting and tincturing of men and women*, 1616, A3ᵛ; Arthur Dent, *The Plaine Mans Path-way to Heauen*, 1601, p. 45; 'A Warning-Piece

to England against Pride and Wickedness,' in *The Works of George Peele*, 1888, I, 77–78; *Poetaster*, II.i. 63–68; Jonson, *Christmas His Masque*, ll. 186–187; Jonson, *The Vision of Delight*, ll. 69–73; *Eastward Hoe*, I.ii. 14–25, 65–72, V.i. 1239–43; *The Scourge of Villainie*, in F. J. Furnivall's notes to Stubbe's *Anatomy*, 1879, p. 272; Greene, *Greenes Vision, Works*, XII, 225–226; W. Harrison, *Description of England in Shakspere's Youth*, ed. Furnivall, 1877, p. 170; *Greenes Never too Late, Works*, VIII, 53; *The Devil is an Ass*, I.i. 126–130; *Bartholomew Fair*, IV.v. 36–37; Richard Brathwait, *The English Gentlewoman*, 1631, p. 15. See especially the excellent work by Marie Channing Linthicum, *Costume in the Drama of Shakespeare and his Contemporaries*, Oxford, 1936.

2 *Epicoene*, II.iv. 67–80; Harrison, *loc. cit.*; Richard Brathwait, *The English Gentlewoman*, in *The English Gentleman; and the English Gentlewoman*, 1641, p. 276; Greene, *Mamillia, Works*, II, 220; John Lyly, 'The Lottery,' *Entertainments at Harefield, Works*, ed. Bond, Oxford, 1902, I, 503; Greene, *Greenes Vision, Works*, XII, 225–226; Lyly, *Euphues and His England, Works*, II, 10.

3 *The Devil is an Ass*, I.i. 126–130; Anne Clifford, *Diary*, ed. V. Sackville-West, 1923, p. 80; Lyly, *The Honorable Entertainement, gieuen to the Queenes Maiestie in Progress, . . . by the right Honorable the Earle of Hertford. 1591, Works*, I., 439; Greene, *Mamillia, Works*, II, 220; Lyly, *Euphues and His England, Works*, II, 10, 199; *Women Pleased*, III.iii; *Bartholomew Fair*, III.vi. 93–95, IV.v. 36–37; *The Taming of the Shrew*, IV.iiii. 142; *Eastward Hoe*, I.ii. 14–25, V.i. 139–143; Agrypnia in Jonson, *King's Entertainment in Passing to His Coronation*, ll. 169–171; *The New Inn*, II.ii. 40–43; Segar's *Honor* in *The Works of George Peele*, ed. Bullen, 1888, II, 283; Greene, *Greenes Never Too Late, Works*, VIII, 53; Louise Labé, *Debate between Folly and Cupid (Oeuvres*, Lyons, 1555), ed. Cox, 1925, p. 44; Brathwait, *The English Gentlewoman* (1631), pp. 15–16; *Epicoene*, II.v. 67–80; Harrison, p. 170; *Poetaster*, IV.i. 3–22.

4 Fynes Moryson, *An Itinerary* (1617), Glasgow, 1907–1908, IV, 234–235; C. Pyrrye, *The praise and Dispraise of Women*, 1569?, B3; Barnaby Rich, *Faultes, Faults, and nothing else but Faultes*, 1606, fol. 23; Thomas Tuke, *A treatise against painting*, 1616, A3ᵛ, B2ᵛ, B3, p. 31; Thomas Nashe, *Christs Teares, Works*, ed. McKerrow, 1910, II, 137; John Downame, *Lectures vpon . . . Hosea*, 1608, pp. 162, 165, 203; *Amoretti*, lxiv, lxxvi, lxxvii; *Epithalamion*, ll. 171–180; *Faerie Queene*, II.iii. 29, II.xii. 20, 66. See *Beaute of women*, 1525?, A2ᵛ; Vaughan-Burdet, *A Dyalogue defensyue*, 1542, C3; William Averell, *Foure notable Histories*, 1590, C2ᵛ; Gosson, *Quippes*, A4; Robert Cleaver, *A Godlie Forme of Household Government*, 1598, p. 238; Dent, p. 46; *Everie Woman in her Humor*, 1609, A3ᵛ; Alexander Niccholes,

A Discourse, of marriage and wiuing, 1615, p. 21; John Donne, Sermon XIV, *Fifty Sermons*, 1649; Joseph Hall, *Works*, 1618, p. 670; *Muld Sacke*, 1620, B1ᵛ; *Haec-Vir*, 1620, A4; *Hic Mulier*, 1620, B3ᵛ; Robert Burton, *The Anatomy of Melancholy*, New York, 1924, p. 522; Hanniball Gamon, *The praise of a godly woman*, 1627, p. 6; Thomas Hall, Appendix, *The Loathsomeness of Long Haire*, 1654; *Cynthia's Revels*, III.iv. 66–70; *The Masque of Beautie*, ll. 179–180; Jonson, *Part of the King's Entertainment*, ll. 151–155; Matthew Griffith, *Bethel*, 1633, p. 259; Richard Brathwait, *The English Gentlewoman*, 1631, p. 8. Interestingly enough, there are a few references to 'false breasts': Brathwait, p. 300; Drayton's *Muses' Elysium* (1630), Nymphal VII, in Furnivall's notes to Stubbes, p. 257; and Brathwait, *The English Gentleman*, 1630, p. 28.

5   *Bartholomew Fair*, II.v. 85–88; Samuel Rowlands, *Looke to it: For, Ile Stabbe Ye*, 1604, D2ᵛ; *Volpone*, III.iv. 2–3; *Poetaster*, IV.i. 3–22; Marston, *The Scourge of Villanie*, from Furnivall's notes to Stubbes, 1879, 272; *The Alchemist*, IV.iv. 362–365; Lyly, *Euphues and His England*, *Works*, II, 199; Greene, *Mamillia*, *Works*, II, 220; *Women Pleased*, III, iii; *The New Inn*, II.i. 42; *The Merry Wives of Windsor*, III.iii. 62, IV.ii. 74; Thomas Nashe, *The Anatomie of Absurdity*, *Works*, ed. McKerrow, 1910, I, 18; *Cynthia's Revels*, V.iv. 348–354.

6   Lyly, *Midas*, I.ii. 76–87; Rowlands, D2ᵛ; *The New Inn*, II.ii. 40–43; *Bartholomew Fair*, IV.v. 65–71; Philip Stubbes, *The Anatomy of Abuses* (1583, etc.), ed. Furnivall, 1877, pp. 68–69; *The Alchemist*, II.vi. 696–699; Mary Bateson, 'Manners and Customs,' in Traill's *Social England*, vol. III, sec. II, New York, 1909, p. 533; *A Proclamacion concernyng hattes and cappes*, *(By the Queene)*, 1573; 'An acte for the makyng of cappes,' *At the parliament begunne*, etc., 1571, F1ᵛ–F2ᵛ; *Every Man in His Humour*, III.iii. 30–38; *A Tale of a Tub*, II.iv. 78–85; *Eastward Hoe*, I.ii. 14–25; Lyly, *Euphues and His England*, *Works*, II, 107; Lyly, *Entertainments at Harefield*, *Works*, I, 502.

7   William Brenchley Rye, *England as Seen by Foreigners*, 1865, pp. 69–70, 73; *The Magnetick Lady*, V.ii. 18–19; *Midas*, I.ii.76–87; Greene, *Mamillia*, *Works*, II, 220; Lyly, *Euphues and His England*, *Works*, II, 10; Brathwait, *The English Gentlewoman* (1641), p. 305; Stubbes, *Anatomy* (1877), p. 69.

8   Gosson, *Quippes*, A4; Daniel Tuvil, *Asylum Veneris, or A Sanctuary for Ladies*, 1616, p. 54; Stubbes, *Anatomy* (1877), p. 69; *Midas*, I.ii. 76–87; John Donne, 'The Token,' *The Complete Poetry and Selected Prose*, ed. Hillyer, New York, 1941, p. 50; *Eastward Hoe*, V.i. 139–143; Van Meteren in Rye, *England as Seen by Foreigners*, p. 69; *The Arraignment of Paris*, V.i. 75–78; passage from Segar's *Honor*, in *The Works of George Peele*, ed. Bullen, 1888, II, 283.

9 Linthicum, pp. 238–255; Labé, p. 44; *Edward I*, vi.1; *Endimion*, II.ii. 32–35; *The Devil is an Ass*, I.i. 126–130; Greene, *Greenes Never Too Late*, *Works*, VIII, 53.

10 Lyly, *Euphues and His England*, *Works*, II, 'To the Ladies of Italy'; Marlowe (and Nashe?), *The Tragedie of Dido*, III.i. 24–25; *The Arraignment of Paris*, I.i. 91–94, III.ii. 115; *Gynthia's Revels*, II.ii. 46–47, II.iv. 1–2; *Every Man Out of His Humour*, III.iii. 33–44; Rowlands, D2ᵛ; Lady Brilliana Harley, *Letters*, Camden Society, London, 1854, p. 76; *The Alchemist*, IV. iv. 362–365; Rye, pp. 69, 73; *Edward I*, vi. 1–5; *Poetaster*, IV.i. 3–22.

11 Ben Jonson, *Works*, ed. Herford and Simpson, Oxford, 1941, III, xvi (between pages 208–209).

12 *The Praise and Dispraise of Women*, 1579, cap. 5, fol. 75ᵛ; Thomas Becon, *The booke of Matrimony*, *Worckes*, 1560–1564, CCC1–CCC1ᵛ; Brathwait, *The English Gentlewoman* (1631), pp. 3–4; John Taylor, *Superbiae Flagellum, or The Wip of Pride* (1621), *Works*, Spenser Society, 1868, part I, vol. II, 32–33; *King Lear*, II.iv. 267–273, III.iv. 105–113. See Hanniball Gamon, *The praise of a godly woman*, 1627, p. 6; John Aylmer, *An harborowe for faithful and trewe subiectes*, Strasburgh, 1559, N1–N1ᵛ.

13 Brathwait, *The English Gentlewoman* (1641), p. 279; William Austin, *Haec homo wherein the excellency of the creation of woman is described by way of an essaie*, 1637, p. 69; Thomas Becon, *The Iewel of Ioy* (1553), in Furnivall's notes to Stubbes' *Anatomy*, 1879, p. 255; Tuke, p. 59, Sir Thomas Overbury, 'A very Woman,' *Miscellaneous Works*, ed. Rimbault, 1856, p. 51; *The proude wyues Pater noster*, 1560, A2; Giovanni Michele Bruto, *The necessarie, fit, and conuenient Education of a yong Gentlewoman*, 1598, K2–K4; Barnaby Rich, *The Excellency of good women*, 1613, pp. 18–19; Rye, p. 71. See Rich, p. 14.

14 Brathwait, *The English Gentlewoman* (1631), p. 8; Thomas Carter, *Carters Christian Common Wealth*, 1627, p. 79; Lyly, *Euphues and His England*, *Works*, II, 194; Jacques Du Bosc, *The compleat woman*, 1639, p. 32 (italicized in the text); Brathwait, *The English Gentlewoman* (1641), pp. 276, 368; Harrison, p. 172. See Tuvil, p. 15; Barnaby Rich, *Faultes, Faults, and nothing else but Faultes*, 1606, fol. 23.

15 Rye, pp. 7–8; Harrison, p. 172; Richard Brathwait, *A Ladies Love-Lecture*, in *The English Gentleman; and The English Gentlewoman*, 1641, p. 450; *Articles for the due execution of the Statutes of Apparell*, 1562; Proclamation by the Queen [Against excess in apparel], 1577; Bateson (Traill's *Social England*), p. 533.

16 Rich, *The Excellency of good women*, p. 21.

CHAPTER IX

1   The edition published by Thomas Petyt bears the date 1561, but Dibdin, Corser, Hazlitt, Miss White, and Stein all believe that 1541 is the correct date. (See Francis Lee Utley, *The Crooked Rib*, Columbus, 1944, pp. 251–257.) Other editions are by Robert Wyer (1542?, not in the *Short-title Catalogue*), John Kynge (1560), and John Allde (1572). Gosynhill is named as the author by the *Short-title Catalogue*, Collier, and Corser, presuming that he names himself in the *Mulierum Pean* as the author of both works; Hazlitt, Miss White, and Stein argue against this assumption. Utley leaves the matter doubtful. A considerable difficulty is encountered in some lines on signature A1ᵛ of *the Schole house*:

> *A foole of late, contryued a booke*
> *And all in prayse, of the femynye*
> *Who so taketh labour, it to ouer loke*
> *Shall proue, all is but flatterye*
> *Pehan he calleth it, it may well be*
> *The Pecocke is proudest, of his fayre tayle*
> *And so be all women of theyr apparayle.*

A possible solution to the problem is that Gosynhill wrote both works at the same time and included in each a reference to the other. C. L. Powell (*English Domestic Relations*, New York, 1917, p. 165) says that *the Schole house* was written in reply to the *Mulierum Pean*.

2   The passages quoted are in order from signatures A2, A3, A3ᵛ, B1ᵛ, and B3.

3   The Huntington Library edition which I have used is conjecturally dated 1560. See Utley, pp. 291–294.

4   See Utley (pp. 272–276), who suggests that a closer parallel than *the Schole house* may be found in Thomas Feylde's *Contrauersye bytwene a louer and a Jaye* (1522?).

5   I have used the microfilm of the copy in the British Museum. See Utley, pp. 284–285.

6   Huntington Library copy.

7   The tract by C. Pyrrye seems to have been composed between 1563 and 1571, both the *Short-title Catalogue* and the *Cambridge Bibliography* dating the extant edition [1569?] (Utley, pp. 205–207). The Folger copy is unique.

8   Utley suggests (p. 156) that 'W' may be 'Wooer' and 'C' may be 'Counsel,' or *W*. How, the printer and *C*. Pyrrye, the author.

9   The ballad *In Praise and Dispraise of Women* is dated by Rollins 1557–1565; it was printed in Richard Johnson's *A crowne garland of goulden roses* of 1612 (Utley, p. 311).

10   Huntington Library copy of *The First Blast*. Arber, in the introduction to his reprint in the *English Scholar's Library*, has an interesting passage which elaborates Knox's motivation: 'At the time this tract was written the destinies, immediate and prospective, of the Protestant faith seemed to lay wholly in the laps of five women, viz.: Catherine de Medici, Queen of France; Marie de Lorraine, Queen Regent of Scotland, whose sole heir was her daughter, Mary, afterwards Queen of Scots; Mary Tudor, Queen of England, having for her heir-apparent the Princess Elizabeth. Of these, the last – also of least account at this moment, being in confinement – was the only hope of the Reformers.'

11   Christopher Goodwin, who was minister to the same congregation, published in Geneva in the same year *How superior powers oght to be obeyd of their subjects*, where he too briefly characterizes the rule of women as monstrous in nature. See Robert Louis Stevenson, 'John Knox and His Relations to Women,' *Familiar Studies of Men and Books, Works*, Collier, New York, n.d., VII, 279–334; and for an excellent discussion of the whole controversy see especially James E. Phillips, Jr. 'The Background of Spenser's Attitude toward Women Rulers,' *The Huntington Library Quarterly*, V (1941), 5–32.

12   On the title page the place of publication is Strasborowe, but the *Short-title Catalogue* lists it 'Strasborowe [J. Daye, London].'

13   See Edwin Arber's reprint of the *First Blast*, pp. vii–viii; and Celeste Turner Wright, 'The Amazons in Elizabethan Literature,' *Studies in Philology*, XXXVII (1940), 454–456.

14   Other controversies over women, or rather controversies between men, took place, which are not of sufficient importance to be included here. One may be mentioned briefly – that between Philip Stubbes and Thomas Nashe. In 1583 (other editions in 1583, 1585, and 1595) was published Stubbes' *The Anatomie of Abuses*. Among the many abuses of the time which he singles out for need of correction in the land of Ailgna (Anglia backwards), are the use of cosmetics, the extravagant feminine headdress, and the inordinate attire of women (pp. 64–78 in Furnivall's edition of 1877). Thomas Nashe calls his work *The Anatomie of Absurdities: Contayning a breefe confutation of the slender imputed praises to feminine perfection, with a short description of the seuerall practices of youth, and sundry follies of our licentious times* (1589). Nashe must have seen the success of Stubbes' book and have realized that a satirical attack on women would go much better than a defence of that sex. At any rate he contributes briefly to the attack on woman's foibles; and yet he strikes a blow or two at Stubbes as well: 'I leaue these in their follie, and hasten to other mens furie, who make the Presse the dunghill, whether they carry all the much of their mellancholicke imaginations,

pretending forsooth to anatomize abuses, and stubbe vp sin by the rootes (B2).'

15   See Louis Wright, *Middle-Class Culture in Elizabethan England*, Chapel Hill, 1935. I have used the Huntington Library copy of the 1622 edition of Swetnam, but have also consulted the 1616 and 1617 editions.

16   Wright, pp. 487–488.

17   Apparently copied from Barnaby Rich, *Faultes, Faults, and nothing else but Faultes* (1606), fol. 23: 'Men you see are full of Faults, but amongst women (some will say) there is but two Faults, and these are, they can neither doe nor say well.'

18   Professor Wright (p. 488) thinks she is probably the daughter of Thomas Speght, and under twenty when she wrote this work.

19   Of course there had been complaints on this matter before the series of 1620. William Harrison, in his *Description of England* (1577), observed that 'women are become men, and men transformed into monsters,' although he does not explain his meaning (ed. Furnivall, 1877).

20   Wright, pp. 492–493.

21   Professor Wright (pp. 495–497) believes that this important work deserves much more recognition than it has received. He feels that the conventional Elizabethan theme of mutability is here applied to 'a dignified defense of social progress.'

22   Italics have been omitted here, since most of the passage is italicised.

23   The *Iuniper Lecture* was entered on August 4, 1638, and the only extant edition is labeled on the title page as 'the second impression, with many new additions'; *Divers Crab-tree Lectures* was entered on April 24, 1639. Professor Wright (p. 504) apparently considers the *Divers Crab-tree Lectures* as having been printed first.

24   Wright, p. 504.

25   A note in the margin of this work (p. 5) presumably indicates that Richard Brathwait's 'boulster lecture' (*Ar't asleepe Husband? A Boulster Lecture*, 1640 – entered November 25, 1639) is to be included in the attack. Reference to Brathwait and to this work, however, shows no evidence of anything attacked; there is also a conflict in the dates of the two works. I have used a microfilm of the copy in the Bodleian Library.

26   See Lu Emily Pearson, *Elizabethan Love Conventions*, Berkeley, 1933, pp. 75–201, 252–261.

Bibliography

ABBOT, ROBERT, *A Wedding sermon*, London, 1608.

AGRIPPA, HENRY CORNELIUS, *The Commendation of Matrimony*, London, 1545.

ALBERTI, LEON BAPTISTA, *The Arte of Loue. Or, Loue discouered in an hundred seuerall kindes*, London, 1598.

ALBERTUS MAGNUS, *Secreta Mulierum*, London, 1485.

ANDREWE, THOMAS, *The Vnmasking of a feminine Machiaueli*, London, 1604.

ANGER, JANE, *Iane Anger her protection for Women. To defend them against the Scandalous Reportes of a late Surfeiting Louer, and all other like Venerians that complaine so to bee ouercloyed with womens kindnesse*, London, 1589.

The Answere of a mother vnto hir sedvced sonnes letter, London, 1627.

AUGUSTINE, *The Glasse of vaine-glorie (out of S. Augustine his booke, intituled, Speculum peccatoris) into English*, London, 1585.

—— *A woorke of the holy bishop S. Augustine concernynge adulterous mariages written by him to Pollentius*, London, 1550.

AUSTIN, WILLIAM, *Haec Homo Wherein The Excellency of the Creation of Woman is described, By way of an Essaie*, London, 1637.

An Apology for Lovers, London, 1651.

AVERELL, WILLIAM, *Foure notable Histories, applyed to foure worthy examples: As, 1. A Diall for daintie darlings. 2. A spectacle for negligent Parents. 3. A glasse for disobedient Sonnes. 4. And a myrrour for virtuous Maydes. Whereunto is added a Dialogue, expressing the corruptions of this age*, London, 1590.

AYLMER, JOHN, *An Harborowe for faithful and trewe Subiectes, agaynst the late blowne Blaste, concerninge the gouernmēt of women*, Strassburg [J. Daye, London], 1559.

B., R., *A Watch-word for Wilfull Women*, London, 1581.

B., Sk., *Counsel to the husband: To the wife Instruction*, London, 1608.

BACON, FRANCIS, *Philosophical Works*, ed. J. W. Robertson, London, 1905.

— *Essays and New Atlantis*, ed. G. S. Haight, New York, 1942.

BALDWIN, T. W., *William Shakspere's Small Latine & Lesse Greeke*, Urbana, Ill., 1944.

BALLARD, GEORGE, *Memoirs of Several Ladies of Great Britain*, Oxford, 1752.

BANSLEY, CHARLES, *A treatyse, shewing and declaring the pryde and abuse of women now a dayes*, London [1550?].

BASKERVILL, CHARLES READ, *The Elizabethan Jig*, Chicago, 1929.

BATESON, MARY, 'Manners and Customs,' Traill's *Social England*, vol. III, sec. II, New York, 1909.

BATTY, BARTHOLOMEW, *The Christian mans Closet*, London, 1581.

BEAUMONT, FRANCIS, and FLETCHER, JOHN, *Works*, Cambridge, 1905–1912.

Beaute of women, Here foloweth a lytell treatyse of the, London [1525?].

BECON, THOMAS, *Worckes (The booke of Matrimony* and *An homely against whordome)*, London, 1564–60–63. See Bullinger.

BENTLEY, THOMAS, *The Monument of Matrones*, London, 1582.

BERCHER, WILLIAM, *The Nobylytye off Wymen* (1559), ed. Warwick Bond, London, 1904.

BOAISTUAU, PIERRE, *Theatrum Mundi, The Theatre or rule of the world*, London [1566?].

BODENHAM, JOHN, see Ling.

BODIN, JEAN, *The Six Bookes of a Commonweale*, London, 1606.

BRADFORD, GAMALIEL, *Elizabethan Women*, Cambridge, 1936.

BRATHWAIT, RICHARD, *Ar't asleepe Husband? A Boulster Lecture*, London, 1640.

— *The English Gentleman*, London, 1630.

— *The English Gentleman; and the English Gentlewoman: Both In one Volume couched*, London, 1641.

— *The English Gentlewoman, drawne out to the full Body*, London, 1631.

— *The Good Wife: or, A rare one amongst Women*, London, 1618.

— *A Ladies Love-Lecture*, in *The English Gentleman; and the English Gentlewoman*, London, 1641.

BRETON, NICHOLAS, *Pasquils Mistresse: Or The Worthie and vnworthie woman*, London, 1600.

BRINSLEY, JOHN, *A Looking-Glasse for Good Women*, London, 1645.

BROOKE, C. F. TUCKER, and PARADISE, NATHANIEL BURTON, *English Drama 1580-1642*, New York, 1933.

BRUTO, GIOVANNI MICHELE, *The necessarie, fit, and convenient Education of a yong Gentlewoman*, London, 1598.

BRYSKETT, LODOWICK, *A Discourse of Civill Life*, London, 1606.

BULLINGER, HEINRICH, *The goldē boke of christen matrimonye, moost necessary & profitable for all thē, that entend to liue quietly and godlye in the Christen state of holy wedlock newly set forthe in English by Theodore Basille* [Thomas Becon] [London, 1543]. Translated by Miles Coverdale.

BULWER, JOHN, *Anthropometamorphosis: Man Transform'd: or, The Artificiall Changling Historically presented*, London, 1653.

BUNNY, EDMUND, *Of Divorce for Adulterie, and Marrying againe*, Oxford, 1610.

BUONI, TOMASO, *Problems of Beautie and all humane affections*, trans. Samson Lennard, London, 1606.

BURDET, ROBERT, see Vaughan.

BURTON, ROBERT, *The Anatomy of Melancholy* (1628), New York, 1924.

BYRNE, M. ST. CLARE, *Elizabethan Life in Town and Country*, London, 1925.

The Cambridge History of English Literature, Cambridge, 1908, etc.

CAMDEN, CARROLL, 'The Elizabethan Imogen,' *The Rice Institute Pamphlet*, XXXVIII (1951), No. 1, 1–17.

— 'Iago on Women,' *Journal of English and Germanic Philology*, XLVIII (1949), 57–71.

CARTER, THOMAS, *Carters Christian Common Wealth; Or, Domesticall Dutyes deciphered*, London, 1627.

CAWDREY, ROBERT, *A Treasurie or Storehouse of Similies*, London, 1600.

CHARRON, PIERRE, *Of Wisdome* (ent. 1606), trans. Samson Lennard, London, 1670.

CHILD, FRANCIS JAMES, *The English and Scottish Popular Ballads*, Boston, 1883–1898.

CINTHIO, GIRALDI, see Bryskett.

CLARK, ALICE, *The Working Life of Women in the Seventeenth Century*, New York, 1920.

CLEAVER, ROBERT, *A Godlie Forme of Household Government*, London, 1598.

— *A godlie forme of householde government*, London, 1600.

CLERKE, WILLIAM, *The Triall of Bastardie*, London, 1594.

CLIFFORD, ANNE, *Diary*, ed. V. Sackville-West, London, 1923.

COLLINS, THOMAS, *The Teares of Love: Or, Cupids Progresse*, London, 1615.

COLONNA, FRANCESCO, *Hypnerotomachia. The Strife of Loue in a Dreame*, London, 1592.

COPLAND, ROBERT, *A Complaynt of them that be to soone maryed*, London, 1535.

— *Here begynneth the complaynte of them that ben to late maryed* (trans. from Pierre Gringoir, *La Complainte de trop tard marié*), London [1535?].

The Court of good Counsell. Wherein is set downe the true rules, how a man should choose a good Wife from a bad, and a woman a good Husband from a bad [London, 1607] (from Stefano Guazzo's *Ciuile Conuersation*).

CRAIG, HARDIN, *The Enchanted Glass*, New York, 1936.

DARCIE, ABRAHAM, *The Honour of Ladies: or, A True Description of their Noble Perfections*, London, 1622.

DAVIES, JOHN, of Hereford, *Works*, ed. A. B. Grosart, Chertsey Worthies Library, 1878.

DAWSON, THOMAS, *The good huswifes Iewell*, London, 1596.

— *The Second part of the good Hus-wiues Iewell*, London, 1597.

DEKKER, THOMAS, *The Batchelars Banquet*, London, 1603 (founded on La Sale, *Les Quinze Joyes de Mariage*).

— *The Non-Dramatic Works* (containing *Dekker His Dreame*, etc., 1620), ed. A. B. Grosart, London, 1885.

DENT, ARTHUR, *The Plaine Mans Path-way to Heauen*, London, 1601.

A Discourse of the Married and Single Life, London, 1621.

A Discovery of the abhominable delusions of those, who call themselues the Family of Loue [London?], 1622.

DOMENICHI, LUDOVICO, see Bercher.

DONNE, JOHN, *The Complete Poetry and Selected Prose*, ed. Hillyer, New York, 1941.

— *Iuuenilia: or Certaine Paradoxes, and Problemes*, London, 1633.

— *Fifty Sermons*, London, 1649.

— *Sermons*, selected and edited by L. P. Smith, Oxford, 1920.

DOVE, JOHN, *Of Diuorcement*, London, 1601.

DOWNAME, JOHN, *Foure Treatises, Tending to Disswade all Christians from foure no less hainous then common sinnes: namely, the abuses of Swearing, Drunkennesse, Whoredome, and Briberie*, London, 1609.

— *Lectures vpon the Foure First Chapters of The Prophecie of Hosea*, London, 1608.

DU BOSC, JACQUES, *The Compleat Woman*, London, 1639.

— *The Secretary of Ladies or a new collection of letters and answers, composed by moderne ladies and gentlewomen*, London, 1638.

DU CASTEL, CHRISTINE, *Here begynneth the boke of the Cyte of Ladyes*, London, 1521.

E., T., *The Lawes Resolutions of Womens Rights: or, The Lawes Provision for Woemen. A Methodicall Collection of such Statutes and Customes, with the Cases, Opinions, Arguments and points of Learning in the Law, as doe properly concerne Women*, London, 1632.

ELYOT, SIR THOMAS, *The Defence of Good women*, London, 1545. See Plutarch.

ENGLAND, *Articles for the due execution of the Statutes of Apparell*, London, 1562.

— Acts, Anno .xiii. Reginae Elizabethe, *At the parliament begunne and holden at Westminster*, etc., London, 1571.

— Proclamation, *By the Queene* [Against excess in apparel], London, 1577.

— Proclamation, *By the Queene, A proclamacion concernyng hattes and cappes*, London, 1573.

ERASMUS, DESIDERIUS, *A modest meane to Mariage, pleasauntly set foorth by that famous Clarke Erasmus Roterodamus, and translated into Englishe* by N. L.[eigh], London, 1568.

— *A ryght frutefull Epystle deuysed by the moste excellent Clerke Erasmus in laude and prayse of matrymony translated in to Englyshe by Richard Tauernour*, London [1530?].

ERASTOPHIL, see *An Apology for Lovers*, London, 1651.

ESTIENNE, HENRI, *A world of wonders*, Edinburgh, 1608.

EVANS, H. A., *English Masques*, London, 1897.

Everie Woman in her Humor, London, 1609.

F., I., *A Sermon preached at Ashby De-la-Zouch ... at the funeral of ... Elizabeth Stanley*, London, 1635.

Family of Love, see *Discovery.*

FENTON, GEOFFREY, *Monophylo, drawne into English by Geffray Fenton. A philosophi-call discourse, and diuision of loue,* London, 1572 (a translation of Étienne Pasquier, *Le monophile*).

FERRAND, JAMES, *Erotomania or A Treatise Discoursing of the Essence, Causes, Symptomes, Prognosticks, and Cure of Love, or Erotique Melancholy,* Oxford, 1640.

FERRERS, RICHARD, *The Worth of Women,* London, 1622.

FETHERSTONE, CHRISTOPHER, *A Dialogue against light, lewde, and lasciuious dauncing,* London, 1582.

FISTON, WILLIAM, *The Schoole of good Manners, or A New Schoole of Vertue, Teaching children and youth how to behane [sic] themselues in all companie,* London, 1629.

FITZHERBERT, JOHN, *The boke of husbandrye,* London, 1548.

FURNIVALL, FREDERICK J., Notes to an edition of Philip Stubbes' *Anatomy of Abuses,* London, 1879.

G., A., *The Widdowes mite* [St. Omer], 1619.

G., C., *The Ladies Vindication: or, The Praise of Worthy Women,* London, 1651.

G., I., *An Apologie for Womenkinde,* London, 1605.

G., R., *A godlie exhortation, and fruitfull admonition to vertuous parents, and modest Matrons. Describing the holie vse and blessed institution of that most honorable state of Matrimonie, and the encrease of godlie and happy children, in training them vp in godly education, and houshold discipline,* London, 1584.

GAMON, HANNIBALL, *The praise of a godly woman. A sermon,* London, 1627.

GARDINER, DOROTHY, *English Girlhood at School,* London, 1929.

GASCOIGNE, GEORGE, *Works,* ed. J. W. Cunliffe, Cambridge, 1910.

GATAKER, THOMAS, *A Good Wife Gods Gift. A Mariage Sermon,* London, 1620.

— *A Good Wife Gods Gift: and A Wife Indeed. Two Mariage Sermons,* London, 1623.

— *A Mariage Praier, or Succinct Meditations: Delivered in a Sermon on the Praier of Eleazer,* London, 1624.

— *Marriage Duties Briefely Couched togither,* London, 1620.

GEREE, STEPHEN, *The Ornament of Women,* London, 1639.

GIBBON, CHARLES, *A Work worth the Reading. Wherein is Contayned, fiue profitable and pithy Questions, very expedient, aswell for Parents to perceiue howe to bestowe their Children in Marriage,* London, 1591.

GIBSON, ANTHONY, *A Womans Woorth, defended against all the men in the world,* London, 1599.

GODFREY, ELIZABETH, *Social Life Under the Stuarts,* London, 1904.

GOSSON, STEPHEN, *Quippes for Vpstart Newfangled Gentlewomen. Or a Glasse, to view the Pride of vainglorious Women,* London, 1595.

— *The Schoole of Abuse,* London, 1579.

GOSYNHILL, EDWARD, *The prayse of all women, called Mulierum Pean*, London [1560?].
— (?), *Here begynneth a lytle boke named the Schole house of women*, London, 1561 [1541?].

GOUGE, WILLIAM, *Of Domesticall Duties*, London, 1622.

GREENE, ROBERT, *Works*, ed. A. B. Grosart, London, 1881–1883.

GRIFFITH, MATTHEW, *Bethel: or, a Forme for Families*, London, 1633.

GRINGOIR, PIERRE, see Copland.

GRYMESTON, ELIZABETH, *Miscellanea*, London [1606?].

GUAZZO, STEFANO, see *The Court of good Counsell*.

GUILLIMEAU, JACQUES, *Child-birth or, The Happy Deliverie of Women*, London, 1612.

GUILPIN, EVERARD, *Skialetheia* (1598), Shakespeare Association Facsimiles, No. 2, London, 1931.

Haec-Vir: Or The Womanish-Man: Being an Answere to a late Booke intituled Hic-mulier, London, 1620.

HALL, JOSEPH, *Works*, London, 1634.

HALLER, WILLIAM, 'Hail Wedded Love,' *ELH*, XIII (1946), 79–97.

HALLER, WILLIAM and MALLEVILLE, 'The Puritan Art of Love,' *Huntington Library Quarterly*, V (1942), 235–272.

HANNAY, PATRICK, *A Happy Husband or, Directions for a Maide to choose her Mate. As also, a Wives Behaviour towards her Husband after Marriage*, London, 1619.

HARDING, DAVIS P., 'Elizabethan Betrothals and "Measure for Measure",' *Journal of English and Germanic Philology*, XLIX (1950), 139–158.

HARLEY, LADY BRILLIANA, *Letters*, ed. T. T. Lewis, Camden Society, London, 1854.

HARRINGTON, WILLIAM, *In this boke are conteyned the comendacions of matrymony the maner & fourme of contractyng solempnysynge and lyuyng in the same*, London, 1528.

HARRISON, G. B., *An Elizabethan Journal*, London, 1928.

HARRISON, WILLIAM, *Description of England in Shakspere's Youth*, edited from the first two editions of Holinshed's *Chronicle* by F. J. Furnivall, London, 1877.

HEALE, WILLIAM, *An Apologie for Women. or An Opposition to Mr. Dr. G. his assertion. Who held in the Act at Oxforde. Anno. 1608. That it was lawfull for husbands to beate their wiues*, Oxford, 1609.

HEBEL, J. WILLIAM, and HUDSON, HOYT H., *Poetry of the English Renaissance*, New York, 1930.

HEGENDORFF, CHRISTOPHER, *Domestycal or housholde sermons*, Part I, Ipswich, 1548; Part II, Worcester, 1549.

HERMAN V [VON WILD], *A brefe and a playne declaratyon of the dewty of maried folkes*, London [1553?].

HEYWOOD, JOHN, *A dialogue conteinyng the number in effect of all the prouerbes in the englishe tongue, compacte in a matter concernyng two maner of mariages*, London, 1546.

HEYWOOD, THOMAS, *A Curtaine Lecture*, London, 1637.

HEYWOOD, THOMAS, *Gunaikeion; or, Nine Bookes of Various History. Concerninge Women*, London, 1624.

Hic Mulier: or, The Man-Woman: Being a Medicine to cure the Coltish Disease of the Staggers in the Masculine-Feminines of our Times, London, 1620.

HOGARDE, MILES, *A Mirrour of loue, which such light doth giue, That all men may learne, howe to loue and liue*, London, 1555.

HUGHEY, RUTH WILLARD, 'Cultural Interests of Women in England from 1524 to 1640 Indicated in the Writings of the Women,' unpublished thesis for the Ph. D. degree, Cornell University, 1932.

In dispraise of women, [*These wamen all*], manuscript ballad, Folger MS. 1186.2, *c.* 1550.

JEAFFRESON, J. C., *Brides and Bridals*, vol. I, London, 1872.

JORDEN, EDWARD, *A briefe discourse of a disease called the suffocation of the mother*, London, 1603.

KAHIN, HELEN ANDREWS, 'Controversial Literature about Women,' unpublished thesis for the Ph. D. Degree, University of Washington, 1934.

KENNEDY, JOHN, *The Ladies Delight*, London, 1631.

KNOX, JOHN, *The First Blast of the Trumpet against the monstruous regiment of Women*, Geneva, 1558.

KOHLER, CHARLOTTE, 'The Elizabethan Woman of Letters,' unpublished thesis for the Ph. D. Degree, University of Virginia, 1936.

LABÉ, LOUISE, *Debate between Folly and Cupid (Oeuvres*, Lyons, 1555), ed. E. M. Cox, London, 1925.

LANE, JOHN, *Tom Tel-Troths message and his pens complaint* (London, 1600), New Shakspere Society, London, 1876.

LANYER, MRS. EMILIA, *Salve Deus Rex Iudaeorum*, London, 1611.

LA SALE, ANTOINE DE, *The fyftene Joyes of maryage*, London, 1509.

LAWSON, WILLIAM, *A New Orchard and Garden: . . . with the Country Houswifes Garden for herbes of common vse, their vertues, seasons, profits, ornaments, varietie of knots, models for trees, and plots for the best ordering of Grounds and Walkes*, London, 1623.

LEGATE, ROBERT, *A briefe catechisme and dialogue betwene the Husbande and his Wyfe*, Wesell, 1545.

LEIGH, DOROTHY, *The Mothers Blessing*, London, 1633.

LEIGH, WILLIAM, *Queen Elizabeth, Paraleld in her Princely vertues, with Dauid, Iosua, and Hezekia*, London, 1612.

LESLIE, JOHN, *A defence of the honour of the right highe, mightye and noble Princesse*

Marie Quene of Scotlande and dowager of France, with a declaration aswell of her right, title & intereste to the succession of the crowne of Englande, as that the regimente of women ys conformable to the lawe of God and nature, London [printed abroad?], 1569.

LEY, JOHN, *A patterne of Pietie,* London, 1640.

LING, NICHOLAS, *Politeuphuia. Wits Common wealth,* London, 1598.

LINTHICUM, MARIE CHANNING, *Costume in the Drama of Shakespeare and his Contemporaries,* Oxford, 1936.

LLOYD, LODOWICK, *The Choyce of Iewels,* London, 1607.

LOMAZZO (LOMATIUS), GIOVANNI PAOLO, *A Tracte Containing the Artes of curious Paintinge Caruinge & Buildinge,* Oxford, 1598.

LOWIN, JOHN, *Conclusions vpon Dances,* London, 1607.

LUPTON, THOMAS, *A Thousand Notable things of sundry sortes,* London [1600?].

LYLY, JOHN, *Works,* ed. Warwick Bond, Oxford, 1902.

M., C., *The Second Part of The Historie, called The Nature of a Woman,* London, 1596.

MACQUOID, PERCY, 'Costume' (chapter XIX), *Shakespeare's England,* Oxford, 1917.

The Man in the Moone, ed. J. O. Halliwell, London, 1849.

MANCINUS, DOMINICUS, *Here begynnyth a treatyse intitulyd the myrrour of good maners,* London [1523?].

MANNINGHAM, JOHN, *Diary,* ed. John Bruce, Camden Society, Westminster, 1868.

MARKHAM, GERVASE, *Country Contentments, or The English Huswife,* London, 1623.

MEXIA, PEDRO, see Milles.

MILLES, THOMAS, *The Treasurie of Auncient and Moderne Times,* trans. from Pedro Mexia, F. Sansovino, etc., London, 1613.

MOFFETT, THOMAS, *The Silkewormes, and their Flies,* London, 1599.

MORE, EDWARD, *A Lytle and bryefe treatyse, called the defence of women, and especially of Englyshe women, made agaynst the Schole howse of women,* London, 1560.

MORYSON, FYNES, *An Itinerary* (1617), Glasgow, 1907–1908.

MULCASTER, RICHARD, *Positions wherin those primitiue circumstances be examined, which are necessarie for the training vp of children, either for skill in their booke, or health in their bodie,* London, 1581.

— *Positions,* London, 1887.

Muld Sacke: or The Apologie of Hic Mulier: to the late Declamation against her, London, 1620.

MUNDA, CONSTANTIA, pseud., *The Worming of a mad Dogge: or, A Soppe for Cerberus the Ialor of Hell. No Confutation but a sharpe Redargution of the bayter of Women,* London, 1617.

MURRELL, J., *Murrels two books of cookerie and carving,* London, 1638.

The Mysteries of Love & Eloquence, Or, the Arts of Wooing and Complementing; as they are manag'd in the Spring Garden, Hide Park, the New Exchange, and other eminent places, London, 1658.

NASHE, THOMAS, *The Anatomie of Absurditie: Contayning a breefe confutation of the slender imputed praises to feminine perfection*, London, 1589.

— *Works*, ed. R. B. McKerrow, London, 1910.

— *Works*, ed. A. B. Grosart, 1883–1884.

NEVILLE, HENRY, *A Parliament of Ladies*, etc., London, 1647.

NEWSTEAD, CHRISTOPHER, *An Apology for Women: or, Womens Defence*, London, 1620.

NICCHOLES, ALEXANDER, *A Discourse, of marriage and wiuing: and of The greatest Mystery therein contained: How to choose a good Wife from a bad*, London, 1615.

NICHOLS, JOSIAS, *An Order of Houshold Instruction*, London, 1596.

NIXON, ANTHONY, *The Dignitie of Man, Both in the Perfections of his Soule and Bodie*, London, 1612.

NORTHBROOKE, JOHN, *A Treatise wherein Dicing, Dauncing, Vaine playes or Enterluds with other idle pastimes &c. commonly vsed on the Sabboth day, are reproued by the Authoritie of the word of God and Auntient writers*, London [1577?].

OECOLAMPADIUS, JOHN, *A Sarmon of John Oecolampadius, to yong men, and maydens*, London [1548?].

ONIONS, C. T., ed., *Shakespeare's England*, Oxford, 1917.

The Order of Matrimony, London, 1548.

OVERBURY, SIR THOMAS, *His Wife*, London, 1632.

— *Miscellaneous Works*, ed. E. F. Rimbault, London, 1856.

PARÉ, AMBROISE, 'Of Poisons' (1575), *Oeuvres*, III, Paris, 1840.

The Parliament of Women. With the merry Lawes by them newly enacted. To live in more Ease, Pompe, Pride, and wantonnesse: but especially that they might have superiority over their husbands, London, 1640.

PARROT, HENRY, *The Gossips Greeting: Or, A New Discouery of such Females meeting*, London, 1620.

PARTRIDGE, JOHN, *The Treasury of commodious Conceits, and hidden Secrets, commonly called The good Huswiues Closet of prouision for the health of hir houshold*, London, 1584.

PASQUIER, ÉTIENNE, see Fenton.

The Payne and sorowe of euyll maryage, London [1509?].

PEARSON, LU EMILY, 'Elizabethan Widows,' *Stanford Studies in Language and Literature*, Stanford, 1941.

— *Elizabethan Love Conventions*, Berkeley, 1933.

PEELE, GEORGE, *Works*, ed. A. H. Bullen, London, 1888.

PERKINS, WILLIAM, *Christian Oeconomie: Or, A Short Survey of the Right Manner of erecting and ordering a Familie, according to the Scriptures*, London, 1609.

— *The Whole Treatise of the Cases of Conscience*, London, 1619.

PHILLIPS, JAMES E., Jr., 'The Background of Spenser's Attitude toward Women Rulers,' *Huntington Library Quarterly*, V (1941), 5–32.

Phillips, James E., Jr., 'The Woman Ruler in Spenser's Faerie Queene,' *Huntington Library Quarterly*, V (1942), 211–234.

Philotus. A Verie Excellent and delectable Comedie, Intituled Philotus. Wherein we may perceiue the great inconueniences that fall out in the mariage betweene olde age and youth, Edinburgh, 1612.

Platt, Sir Hugh, *A closet for ladies and gentlewomen, or the art of preseruing, conseruing, and candying*, London, 1608.

A Pleasant conceited comedie, wherein is shewed, how a man may choose a good wife from a bad, London, 1608.

Plutarch, *The education or bringinge vp of children translated oute of Plutarch by syr Thomas Eliot knyght*, London [1535?].

Pollard, A. W., and Redgrave, G. R., *A Short-title Catalogue of Books Printed in England, Scotland, & Ireland And of English Books Printed Abroad 1475–1640*, London, 1948.

Powell, Chilton Latham, *English Domestic Relations 1487–1653*, New York, 1917.

The Praise and Dispraise of Women, London, 1579.

The Praise of Musicke, Oxford, 1586.

The Proude wyues Pater noster that wolde go gaye, and vndyd her husbonde and went her waye, London, 1560.

Prynne, William, *The Vnlouelinesse, of Loue-Lockes. or, A Summarie Discourse, proouing: The wearing, and nourishing of a Locke, or Loue-Locke, to be altogether vnseemely, and vnlawfull vnto Christians. In which there are likewise some passages collected out of Fathers, Councells, and sundry Authors, and Historians, against Face-painting; the wearing of Supposititious, Poudred, Frizled, or extraordinary long Haire*, London, 1628.

Pyrrye, C., *The praise and Dispraise of Women*, London [1569?].

Resch, Wolfgang, *The vertuous scholehous of vngracious women*, London [1550?].

Rich, Barnaby, *The Excellency of good women*, London, 1613.

— *Faultes, Faults, and nothing else but Faultes*, London, 1606.

— *Roome for a Gentleman, or the Second Part of Faultes*, London, 1609.

Roesslin, Eucharius, *The birth of mankinde, otherwise named The Womans Booke*, London, 1604.

Rowlands, Samuel, *Looke to it: For, Ile Stabbe Ye*, London, 1604.

Ruscelli, Girolamo (Alessio), *The Secretes of reuerende Maister Alexis of Piemount*, London, 1568.

— *The seconde parte of the Secrets*, London [1568?].

— *The thyrde and last part of the Secretes*, London, 1566.

— *A verye excellent and profitable Booke conteining sixe hundred foure score and odde experienced Medicines*, London, 1569.

RYE, WILLIAM BRENCHLEY, *England as Seen by Foreigners in the days of Elizabeth and James the First*, London, 1865.

SADLER, JOHN, *The Sick Womans priuate Looking-glasse*, London, 1636.

SHAKESPEARE, WILLIAM, *Works*, ed. Hardin Craig, Chicago, etc., 1951.

SHERLEY, ANTHONY, *Witts New Dyall*, London, 1604.

SIDNEY, SIR PHILIP, *The Countesse of Pembrokes Arcadia* (1590), ed. Albert Feuillerat, Cambridge, 1912.

SMITH, HENRY, *A Preparatiue to Mariage*, London, 1591.

— *The Wedding Garment*, London, 1590.

— *Works*, ed. Thomas Fuller, vol. I, Edinburgh, 1866.

SNAWSEL, ROBERT, *A looking glasse for Maried Folkes*, London, 1610.

SOWERNAM, ESTER, pseud., *Ester hath hang'd Haman: or An Answere to a lewd Pamphlet, entituled, The Arraignment of Women. With the arraignment of lewd, idle, froward, and vnconstant men, and Husbands*, London, 1617.

SPEGHT, RACHEL, *A Mouzell for Melastomus, The Cynicall Bayter of, and foule mouthed Barker against Evahs Sex. Or an Apologetical Answere to the Irreligious and Illiterate Pamphlet made by Io. Sw. and by him Intituled, The Arraignement of Women*, London, 1617.

SPENSER, EDMUND, *The Complete Poetical Works*, Student's Cambridge Edition, Boston, etc., 1908.

STEVENSON, ROBERT LOUIS, 'John Knox and His Relations to Women,' *Familiar Studies of Men and Books, Works*, Collier, New York, n.d., VII, 279–334.

STOPES, MRS. C. C., 'Sixteenth Century Women Students,' *Shakespeare's Environment*, London, 1918.

STUBBES, PHILIP, *A Christal Glasse for Christian Women*, London, 1592.

— *The Anatomie of Abuses* (1583), ed. F. J. Furnivall, London, 1877–1879.

SWETNAM, JOSEPH, *The Arraignment of Lewd, Idle, Froward, and vnconstant Women: Or, the Vanitie of them; chuse you whether. With a Commendation of the Wise, Vertuous, and Honest Woman. Pleasant for married men, profitable for young men, and hurtfull to none*, London, 1622.

Swetnam, the Woman-hater, arraigned by women. A new comedie, Acted at the Red Bull, by the late Queenes Seruants, London, 1620.

SYMMES, H. S., *Les Débuts de la Critique Dramatique*, Paris, 1903.

SYMONDS, J. A., *Shakspere's Predecessors*, London, 1884.

TASSO, ERCOLE and TORQUATO, *Of Mariage and Wiuing. An Excellent, pleasant, and Philosophical Controuersie, betweene the two famous Tassi now liuing, the one Hercules the Philosopher, the other, Torquato the Poet*, London, 1599.

TASSO, TORQUATO, *The Housholders Philosophie. Wherein is perfectly and profitably described, the true Oeconomia and forme of Housekeeping*, trans. Thomas Kyd, London, 1588.

TATTLE-WELL, MARY, and HIT-HIM-HOME, IOANE (pseud.), *The womens sharpe revenge: Or an answer to Sir Seldome Sober that writ those railing Pamphlets called the Iuniper and Crab-tree Lectures &c. Being a sound Reply and a full confutation of those Bookes: with an Apology in this case for the defence of us women*, London, 1640.

TAYLOR, JOHN, *A Iuniper Lecture. With the description of all sorts of women, good, and bad: From the modest to the maddest, from the most Civil, to the scold Rampant, their praise and dispraise compendiously related*, London, 1639.

— *Works*, Spenser Society, Manchester, 1868.

TAYLOR, THOMAS, *A Good Husband and A Good Wife*, London, 1625.

Tell-Trothes New-yeares Gift (1593), New Shakspere Society, London, 1876.

TILLEY, M. P., 'I Have Heard of Your Paintings Too,' *Review of English Studies*, V (1929), 312–317.

TILNEY, EDMUND, *A brief and pleasant discourse of duties in Mariage, called the Flower of Friendshippe*, London, 1568.

TRAILL, H. D., *Social England*, vols. III–IV, New York, 1909.

TUKE, THOMAS, *A Treatise against Painting and Tincturing of Men and Women*, London, 1616.

TUSSER, THOMAS, *The Points of Huswifery*, appended to *Five Hundred Points of Good Husbandry* (1573, etc.), ed. William Mavor, London, 1812, pp. 233–330.

TUVIL, DANIEL, *Asylum Veneris, or A Sanctuary for Ladies. Iustly Protecting Them, their virtues, and sufficiencies from the foule aspersions and forged imputations of traducing Spirits*, London, 1616.

UTLEY, FRANCIS LEE, *The Crooked Rib*, Columbus, 1944.

VAUGHAN, ROBERT, or BURDET, ROBERT, *A Dyalogue defensyue for women agaynst malycyous detractoures*, London, 1542.

VIRET, PIERRE, *The Schoole of Beastes, Intituled, the good Housholder, or the Oeconomickes*, London, 1585.

VIVES, JOANNES LUDOVICUS, *A very frutefull and pleasant boke called the Instructiō of a Christen womā*, London [1529?].

— *The office and duetie of an husband*, London [1553?].

— See Watson.

A. Warning-Piece to England against Pride and Wickedness (anonymous ballad), *The Works of George Peele* vol. I, London, 1888.

WATSON, FOSTER, *Vives and the Renascence Education of Women*, London, 1912.

WHATELY, WILLIAM, *A Bride-Bush or A Wedding Sermon: Compendiously describing the duties of Married Persons: By performing whereof, Marriage shall be to them a great Helpe, which now finde it a little Hell*, London, 1617.

— *A Care-cloth: Or A Treatise of the Cumbers and Troubles of Marriage: Intended to*

Advise them that may, to shun them; that may not, well and patiently to beare them, London, 1624.

WHETSTONE, GEORGE, *An Heptameron of Ciuill Discourses,* London, 1582.

WHITFORDE, RICHARD, *A werke for housholders or for them y* haue the gydynge or gouernaunce of any company,* London, 1530.

WILSON, VIOLET A., *Society Women of Shakespeare's Time,* New York, 1925.

WING, JOHN, *The Crowne Coniugall or, the Spouse Royall. A Discovery of the true honor and happines of Christian Matrimony Published for their consolation who are married, and their encouragment who are not, intending the benefit of both,* Middelburgh, 1620.

WIRTZUNG (WIRSUNG), CHRISTOPHER, *General Practise of Physick* (1598), London, 1654.

WOLF, EDWIN, 2nd, 'If Shadows be a Picture's Excellence,' *PMLA,* LXIII (1948), 831–857.

WRAGGE, SYBIL, ed., *The Age Revealed,* London and New York, 1929.

WRIGHT, CELESTE TURNER, 'The Amazons in Elizabethan Literature,' *Studies in Philology,* XXXVII (1940), 433–456.

WRIGHT, LEONARD, *A Display of Duty,* London, 1616.

WRIGHT, LOUIS B., *Middle-Class Culture in Elizabethan England,* Chapel Hill, 1935.

Index

Abimelech, 212.

Abraham, 212.

Accessories, of dress, 230–231.

Acne, 183.

Adultery, 97–98.

Advancement of Learning, The. See Bacon, F.

Advantages of marriage, 80–82.

Aeschines, 56.

Age, at marriage, 63, 91, 93–94; of student, 49.

Agrippa, Henry Cornelius, 18; *The Commendation of Matrimony*, 64, 85–86, 96.

Alberti, Leon Baptista, *The Arte of Loue*, 73–74.

Alchemist, The. See Jonson, B.

Alday, John, trans. See *The Praise and Dispraise of Women.*

Alde, Elizabeth, 146.

Alexis, The Secrets of. See Ruscelli, G.

Almain, 158, 166.

Almond for a Parrat, An. See Nashe, T. (?)

Alum, rock and plume, 180–181, 189, 204.

Amadis of Gaul, 51, 170.

Amoretti. See Spenser, E.

Amusements, 153–171.

Anacreon, 50, 153.

Anatomie of Absurditie, The. See Nashe, T.

Anatomie of Abuses, The. See Stubbes, P.

Anatomy of Melancholy, The. See Burton, R.

Anger, Jane, *Jane Anger her Protection for Women*, 32, 58, 214.

Anthropometamorphosis. See Bulwer, J.

Anti-feminist books and pamphlets, 17, 23–29, 241–271.

Antonius. See Herbert, Mary.

Antony and Cleopatra. See Shakespeare, W.

Apology for Lovers, An, 74.

Apology for Women, An. See Heale, W.

Apparel. See Dress.

Apuleius, Lucius, *The Golden Ass*, 51, 153.

Arbeau, Jehan Tabourot, 166.

Archidamus. See Isocrates.

Aretino, Pietro, 55, 153.

Aristeides, 153.

Arnold, Elizabeth, trans., 202.

Arraignment of Lewd, Idle, Froward, and vnconstant Women, The. See Swetnam, J.

Arraignment of Paris, The. See Peele, G.

Arreta, mother of Aristippus, 55, 251.

Ar't asleepe Husband? A Boulster Lecture. See Brathwait, R.

Arte of Loue, The. See Alberti, L.B.

Artes of curious Paintinge, The. See Lomazzo, G.

Artificiality of women, 199, 256, 262.

Art of English Poesy, The, 154–156.

Arts, The, 270.

Arundel, Earl of, daughters Jane and Mary, 57.

Arundel, Mary, 57.

Ascham, Margaret How, 57.

Ascham, Roger, 56.

Astrologers, women as, 147.

Astrophel. See Spenser, E.

Asylum Veneris. See Tuvil, D.

As You Like It. See Shakespeare, W.

Augures, Masque of. See Jonson, B.

Augustus Caesar, 211.

Aurelius, Emperor, 200.

Austin, William, *Haec homo*, 18, 30, 233, 267, 270.

Authority of parents, 39–40.

Autobiography. See Halkett, A.

Averell, William, *Foure notable Histories*, 156, 165, 187.

Aylmer, John, 57; *An Harborowe for Faithful and Trewe Subiectes*, 253–254.

Bacon, Francis, 169; *The Advancement of Learning*, 202; 'Of Marriage and Single Life,' 131.

Badness, of men, 31–32; of a few women, 47, 250.

Bakers, Company of, 146.

Band, falling, ruff, etc., 223, 224–226.

Bandore, 158.

Banns, marriage, 84.

Bansley, Charles, *A treatyse, shewing and declaring the pryde and abuse of women*, 195, 246.

Bartholomew Fair. See Jonson, B.

Cornelia, mother of Gracchus, 56; wife of Scipio Africanus, 55, 251.
Correction, of wife, 114–117.
Correspondence, female, 156.
Cosmetics, 175–215, 266; all women indulge, 176; source, 176–177; why used, 177, 199–200; on face and neck, 178; ceruse, 178–179; red colors, dyes, 179–181; fucus, 179; masks, 181–182, 200; facial waters, 182; freckles, 182; acne, 183; internal remedies for beauty, 183, 187–188; pimples, 183; scurfs, 183–184; bleaches and skin peelers, 183–184; wrinkles, 186; baths, 187; eyes and eyebrows, 188–189; lips, 189; teeth, 189–190; laughing, 190; mouthwashes, 190; hair, 190–194; curled hair, 191; perfumes, 191, 194, 195–196; dyed hair, 191; periwigs, perukes, 191–192, 200; hair styles, 192–193; hands, 194.
Cosmetics, against the use of: Church Fathers, 197; against God, 197–199; artificial, 198–199; evidence of pride, 199–200; used by courtesans, 200–201; time taken from devotion, 201; harmful, 202–204; effect on men, 204–206; do not deceive men, 206–207; colors run, 207–208; what would ancestors think? 208; effect on husbands, 208–209; time taken from household duties, 209; expensive, 209–210.
Cosmetics, in defense of: man is to blame, 211–212; used in Biblical times, 212; use praised, 212–214.
Costume, complete, 219–223. See Clothing.
Costume in the Drama of Shakespeare and His Contemporaries. See Linthicum, M.C.
Counterfeiting, 270.
Country Contentments. See Markham, G.
Courant, 166.
Courtesans, use of cosmetics by, 200–201; style of dress of, 224.
Court of Good Counsell, The, 191, 209.
Courtship, 72–73, 74–75.
Creation, 17–18.
Crooked Rib, The. See Utley, F.
Culture, a fashionable occupation, 56.
Curtaine Lecture, A. See Heywood, T.
Customs, marriage. See Marriage customs.
Cymbeline. See Shakespeare, W.
Cynthia's Revels. See Jonson, B.

Dairy, 44, 140.
Dakins, Margaret, 48, 141, 153.

Dancing, 162–169.
Daniel, Samuel, *Vision of the Twelve Goddesses*, 169.
Dante Alighieri, 153.
Danvers, Lady. See Donne, J.
David, the psalmist, 249.
Dawson, Thomas, *The good huswifes Iewell*, 135.
Debate betweene Follie and Loue, The. See Greene, R.
Deborah, 31.
Decameron, The. See Boccaccio, G.
Deceit, of women, 27, 31–32, 248.
Deceyte of Women, The. 25, 65.
De cultu feminarum. See Tertullian.
Defence of Good women, The. See Elyot, T.
Defence of the honour of ... Princesse Marie, A. See Leslie J.
Defence of women, The. See More, E.
'Defence of Womens Inconstancy, A.' See Donne, J.
De futuro spousals, 86–91.
De habitu muliebri. See Tertullian.
Dekker, Thomas, 129–130; *The Batchelars Banquet*, 129–130; (with Webster, J.) *Westward Ho*, 179, 183. See La Sale, A. de.
Demosthenes, 56.
Dent, Arthur, *The Plaine Mans Path-way to Heauen*, 71, 193, 195, 198, 220.
De praesenti spousals, 86–91.
Description of England. See Harrison, W.
Devil is an Ass, The. See Jonson, B.
Dewty of maried folkes. See Herman V.
Dialing, 153.
Dialogue agaynst ... dauncing, A. See Featherstone, C.
Diary. See Clifford, A.; Manningham, J.
Differences between men and women, 17–20.
Dignity of Man, The. See Nixon, A.
Diponares, 83–84.
Discourse, of marriage and wiuing, A. See Niccholes, A.
Discourse of the Married and Single Life, A., 63, 99.
Diseases, women subject to, 19–20.
Display of Duty, A. See Wright, Leonard.
'Disposition of Most Women, The Natural.' See Wright, Leonard.
Disputation betweene a Hee and a Shee Conny-Catcher. See Greene, R.
Distichs. See Cato.
Divers Crab-tree Lectures. See Taylor, J.
Divorce, 96–97.

Health of household, in wife's care, 135–136, 243–244, 250.

Henry VIII, 48, 168.

Heptameron of Ciuill Discourses, An. See Whetstone, G.

Herbert, Mary, Countess of Pembroke, 57; *Antonius*, 156; *The Doleful Lay of Clorinda*, 156.

Hercules, 249.

Herford, C.H., 245.

Herman V (von Wild), *A brefe and a playne declaratyon*, 130.

Herodotus, 68.

Herrick, Robert, 'A Sweet Disorder,' 207.

Hesiod, 153.

Hester, 31.

Heywood, Thomas, *A Curtaine Lecture*, 33, 86, 126, 267; *Gunaikeion*, 31, 120; *The Wise Woman of Hogsdon*, 147.

Hic Mulier: or, The Man-Woman, 199, 263, 265–266.

His Wife. See Overbury, T.

Hoby, Lady. See Dakins, M.

Hodsall, Anne, 147.

Holinshed, R., 177.

Home, care of, 43; wives to stay at, 125.

Homer, 46, 51, 153.

Honorable Entertainement, The. See Lyly, J.

Hood, 225–226, 228, 264.

Horace, 153.

Horman, William, *Vulgaria*, 178.

Horsetrick, 166.

Hosea. See Downame, J.

Household duties, time taken from by cosmetics, 209.

Housekeeping, neat, 125.

Housholders Philosophie, The. See Tasso, T.

Howard, Henry, Earl of Northampton, *A Dutifull defence of the lawfull Regiment of women*, 255.

Howard, Jane, 57.

Hudibras. See Butler, S.

Hue and Cry after Cupid, The. See Jonson, B.

Humanities, education in, 44–49.

Humourous Day's Mirth. See Chapman, G.

Huntingdon, Countess of, 48.

Husband, duties of. To the Wife: give orders, 110; responsible for her actions, 112; love her, 112, 259; rule her, 112–113; speak softly to her, 113, 256; be merry and pleasant, 114; be generous, 114; love her relatives, 114; correct her mildly and in private, 116; whipping her approved and disapproved, 116; avoid

causing jealousy, 117; avoid jealousy, 117–118; place no temptation before her, 118; be a companion to her, 118–119, 256; tell her his secrets, 119–120; keep wine from her, 120. To the household: control it, 120; provide for it, 120; do not perform wife's duties, 120; keep out of kitchen, 120, 256; control male children and male servants, 120–121; instruct the family in religion, 121; entertain Christian strangers, 121.

Husbandry, Five Hundred Points of Good. See Tusser, T.

Husbandrye, The boke of. See Fitzherbert, J.

Husbands, effect of use of cosmetics on, 208–209.

Huswifery, The Points of. See Tusser, T.

Hymenaei. See Jonson, B.

Hypnerotomachia. See Colonna, F.

Idleness of women, to be avoided, 42, 153.

Ile Stabbe Ye. See Rowlands, S.

Impediments to marriage, 84, 94–96.

Inconstancy of women, 34, 248.

In dispraise of women, 28–30.

Inferiority of the wife, 121–122.

Inglis, Esther, 58.

In laude and prayse of matrymony. See Erasmus, D.

Innkeepers, women as, 147.

In Praise and Dispraise of Women, 250.

Instructiō of a Christen womā. See Vives, L.

Ipomedon, 51.

Isabella, Queen, 47.

Isocrates, 56; *Archidamus*, 57.

Itinerary, An. See Moryson, F.

Iuniper Lecture, A. See Taylor, J.

Iuvenilia. See Donne, J.

James I, 43, 105, 263, 266.

Jeaffreson, J.C., *Brides and Bridals*, 99–100.

Jealousy, 27, 117–118, 255.

Jig, The Elizabethan. See Baskervill, C.

'John Knox and His Relations to Women.' See Stevenson, R.L.

Jones, Inigo, 168.

Jones, Robert, 158.

Jonson, Ben, 168–170; *The Alchemist*, 226; *Bartholomew Fair*, 71–72, 73, 222, 225; *The Case is Altered*, 43; *Cynthia's Revels*, 175, 184, 193; *The Devil is an Ass*, 170, 179–180, 184–186, 208, 219; *An Entertainment at the Blackfriars*, 147–148; *Epicoene*, 95–96, 100–102, 113–114, 129, 147,

Luther, Martin, [*Matrimony*], 246.

Lyly, John, *Campaspe*, 141, 191; *Endimion*, 230; *Entertainments at Sudeley*, 33; *Euphues*, 42, 43, 49, 63, 118, 124, 160, 162, 205–206; *Euphues and His England*, 40, 120, 125, 157–158, 162, 222, 227, 235; *Gallathea*, 141; *The Honorable Entertainement*, 222; 'Later Love Poems,' 126, 141, 182, 211–212; *Midas*, 85, 162, 192–194; *Sappho and Phao*, 72, 162; *The Woman in the Moone*, 71.

Lynn, Walter, trans., 245.

Lytle and bryefe treatyse, A. See More, E.

Macbeth. See Shakespeare, W.

Madder, 180.

Madonese, John, *The Ornaments of Woemen*, 203.

Magnetick Lady, The. See Jonson, B.

Maids, household, 133–134, 145–146.

Malcontent, The. See Marston, J.

Male attire, assumed by women, 221, 263–267.

Mamillia. See Greene, R.

Man in the Moone, The. 206.

Manners, good, 42–43.

Manningham, John, *Diary*, 114, 117.

Mantua-makers, woman as, 147.

Manufacturers, women as, 146–147.

Marcus Aurelius, 210.

Margaret, Countess of Richmond and Derby, 47.

Margarite of America, A. See Lodge, T.

Mariage, A modest meane to. See Erasmus, D.

Markham, Gervase, *Country Contentments*, 137, 140.

Marriage, of minds rather than of bodies, 79; four ends of, 80; forced, 79–80, 85–86; advantages of, 80–82; ordained by God, 80, 246; offenders against, 80–81; too expensive, 81, 83; too restraining, 82; changes way of life, 83; sacrament of, 84; contract of, 84, 87; banns, 84; impediments to, 84, 94–96; parents obeyed in, 85–86; *de futuro* spousals, 86–91; *de praesenti* spousals, 86–91; spousals, 86–91; bond required in, 88; ceremony of, 90, 99–100; child, 91–92; age at, 91, 93–94; clandestine, 92–93; breaking of sacrament of, 96–98; separation, 97; divorce, 96–98; adultery, 97–98; dowry, 98–99, 104–105; ring, 99–100, 121; bridal costume, 99; customs of, 100–105; wedding feast, 100–102; con-

summation of, 102; legal problems of, 103–105.

Marston, John, 21; *The Malcontent*, 21, 176, 188, 214; *The Scourge of Villanie*, 225.

Mary, Princess, 153, 160, 168.

Mary (Tudor), Queen, 252, 254.

Mary of Guise, 252.

Mary Queen of Scots, 187.

Masculinity, in women, 221, 263–267, 270.

Mask, 181–182, 200, 226, 231.

Masque, 168–169.

Masque of Augures. See Jonson, B.

Masque of Beauty. See Jonson, B.

Masque of Flowers, 169.

Masque of Owles. See Jonson, B.

Massinger, Philip, *The Guardian*, 154.

Mastic, 190.

[*Matrimony*]. See Luther, M.

May dances, 168.

Measure for Measure. See Shakespeare, W.

Medea, 31.

Medical practitioners, women as, 147.

Medicines, for beauty, 183, 187–188.

Melanchthon, 97.

Melusina, 51.

Men, attitude of, toward cosmetics, 204–210; blamed for cosmetics, 211–212; vices of, 32.

Menaphon. See Greene, R.

Merchant of Venice, The. See Shakespeare, W.

Mercuric sulphide, 180.

Mercury, sublimate of, 183–184, 202–204.

Merry in bed, wifely duty to be, 126–128.

Merry Wives of Windsor, The. See Shakespeare, W.

Mexia, Pedro, 184.

Michelangelo Buonarroti, 40.

Midas. See Lyly, J.

Middle-class, 148, 255.

Middle-Class Culture in Elizabethan England. See Wright, L.B.

Middleton, Thomas, 169.

Midwives, 147–148.

Milliners, women as, 147.

Mind and body, go together, 260.

Mirror, 176, 209, 230–231.

Miscellanea. See Grymeston, E.

Miseries of Inforst Mariage, The. See Wilkins, G.

Modest meane to Mariage, A. See Erasmus, D.

Monkey-waist, 195.

Monophylo. See Fenton, G.

Montaigne, 55, 153.

Vices, of men, 31–32; of women, 23–29, 241–242, 257–258, 261.
Vigo, 32.
Viol, 158.
Virgil, 46, 51.
Virginals, 158.
Virtues, of women. See Women, Virtues of.
Virtues, The four cardinal, 31, 270.
Vision, Greenes. See Greene, R.
Vision of the Twelve Goddesses. See Daniel, S.
Vives, Ludovicus, *Instructiō of a Christen womā,* 19, 46–47, 51, 54, 66, 67, 94, 102, 118, 137, 153; *The office and duetie of an husband, The,* 33, 41, 49, 50, 51, 154, 165, 189, 195, 199, 208. See Watson, F.
Vives and the Renascence Education of Women. See Watson, F.
Vnlouelinesse of Loue-Lockes, The. See Prynne, W.
Volpone. See Jonson, B.
Volte, 166.
Voragine, Jacobus de, 82.
Vulgaria, See Horman, W.

Warning-Piece to England against Pride and Wickedness, A, 220.
Warres of Cyrus, 19, 20.
Washing clothes, 44.
Waters, cosmetic, 182, 187.
Watson, Foster, *Vives and the Renascence Education of Women,* 198, 205.
Wax-chandlers, women as, 147.
Weaknesses, of women, 19–20, 23–24, 30.
Wealth, necessary in a wife, 62–63, 79–80, 256.
Webster, John, *The Duchess of Malfi,* 90. See Dekker, T.
Wedding feast, 100–102.
Weelkes, Thomas, 158.
Weston, Elizabeth Jane, 58.
Westward Ho. See Dekker, T.
Whately, William, *A Bride-Bush,* 97, 116, 130–131; *A Care-cloth,* 24, 71, 97, 111, 113–114.
Whetstone, George, *An Heptameron of Ciuill Discourses,* 99.
Whipping, 42, 116.
Wiclif, J. See *Of Weddid Men.*
Widow, 64–65, 102–103, 146, 256, 268.
Wife, choice of a, 61–75.
Wife, courtship of, 72–73.
Wife, duties of. To household: take care of property, 132–133, 243, 259; instruct and govern maids, 133–134; rear daugh-

ters and young sons, 134–135; guard health, 135–136; take care of needy, 136; grow food and prepare drink, 136; cook, 137–140; govern kitchen, 137; know offices of butler, pantler, etc., 139–140; care for garden, 140; oversee dairy, 140; oversee making of cloth, 140–141; sew, 141–142; make perfume, 142.
Wife, duties of. To husband: obey his orders, 110, 121–122, 259, 266; share his troubles, 119–120; love and revere him, 121, 258; be in subjection to him, 121, 246, 259; be inferior to him, 121; avoid contention, 121–122; be silent, 123, 257; let her mood correspond to his, 123; admit a guiltless guilt, 123–124; let him think he rules, 124; guard her reputation, 124–125, 257; stay at home, 125; keep house neat, 125–126; be merry in bed, 126–128; put husband first, 128; avoid improvidence, 128–130; be chaste, 130, 257; be responsible for modest sexual conduct, 130–131.
Wife, qualifications of: good parentage, 62; wealth, 62–63, 79–80, 256; education, 63; same status in society as husband, 63–64; same age as husband, 63; same religion, 64; not a widow, 64–65, 256; in love, 65–66; beautiful, 66–68, 256, 257; chaste, 68–70, 257; silent, 70; without pride, 70–71; serious, 71.
Wife for a Month, A. See Fletcher, J.
Wild, von. See Herman V.
Wild-Goose Chase, The. See Fletcher, J.
Wilfulness, of women, 24–26, 28, 256.
Wilkins, George, *The Miseries of Inforst Mariage,* 86.
Wimple, 225.
Winter's Tale, The. See Shakespeare, W.
Wirtzung (Wirsung), Christopher, *General Practise of Physick,* 183–184, 187–190, 194.
Wise Woman of Hogsdon, The. See Heywood, T.
Wits Miserie. See Lodge, T.
Witts New Dyall. See Sherley, A.
Wolfe, R., widow of, 146.
Woman Hater, The. See Fletcher, J.
Woman in the Moone, The. See Lyly, J.
Womans Lawier, The. See E., T.
Womans Prize, The. See Fletcher, J.
Womans Woorth, A. See Gibson, A.
Women, controversies over, 241–271; education of, 39, 58, 258; English, dif-

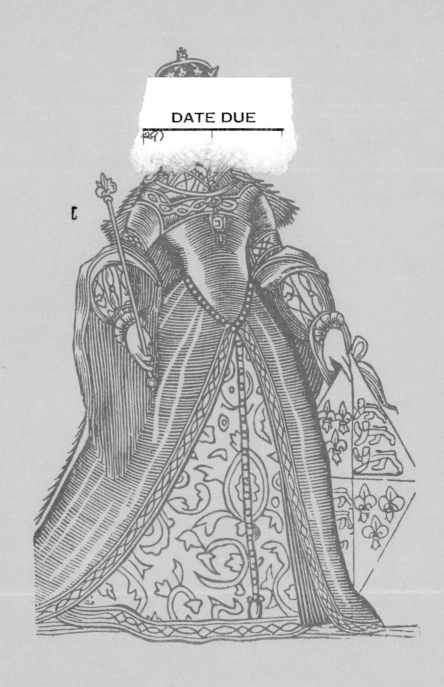